Famine In the Bullpen

a software engineer reviews
America's creativity crisis

Also by Julian S. Taylor:
The Flying Crossbeam

Famine In the Bullpen

Julian S. Taylor

Sockwood Press • Nederland, Colorado

Copyright © 2018 Julian S. Taylor
The moral right of the author has been asserted.
All rights reserved.

No part of this book may be reproduced, stored in a retrieval system or transmitted in any form or by any means without the prior written permission of the publisher, except by a reviewer who may quote brief passages in a review to be printed in a newspaper, magazine or journal.

My sincere thanks to The Train Cars and Very Nice Brewing Company in Nederland, Colorado where much of this book was written.

Cover photograph courtesy
Harris & Ewing collection
U.S. Library of Congress

Published by
Sockwood Press
PO Box 706
Nederland, CO 80466
https://sockwood.com

LCCN: 2018909517
ISBN: 978-1-944572-06-8

Printed in the United States of America
1st edition

Dedicated to
Mahima Mallikarjuna
Terence Leong
Willy Hui
Precious friends and inspiring engineering team.

Disclaimer

Throughout this book, I make mention of commonly used frameworks and tools — systems designed to facilitate good software practices especially as regards the Java complex. The names should be familiar to anyone experienced with software. I wish to emphasize here, as I do in the body of this work, that I do not hold any of these tools or frameworks in contempt; but instead, recognize that each serves its purpose well when properly assessed for the target environment.

My aim is to critique how modern methods misuse these systems, not the systems themselves. These well-conceived and useful systems should definitely be applied to appropriate well-designed software architectures. I will insist upon a solid and disciplined design prior to specification of the various third-party systems. It is the ill-conceived leap to apply a third-party system without first designing the overall solution which I hold in contempt.

Introduction

I wrote this book because I had been going from company to company writing software for newspaper publishing, satellite imaging and banking following a long tenure at the enterprise software powerhouse Sun Microsystems. During that time I started to realize that something was wrong. I was no longer enthused. I used to wake up in the morning anticipating the challenge of the day; unsure how I would address the problem at hand; and enjoying the tantalizing hint of fear that I would fail to resolve it. That experience has become disconnected from my professional life and I thought that an analysis was warranted. There are plenty of programming jobs out there but there are almost no jobs in software engineering. One may begin as a programmer, typing up code to make machines do our bidding; but, eventually, once coding has become second nature, one will crave to do something truly interesting.

The welder may become a specialized precision welder. The seamstress may become a fashion designer. The carpenter may become a master builder. The programmer may become a senior programmer but there will never be a time when the programmer will be challenged to do what no one else has ever done. The software term "architect" does not refer to one who applies discipline to the design of structures which have not heretofore been conceived. That doesn't happen in software. The architect figures out what standard frameworks will be used to build out another standard web application. The industry has abandoned the correction of serious problems. This book examines why that is and how we might explore options which reintroduce engineering as a respectable occupation.

Solving problems is a complicated process. It isn't as simple as many suspect. When taking on the sort of problem that engineers tend to get, the solution isn't selected from a multiple-choice list. No one knows what the solution is and the engineer has to dredge it up from a fog of symptoms, uncertainty and doubt. My astute reader may suspect that this is a common topic for me; and, in fact, it is. When my droning becomes too tedious for my listener I will sometimes illustrate with this anecdote, or something very similar.

Roughly 13 billion years ago everything we know began when it exploded rapidly into existence from an infinitesimal point of infinite density. At the moment of creation, matter and anti-matter came spontaneously into existence and then, as would be expected, ninety nine percent of the matter was destroyed by its corresponding anti-matter. Fortunately, due to quantum asymmetries on a cosmic scale, much of the matter remained to form all of the things we see around us. By means which are still in dispute, the anti-matter went elsewhere, perhaps to a different universe – a universe much like ours except much more anti than matter.

What few mention regarding this process is that from that primordial atom there also came into existence an equal number of problems and solutions. In the first few nanoseconds, ninety-nine percent of all problems were spontaneously resolved by their corresponding solutions. In those same few nanoseconds, the cosmic asymmetry that drove the anti-matter to the anti-matter universe forced a fundamental split between problems and solutions. The solutions appear to have accompanied the anti-matter into the alternate universe. This assertion may be easily verified by simply observing the number of unresolved problems in your immediate environment.

This theorized alternate universe, constructed from anti-matter and solutions, is permanently isolated from our universe. In that universe anti-people are granted anti-loans instantly with no anti-paperwork. They anti-collide in anti-intersections with no damage to either anti-vehicle. Their universal anti-healthcare is the envy of all matter universes. To discover a problem is an anomaly worthy of a major news release and billions of anti-citizens watch their mass media video anti-monitors in rapt amazement as the authorities dip into the abundance of solutions to resolve it with ease.

This means that we, in our universe, must apply our efforts to the resolution of problems through creative guile in much the same way that physicists annihilate matter in a nuclear accelerator: by converting the problem itself into some form of the solution. The method is not trivial and requires an application of discipline and training in order to assure a sustainable resolution. A company seeking to solve an actual problem has to commit to an environment which supports problem-solving and, in my experience, such environments are rare.

Most people simply assume that they will be wasting a third of their lives working at a pointless job for some rich guy. Some few find themselves doing what they always wanted to. Many of these satisfied workers will find that what they do demands not only rewarding labor but also the occasional creative challenge. The happy human being requires interaction with other humans, labor yielding goods of recognizable value and challenge yielding creative solutions worthy of praise.

The human being is a creative animal. I suspect that *defines* the human being. There have been cases wherein a new worker was presented to my team as a dullard and, sometimes out of desperation, I gave him a job that I feared was beyond him. Every time, I have been shocked and gratified to find that the person was thought to be a dullard simply because of a blatant misapplication of talents. Human beings deserve to solve grand problems and receive the accolades commensurate with their accomplishment.

I only hope that my clumsy attempt to persuade introduces at least a few concepts that are new. I may shock and distress, but I may also reinforce what you already suspect. If so, welcome to the revolution!

Table of Contents

1: Scope 1
2: Definitions 15
3: A Prestigious Failure 31
4: Bound Fast 42
5: Feature Factory 55
6: What Is Rigorous... 76
7: Common Knowledge 85
8: Fast Follower 96
9: Unless God Builds the House... 105
10: A Failed Experiment 114
11: Playing With Paradigms 127
12: The World as Object and Representation 139
13: On Reading the Tractatus 150
14: Software As a Surface 166
15: The Science of Desolation 182
16: Root Cause Analysis 189
17: Not Google Timber 195
18: Runner's High 206
19: Onramp 219
20: A Culture of Innovation 228
21: PROSE 239
22: Informal Methods 251
23: Health and Wholeness 263
Appendix A: The Toyota Way 275
Bibliography 276
Index 278

1: Scope

> *A man can stand anything except a succession of ordinary days.*
>
> Johann Wolfgang von Goethe

Engineering is a very old profession. People often date its origins to Imhotep in the Twenty Seventh Century BCE[1]. Imhotep planned and executed the massive Stepped Pyramid at Saqqara in Egypt for King Djoser. It was an amazing feat and it involved not only an ingenious architectural design but also the contributions of well-schooled artisans who cut the stones and placed them with phenomenal skill.

We remember Imhotep largely because his contribution was so glorious. What he produced was a single structure of literally monumental proportions that remains largely intact today. Imhotep is credited with this marvel and he was, without question, a brilliant polymath; but his genius was not born grown. It was built upon the works of other ingenious people who developed the early concepts of physics, geometry and administrative principles upon which he relied for his work.

Imhotep was acting as adviser and physician to the Pharaoh in an innovative nexus of the ancient world. His great work was certainly an example of engineering acumen, but engineering provides solutions that are both large and small. Large engineered structures include tall buildings and commercial aircraft. Small engineered structures include the white light LED, the sonic flow nozzle and the fuel injector. Indeed,

---

[1] Since this precedes the first evidence of currency by seven centuries, it means that prostitution may actually be the *second* oldest profession.

the large engineered structure would not be possible without exploiting the smaller engineered components developed prior to it. To some degree, the larger project is only *conceivable* because of the well-tested components that allow the engineer's mind to fill in a reasonably complete picture of the final product.

Engineering, at its base, is the disciplined solving of problems. People solve problems every day and many times those solutions would be correctly described as engineering solutions (to some, engineering is second nature). The key difference between a technical solution and an engineering solution is that the engineering solution is simpler and more stable. It takes into account the long term goal and the actual root cause of the observed problem.

Imhotep's place in history is well deserved, but let us also acknowledge that this was not actually the origin of engineering. He made direct use of prior engineered techniques developed over the previous centuries including stone cutting and cladding; and, he astutely applied established technologies such as the wheel and the lever. Long before that, a clever mind realized that a cord could be drawn into tension across a bow in order to propel a pointed projectile into the flesh of a game animal. Of course, prior to that, another clever person figured out that a pointed tip would pierce the flesh of an animal and render it immobile. Without that, the hungry hominid would have had to just wait for the creature to die.

Cooking the animal was also a key advance: predigesting and disinfecting the food prior to eating; and, before that, fire itself: recognizing that what came from the skies during thunderstorms could be replicated locally. In each case, there was a problem; and, its solution was not obvious to the casual observer. Most people in the tribe simply accepted that the occasional dead antelope provided a satisfying protein boost. The body would crave that rare boon and the ape-like gut would process it through its lengthy intestine. With the invention of cooking, much of that gut could evolve away since the food was partially broken down already. Hominid to Man was at least in part driven by clever individuals building on the cleverness of prior individuals who resolved

1: Scope

perceived problems using disciplined methodology. This is what we expect from Engineering.

———•———

These were not mere discoveries. Engineering is not science because it goes beyond discovery[2]. Engineering requires that one recognize the problem and associate the observed phenomenon with a new environment in which the problem no longer exists. When Alexander Flemming found that Penicillium mold delineated areas within a petri dish forbidden to Staphylococcal bacteria, he didn't comprehend the long term repercussions. Fortunately, he explained it to a few people who better recognized its practical application. Flemming was not the engineer, here. It was Cecil George Paine and Howard Florey who associated the phenomenon with the problem and developed penicillin and the mechanism for its manufacture. Engineering recognizes a problem, finds its root cause and resolves it.

Prior to penicillin, numerous precisely targeted chemicals such as Salvarsan and various sulfonamide drugs were pumped into the body to address very specific bacterial invasions. Each drug addressed a particular type of infection. These were technical solutions addressing specific problems in a one-off fashion. It was not until penicillin that a general-purpose chemical capable of disrupting the reproductive cycles of a large class of bacteria could be applied against a wide variety of diseases and localized infections.

The word *engineer* derives from the Latin *ingeniatorem* which means *one who excels at contriving*. You may notice that the word appears to share a familiar fragment with the word *genius* and it is actually from the same root as the words genius and genie. In the Roman empire the genius was the essence of the being; not the soul, in the Christian sense, but certainly the thing that makes the man. Engineering is not a procedure, it is too personal for that. It demands an investment of the spirit.

---

[2] See *Engineering Science as Opposed to Natural Science* at
http://arrow.dit.ie/cgi/viewcontent.cgi?article=1008&context=engineducpres, a Dublin Institute of Technology presentation explaining this distinction in good detail.

While not all engineering has the goal of accomplishing the apparently impossible, it must always be open to this.

An engine is different from a motor because the engine is *ingenious*: it converts a liquid (vegetable oil) or a solid (wood) into energy and then motion. A motor takes something already recognized as energy, like electricity, and converts that into motion. The development of the electric motor required the mind of the engineer, but what the motor itself does is quite simple. It is a specialized transducer; it is not ingenious.

Companies hire engineers to exercise their state-licensed discipline in the design and assurance of safety-critical equipment such as elevators or technically challenging systems such as electrical networks within large buildings. They also hire engineers to address complex technical problems with practical solutions. The latter is the form of engineering with which I am most familiar and it is the form to which this book will be primarily limited.

The licensed engineer plays an important role worthy of respect. The licensed engineer may engage in the full spectrum of the engineering discipline but it is not the state-licensed procedural component with which we are concerned. The form of engineering upon which we will be primarily focused is that of *problem solver*; solving both simple and complex problems using a method that is largely unchanged since Imhotep: decompose, analyze, recompose, resolve. It looks like a procedure but it is not; it is a method.

One familiar with the engineering discipline will approach the problem in a way that is fundamentally different from that of a technician who takes the commonsense approach of examining the problem and fixing it. When confronted with a problem, the engineer will first ask *what the problem is*, knowing that the problem presented is never the actual problem. The technician will determine what existing component or combination of components will solve the problem as presented.

The technician will probably develop a solution; but, it will only work for that one problem and will not apply well to other similar

1: Scope

problems. The engineer will recognize the side-effect for what it is and trace back to the side-effect that caused it and then back and back until the root cause is identified. The resolution of the root cause will resolve the identified "problem," but will also resolve the other problems arising from that same root cause. The engineering approach seems much more complicated; but, the solution to the root cause is typically much simpler than the solution to the side-effect.

The engineering solution is of greater value than the technical solution because it will address more perceived problems. It will require less maintenance and will also apply effectively to other similar root causes. The technical solution will tamp down the side-effect that was annoying the user, but all of the other side-effects remain and will each require their own technical solution.

The engineering solution requires detective work. It applies scientific method to the presented problem. It applies a hypothesis and tests it. Failing that, the next hypothesis may advance the cause. Eventually the hypothesis is proved and the resulting theory may point to the root cause. Further scientific review uncovers the nature of the root cause and we begin to move from science to problem solving. Taking into account the pieces comprising the root cause, the engineer seeks to pull the entire problem to mind. The fact that the presented problem is not the problem to be solved is acknowledged by Charles Kettering, former head of research at General Motors, when he said, "A problem well-stated is half-solved." The understanding of the initial problem must be assessed and analyzed. It must be repeatedly reviewed and revised. The understanding itself must be *crafted*. Crafted with the same care as the eventual solution.

Henri Bergson agrees that "A well-posed problem is a problem solved." Most engineers have had the experience of confronting the problem and analyzing it until it is all you can think about during a movie outing. It's what you are pondering while driving home and you awake in the morning having dreamt about it. The problem becomes solid and tangible. It becomes a comprehensible body and one day you behold it only to realize that the problem is actually the solution in disguise.

This is invariably the process that leads to the engineering solution. The solution often arises from the unconscious mind after sometimes interminable days of labor. The process is tedious, uncertain and painful. It is this process that I miss like a severed limb.

———•———

In my penultimate year as a senior staff engineer at Sun Microsystems I was exposed to what had happened to the software development process while I was preoccupied with wonderfully intractable engineering challenges in my cozy isolated office working with my dedicated and focused team. When I saw the ritual in action, it was so bizarre that I dismissed it as an aberration. Now I live it every day.

My team had produced a tool that would assess Sun computer systems in the field, determine what corrections or upgrades were required and then deliver and install those changes. The operation of the tool was simple but its development was very involved. Numerous problems had to be solved.

How, without downloading any information about the remote system, could we determine if any corrections were required? How could an engineer at Sun describe the anomalous or sub-optimal state that would signal the need for correction or upgrade? How, when Sun encouraged its customers to modify their systems in any way that they liked, could we distinguish between our original software and some modification provided by the customer? How, in the days before the modern application server, could the necessary corrections be delivered and installed to functioning Solaris systems that could not be rebooted?

After this service had been deployed for a couple of years, a senior manager from our division and I were called to Santa Clara for a meeting about patch automation. The director in charge of the meeting began by talking about how Red Hat was making us look like fools in the area of software updates. Red Hat systems were easily patched over the network and Solaris would need to catch up.

1: Scope

I had been in other meetings with this director. I knew that she knew about our fully operational patch automation solution. She had analyzed it and had complained that we weren't using some of her preferred cutting-edge frameworks like the briefly-popular *SOAP*. We had discussed this at length and I had argued in support of our light weight REST-like approach. Since the discussions had always ended amicably, I simply assumed that I didn't actually understand her concern. I decided to wait it out until I understood what she was talking about.

Just before lunch, she called upon one of her associates to demonstrate the Red Hat system. The fellow plugged in his notebook computer and showed everyone what was happening on the big screen. We watched the screen as he spoke.

"Look," he said selecting an icon, "it's now analyzing my system." After a few moments, he said, "Now it's done." He pointed at the screen as he selected another icon. "Now I'm downloading the required patches. They're being installed. Now I reboot and the Red Hat system is patched."

There was a moment of silence and suddenly the room was awash with noise. "How do they determine what patches are needed?" "What kind of data would be required to enable such an analysis?" "How would they keep such a knowledge base up-to-date?"

I now realized that they were talking about *exactly* what Sun was already doing as if it were not doing it. The shock was so intense that I was speechless. Was she so upset about our early REST implementation that she was intent on dismantling it just to promote her own ideas? I could certainly speak up and say that we were already doing this but, of course, she and half of the people in the room already knew that. Maybe they had never seen the actual product in action. I watched in stunned silence as they undertook to solve the problem using the approach we all use today: matching up stated problems to popular tools and frameworks. This was, of course, not the approach we had taken to solve this problem the first time.

Famine In the Bullpen

Twenty senior managers and engineering directors guided a block diagram being constructed on the large white board outlining all of the frameworks that would be required to solve the problem the way Red Hat had. The director's favorite tools were all there: SOAP, XSLT, Perl and various odd acronyms with which I had no experience. Since they had done no research to actually understand the problem, they were drawing their boxes around and aligning their tools against assumed symptoms, believing they were problems, and drawing lines between the boxes as though an interaction between the symptoms would somehow construct the solution.

The actual genius of the problem remained unclear since they were only addressing side-effects. The questions repeated over and over through the room as the diagram was forming, "What sort of database...", "Would a NoSQL database work for...", "How many data points would..." A cacophony of questions and popular products rang out while the boxes and lines marched across the whiteboard.

They were making the problem sound so complex and inscrutable that I was losing confidence in our well-proved design. Could it be that our solution hasn't actually been working all this time? Do these people understand some scholarly higher-level problem that I simply don't grasp? Was I just a dunce with no real understanding of engineering method? While I couldn't fathom what they were doing, the process, as they conducted it, seemed so natural, so routine. They approached this cryptic process as if it were child's play – calling out problems and drawing boxes and lines. Was I confused about what engineering was?

It was clear that the director in charge was familiar with the trivial routine that is engineering; she had done this before. She knew that the final diagram would convey a solution with the simplicity of an algebraic equation. It was the claim that a wino pulled out of a Newark alleyway could be taught this procedure and do engineering. As I started to see boxes and words on the board that revealed actual serious misunderstanding of the problem, I began to regain some confidence. I turned to our manager and asked if he had brought the Solaris notebook computer.

1: Scope

He had.

After lunch, our manager opened his Solaris notebook before the assembled crowd. He said that he was going to use the Sun patch architecture to update his Solaris notebook computer. He selected the icon and said, "It's downloading the analysis software. It's performing the analysis." The big screen showed the progress bar advancing steadily. "It's downloading the patches. It's installing all patches that don't require reboot and setting aside the other patches for the next reboot operation." He looked around the room and concluded, "Now it's done. The Solaris system is up-to-date."

He closed the notebook and returned to his seat.

After a moment of silence, the attention simply returned to the whiteboard. "How would we gather the kind of data necessary to...", "The UX should be all drag-and-drop...", "We'd need a whole lab and new..."

The manager and I exchanged a puzzled stare. We sat in silence through the rest of the discussion, unable to grasp what had just happened. I knew that my stated opinion would have had no effect, but I couldn't imagine that an actual live demonstration would fail to draw this pointless exercise to a close. I remain puzzled but I have a hypothesis. I believe that the participants in that exercise did not object to our solution, they objected to our method and this was merely a demonstration that our engineering method was flawed and that their procedural method could produce equivalent or better results.

After the zero-impact demonstration, I was utterly demoralized. I sat quietly through a second day of discussion and whiteboarding. At no point did anyone bring up any of the actual intractable problems that would need to be tackled to provide what they were intending to provide – the intractable problems my team had already resolved in such a simple and effective way. About an hour before the meeting adjourned, I finally, reluctantly, raised my hand and asked the director in charge, "How do you analyze the state of the target host and generate the correct request for updates?"

She turned to me and fixed her gaze. Her voice was confident. It was the confidence of a parent explaining a coffee grinder to a five year old: "WSDL."

———— • ————

This approach is fundamental to the degradation of software engineering. If this is actually how software is developed, then I agree with Ben Christensen[3] who demands that the word "engineer" no longer be associated with what software people do. What I saw in this supposedly technical meeting was a group of supposedly technical people exposing their firm belief that solving an engineering problem is a simple step-by-step procedure. It involves a mapping between observed bad behavior and basic frameworks that can be simply plugged together to yield a solution.

That meeting in Santa Clara resulted in employment for nearly one hundred technical people. They set up a lab and quite literally installed our patch automation software behind layers of support servers. To use the service, one simply needed to penetrate a layer of glitz to finally expose the service that my team had assembled long ago and had maintained until the director's team took it over. The lab, chock-full of servers using their uncommonly talented WSDL, comprised nothing more than a thin façade between the user and the patch automation solution the director had so vehemently derided.

This project wasted millions of dollars at a time when Sun could ill afford it. After about a year of operation, the lab was shut down and most of the director's team was laid off. The director moved on to another company and the panic over Sun software updates dissipated like a vapor.

Why would a company waste this kind of money? Why has this behavior, an aberration at Sun, become the industry norm? Since the job of a company is to make money, the answer must be that this is more profitable than the alternative. If the alternative – developing new and

---

3   See http://benjchristensen.com/2009/08/11/software-development-is-not-engineering/. I saw this essay on a Huffington Post site.

1: Scope

useful products to satisfy real needs – is no longer the preferred mode in the software industry, what has changed, why and when did that happen?

———•———

Pearls and ideas often begin with an irritant and my irritant was the rigid procedural world that arose outside the confines of Sun Microsystems' intellectual bunker during the early 2000s – a world constructed with my own witless participation. I mean *witless* in its most degrading sense. Many other engineers at Sun understood precisely what was happening on the outside. There was a clear plan that I simply could not fathom. After being laid off, in 2006, I had to confront this belief system directly. I moved from a chaotic and godless world of challenge and invention to a highly structured world involving the ritual assembly of components within standard frameworks. This book will seek to understand that state of affairs.

This unexpected shift from what seemed glorious to what seems mundane compels me to undertake an analysis of the phenomenon. I seek, in this book, to assess the software industry as I have seen it and try to either explain and accept this bold new understanding of the nature of engineering or define a mechanism whereby the engineering with which I was once familiar may become possible again.

This tome will seek to explore how the software industry has changed over my lifetime from a competition-driven scramble for the next profitable solution to a community of lethargic watchers monitoring competitors for the next big idea only to find that the competitors themselves are simply watching back with the same hopes.

In order to understand this transformation, we will need to examine the mechanisms which sustain it. Business chooses the predictable over the unknown, prompting a natural tendency to limit inspiration using the step-by-step procedure. We will need to review with care the structure and motivations behind the modern business and its cowering aversion to the risk of invention; but, this is not a business text. While the way we do business plays a role, the underlying software methodologies are inextricably entwined with the elements of the structure. For this reason, we will need to explore the modern development process and assess its role in facilitating modern corporate goals; but, this is not a book about methodology. While methodology is key, the language influences the methodology and the attitudes that entrench the belief system. Thus we will examine languages, the frameworks that support such languages and the beliefs and prejudices that are required to best apply such languages. Nevertheless, this is not a language manual. Although the language drives the attitudes, there is an overarching culture that influences the business that designates the method that selects the language which demands the support structure defining the underlying belief system.

This book is about that entire process.

As with any engineering problem, there are a number of threads that must be pulled together if a solution is to present itself. What we perceive, when we find ourselves frustrated by the monotonous press of ordinary deliverables, are side-effects. Each one seems to be the cause of the pain, but behind each is a deeper cause and unless that cause is understood, *its* cause will not become clear and the eventual root cause will never be brought to book.

There will be a certain amount of exploration since that is fundamental to engineering methodology. The engineer is an explorer: a scientist and a mathematician and a dabbler and a child at play. I invite you to explore with me as we assess an industry practice and either refine our respect for it or isolate its cause and propose a solution.

———•———

In the modern world of software, problems tend to be solved with prefabricated frameworks. New developers are trained to identify the framework as soon as the problem is described. Do you need to break an operation into multiple threads acting cooperatively to accomplish a task quickly? Use Akka. Do you need to configure a number of Java objects? Use Spring Inversion of Control (IoC). Are you unable to fully test your software until it's finally in production? Use Bamboo and Chef to

1: Scope

implement continuous delivery (CD). Since every employer has a penchant for the simple predictable process, they're all looking for people with these frameworks on their resumés. Since knowledge of these frameworks distinguishes between the successful software engineer and the unemployed iconoclast, every employee will sing the praises of these modern prepackaged solutions. That means your company is going to be using plenty of frameworks whether it needs them or not because these are the tools with which the skilled developer will acquire his next job.

This notion that there is a simple mapping from any problem to a specific existing solution has inspired the Agile process of *Scrum* which not only exemplifies but promotes the current belief that engineering is a simple procedure. In Scrum, every problem is presumed to be easily corrected in a predictable fashion. The typical time allocated for solving such a problem is two weeks, at the end of which your solution must be demonstrated to the waiting customer.

As a general rule, a big problem to which no one can imagine a solution is relegated to the hall-of-shame called the *epic*. "Epic" is the term Scrum folks use for a problem that cannot be solved in two weeks (a problem that is not a simple mapping). It is typically set aside to be broken into stories and addressed later. Often, though, Scrum teams are conditioned to simply avoid epics until they ripen, rot and can be finally composted as *will not fix*.

To be fair, how do you plan an unknowable into a rigid time-critical procedure? I've seen such problems manifested, investigated for two weeks, renewed for two more weeks and finally dropped because, honestly, if you can't predict your completion date, you can't show progress. You can't demonstrate a great idea, you can only demonstrate completed software.

———•———

If your job is just to code up what the customer wants, it really does look simple. Customers tend to ask for what they believe you can provide; and, most of your customers already have a preconceived notion of what that is. The customer learns to settle for what is possible based on past experience with your team – you cannot grow, the customer cannot grow. So what is the role of the visionary? How many customers turned to the lead engineer at Sony and told him that they wanted a way to listen to their music while they were jogging? How many customers went to Preston Tucker and told him that they needed the automobile's headlights to track their steering wheel? How many customers were telling Steve Jobs that their telephone wasn't running enough computer programs?

Yes, you can pull in skilled and disciplined engineers and direct them to do what the customer tells them; but, is that what advances the technology? Does that provide what the customer actually *needs*? Is that a process that adds real value to our world; or does it waste the glorious vitality of the human spirit by treating the manifold wonders of human potential as a mundane set of interchangeable tools?

This is the issue to be assessed. This is the scope of our enterprise.

2: Definitions

I like good strong words that mean something...
Louisa May Alcott

The most important part of a technical document is the definitions. Most technical disputes begin with the misunderstanding of a word. A technical explanation will invariably include numerous words that look commonplace; but, due to the nature of technical description, have very specific meanings.

Consider this example. In an informal conversation, a manager might tell an engineer responsible for curating information in a data store to "maintain a version for each record." Strictly speaking, the manager has instructed the engineer to assign to each record, every time it is created or changed, a dot-delimited ordered array of zero-based revisions (e.g., *4.0.8*) identifying its compatibility with previous embodiments of that record. For example, the version 3.9 identifies the third major revision of the record. The second number (the 9) indicates that this third revision has been augmented nine times in some way. In each case, the augmentation simply added entries such as a new address line or a mobile phone number, it didn't change any of the existing attributes of each entry. Version 3.9 of the record includes all of the entries that were present in version 3.0. Those entries retain exactly the same format used in that version. It is *backward compatible* with all prior records having a major revision of 3.

If any of those modifications were to change the record in a manner that modified any of the existing entries, the version would *roll* to 4.0. This would indicate that the record could no longer be considered compatible with software intended to interpret the format of major revision 3. For instance any product expecting to use a record of version 3.4 will be able to process a record of version 3.10 successfully, but it will not be able to use its new data. Software designed to read version 1.8 of the record may or may not be able to process version 3.9 successfully. The producer of the record will not guarantee that it will work. That is what a *version* is and how it is interpreted.

In all likelihood, what the manager *actually* wanted was for the record to be assigned a simple *revision*: an integer or alphabetic character indicating how many times the record has been changed. He should have insisted that the engineer "maintain a *revision* for each record." A revision indicates nothing regarding the backward compatibility of the record and is generally represented as an integer that is incremented by one each time the record is changed. It indicates only how many times the record has been modified and distinguishes between those modifications.

In the same way, in casual conversation, one may be forgiven for using the terms *senseless* and *nonsensical* interchangeably; but, in a technical philosophical discussion, these words mean completely different things. Something is nonsensical when it is not grounded in reality. Something that is senseless carries no intellectual content. Casual conversation does not demand the same kind of discipline as technical communication. Thus, in common parlance, we may say "Every dog has his day," as opposed to "For every dog there exists at least one day such that the day was had by a unique dog."

In a technical context, the use of the wrong word may drive the production of the wrong part or, if sufficiently vague, may leave the listener to fill in the meaning based upon his experience. This can be particularly problematic when people of differing native tongues are involved. Both communicators may be well-meaning and competent but the

2: Definitions

common vernacular is simply not designed with the discipline required to convey technical content.

———•———

It has been argued that common language may be modified in order to improve its ability to convey meaning. Some philosophers, such as Gottlob Frege, in *On Sense and Reference*, took this problem very seriously and strove to produce a language that could be used to convey with absolute precision the facts of the world. These endeavors often take the form of attempts to unify philosophy and science and are commonly manifested as the explication of a more formal language. Frege was followed by Bertrand Russell who attempted, in *Principia Mathematica*, to use the precise language of logic to explain mathematics. Other great thinkers such as David Bohm[4], in *Wholeness and the Implicate Order*[Bohm_1980], Rudolf Carnap, Willard Van Orman Quine and Nelson Goodman have also sought to discipline the English language so that it could essentially say what it means. Surely, there have been innovative thinkers who have sought to discipline other conversational languages as well; but, to this day, none have succeeded.

For this reason, we are burdened (regardless our native tongue) with a language which does not provide an inherent explication of precise meaning. Our language has arisen in the service of casual conversation. It serves us well when we seek to express our love for our partner or when we seek to explain the error in a coworker's proposal or when we are explaining the need for tolerance and understanding between siblings...

No wait...

It doesn't really work for any of that either. Let's face it, language *evolved*. It was *crowd-sourced*. It was not designed to provide any specific thing, it just *is*. It's all we have to work with and we have to take special

---

[4] David Bohm wrote one of the first textbooks on quantum physics, *Quantum Theory*. A brilliant physicist, he worked closely with Neils Bohr, but sought to find an alternative to the Copenhagen Interpretation, finding it difficult to reconcile it with his personal experience of reality. His book *Wholeness and the Implicate Order* (1980) expresses his view of reality as an interconnected whole.

steps to assure that it can accomplish the task to which it must be applied.

For technical interchange, we strive to use language that we have formalized and restricted in order to assure an improved understanding between participants. We remind the reader at the beginning of the document that *shall* represents an obligation and that *will* represents a preferred option. Since words mean different things in different contexts, we provide definitions, not just to provide the reader with a convenient dictionary, but to remind the writer that he has bolted himself to a particular usage as regards particular words within his document.

Therefore, I bolt myself, as I have done many times before, to specific meanings for specific words within this document. The reader is invited to find all of the cases wherein I violate my own definitions and I will humbly acknowledge the homage I owe for my correction.

In the world of engineering, we must present ourselves for criticism on a regular basis. This is because one person reviewing one problem long enough to resolve it will, in every case, become blind to the obvious as the intricate nuances grow to fill the entire field of view.

A Zen master is recounted to have said, "The sage delights in correction." Although it is difficult, if we seek to do good for the world, we must submit ourselves for correction and if we respond in any way other than delight, we will either live in misery or we will rest comfortably in the ignoble mundane.

Here, therefore, I present the definitions of the key words used in this text.

———•———

accessor		(n) a method returning the value of an attribute of its associated object (e.g., getCount() may return the value of an internal counter)

2: Definitions

agile
: 1. (adj) emphasizing efficiency and minimization of waste 2. (n) a popular software development process conforming to the Agile Manifesto (chapter 5) emphasizing rapid turnaround and early software delivery

ARC
: see Architecture Review Committee

Architecture Review Committee
: (n) a committee of curmudgeons at Sun Microsystems responsible for reviewing all changes to public interfaces

assembly language
: (n) a tool which provides a simpler way than machine code to directly program a particular CPU such that each instruction corresponds directly to the binary instructions understood by the CPU

backward compatible
: (adj) the property of a particular change indicating that it has not rendered its associated interface unusable by existing clients

bare metal
: (n) a euphemism meant to refer to the underlying electronic computing platform prior to the installation of an operating system

bean
: 1. (n) according to the JavaBean specification, any Java object that is serializable, has a default zero-argument constructor, and exposes internal state using accessors and mutators 2. (n) in common parlance, and most commonly applicable in this book, a Java object having state but no behaviors so as to distinguish it from a *machine*

behavior	(n) the rules identifying how a provider may respond to a request (e.g., Given a valid make and model, the corresponding Automobile shall be returned. If the make or model are invalid, an InvalidArgumentException shall be raised. If the make and model are valid but do not correspond to an existing Automobile a NoSuchAutomobileException shall be raised.)
binary	(adj) the property of a number, code or instruction indicating that it is represented in base 2, made up of only ones and zeros (e.g., binary 9 = 1001)
C	(n) an imperative procedural programming language providing an intentionally intimate connection to the underlying computer hardware making it a reasonable next step beyond assembly language
C++	(n) an imperative Object-Oriented programming language extended from and sharing some key semantics with C
central processing unit	
	(n) an electronic circuit, typically an integrated circuit, within a computer which carries out machine code instructions
Change Review Team	
	(n) a loosely associated group of senior engineers at Sun Microsystems responsible for a final review of each software change prior to integration into Solaris
channel	(n) a formal mechanism used to transfer data between a data source and a data consumer
class	(n) an object defining a type from which objects of the given type may be instantiated

2: Definitions

client
: (n) a program that initiates requests for data from a provider using an agreed upon interface

close reading
: (n) the careful, sustained interpretation of a brief passage of a text emphasizing the single and the particular over the general

company
: (n) an organization registered formally with a state entity to do business within that state (e.g., a corporation or LLC)

competence
: (n) the ability to recognize deficiencies in ones own abilities and address them constructively

context-free grammar
: (n) a grammar which may be fully specified as a set of substitution rules from the set of all possible valid terms to a progressively more refined result set comprising, typically, an actionable procedure

CPU
: see central processing unit

creeping elegance
: (n) that process wherein an engineering team may incrementally add new capabilities to an ongoing project expanding its scope and losing track of the original goals

CRT
: see Change Review Team

curmudgeon
: (n) an individual who would write a book like this

DAO
: see Data Access Object

Data Access Object
: (n) an object responsible for transferring data between a conventional object and a remote data source such as a database or a device

Data Definition Language
: (n) that portion of the SQL repertoire which controls the structure of tables such as CREATE, ALTAR and DROP

Data Manipulation Language
: (n) that portion of the SQL repertoire which adds, modifies and removes data in relation to tables such as INSERT, UPDATE and DELETE

Data Transfer Object
: (n) an object designed to serve as a minimized payload describing (typically) only the changed components of a larger object for the purpose of efficient transport over a bandwidth-limited channel

DDL
: 1. see Data Definition Language 2. (n) used to designate a file containing SQL conforming to the Data Definition Language (e.g., "That DDL describes our schema.")

declarative methodology
: (n) one of two generally accepted categories of software development methodologies (see imperative methodology) which emphasizes the definition of the logic of a program as opposed to step by step procedures following from a common starting point

diamond problem
: (n) a problem encountered in OOM when a child object having two parents each with an identical method signature introduces an ambiguity into the child when invoking that method in that it has no way of knowing which of the parents is supplying the method being invoked

2: Definitions

distant reading
: (n) a technique for analyzing text that avoids interpreting particular phrases in favor of the rigorous aggregation of information from the larger corpus

DML
: 1. see Data Manipulation Language 2. (n) used to designate a file containing SQL conforming to the Data Manipulation Language (e.g., "Populate the tables using this DML.")

DTO
: see Data Transfer Object

Eiffel
: (n) an object-oriented computer programming language which supports and promotes a number of widely accepted software engineering principles

emotional intelligence
: (n) the capacity to recognize and respond constructively to the emotional state of ones self and others

engineering solution
: (n) any mechanism which resolves a problem by effectively addressing its root cause

form
: (n) a conceptual model of a precisely delineated state of affairs representing the current state as well as past and likely future states

formal argument
: (n) a parameter provided to a method in order to control its behavior

formal method
: (n) a set of procedures and policies intended to support the prosecution of a technical project including design, development and progress monitoring

fragile base class problem
> (n) a problem encountered in OOM wherein a poorly devised parent class imparts its own inadequacies to its children

functional methodology
> (n) a declarative software development methodology which seeks to resolve problems by modeling the solution as data sets which may be mapped through functions to other data sets while minimizing side-effects

generative grammar
> (n) a grammar the rules of which support the generation of valid sentences which carry meaning despite being difficult to anticipate from the basic grammatical rules and which might be fully specified only within the context of the interaction between a mytho-poetic culture and a universal grammar defined by human brain structures

grammar
: (n) a set of rules governing the composition of lexical tokens into structures that convey information or instructions

halfpager
: (n) a detailed explanation of a perceived problem

hermeneutics
: (n) a theory of text interpretation, later broadened to questions of general interpretation, emphasizing an innocent approach to the body of work which minimizes bias and improves fidelity to the original intent

imperative methodology
> (n) one of two generally accepted categories of software development methodologies (see declarative methodology) which emphasizes step by step procedures beginning from an initial state

2: Definitions

interface
: (n) a mechanism for gaining access to the capabilities of a software program through a well-defined signature and behaviors

IoC
: See Inversion of Control

Inversion of Control
: (n) a software technique wherein the dependencies of an object are provided through automation in response to a specification identifying those dependencies

Java
: (n) a general purpose computer programming language made popular by Sun Microsystems and used primarily to build web-based services

life cycle
: (n) a term used in software to describe the arc of a project having a beginning middle and end, each with distinct characteristics (e.g., early in the life cycle is the proposal, late is maintenance-only then discontinuance)

machine
: (n) in common parlance, any Java object having behaviors but no state so as to distinguish it from a *bean* (def 2)

machine code
: (n) the most primitive sort of computer program wherein each binary number or group of numbers translates directly into an operation within the CPU

maintenance mode
: (n) that portion of a project life cycle wherein it has been delivered, is providing the intended capabilities and requires no more innovative modifications

management
: (n) those individuals involved in supervision of productive workers without themselves directly producing value

method	1. (n) a body of disciplined techniques intended to accomplish a specific purpose 2. (n) in OOM that component of an object providing control over or access to its internal operations (e.g., start() may be a method which causes an object to begin some operation)
mixin	(n) an object with specific behaviors intended for use by another object without requiring that the other object inherit it
mock	(n) a software component designed to provide an emulation of a declared interface usually for the purpose of testing.
mutator	(n) a method which modifies the value of an internal attribute of its associated object (e.g., setCount(6) may initialize a counter in an object to 6)
object	(n) the realization of a type
Object-Oriented Methodology	(n) an imperative software development methodology wherein the problem is resolved by considering what thing will take on what task in cooperation with other things as opposed to what actions must be performed
onepager	(n) a halfpager to which a solution has been appended
OOM	see Object-Oriented Methodology
Operating System	(n) software that mediates between user application software and the underlying bare metal usually providing general purpose software resources
organization	(n) an identifiable assembly of people working together in pursuit of a common goal (e.g., building housing for low-income occupants or making money)
OS	see operating system

2: Definitions

panopticon — (n) a type of building so constructed as to assure good behavior on the part of all occupants by making it impossible for any to know when they are or are not being observed thereby defaulting to the assumption that they are under constant observation

persistent store
 — (n) a repository having a well-defined interface allowing insertion and extraction of data guaranteed to be retained in relative perpetuity (e.g., a relational database)

problem space (n) that state of affairs in which the problem is manifested

problem statement
 — (n) an attempt to define a problem unambiguously with minimum reference to any potential solutions

procedural methodology
 — (n) an imperative software development methodology wherein the problem is resolved by constructing procedures which manipulate data structures

procedure — 1. (n) a step-by-step process which, if observed faithfully, will yield a well-defined result 2. (n) an access point within a program which invokes an action or change of state

provider — (n) a program which responds to requests using a well-defined interface

Python — (n) a computer programming language supporting multiple styles, primarily object-oriented but also lending itself to more nearly functional methodology

red flag review
 — (n) a process for resolving problems before they happen by anticipating likely problems and establishing resolutions before-hand

root cause	(n) the practical first mover for an observed problem, not the origin of existence itself, which would not be practical; but the problem's origin such that to find *its* origin would provide no value in correcting the class of problems as defined
realization	1. (v) the process of constructing an instance of a type 2. (n) an instance of a form
requirements	(n) a document representing an expression of what the world would be like if the problem were resolved, often including elements of the problem and a proposed solution
REST	(n) a network architectural style proposed by Roy Fielding which strives to fully exploit the stateless underpinnings of the HTTP protocol
revision	(n) an indicator (usually an integer) representing how many times an entity has been modified (e.g., revision 7 was created and then revised six times, each revision being assigned the next integer in sequence)
SDF	See Software Development Framework
server	1. (n) a network-facing provider responding to client requests with one or more services 2. (n) a physical computer designed to support the processes identified in definition #1
service	(n) any well-defined interface into a server providing data, registries or other value in response to a well-defined request, often using an HTTP protocol
side-effect:	(n) any behavior visible outside of an invoked method, function or procedure which is not that operation's return value such as a change in program state, the initiation of a print job or the delivery of an XML message to a remote client

2: Definitions

signature
: (n) a simple communication pattern identifying the data to be provided to and returned from a program (e.g., Automobile getAutomobile(String make, String model))

skill
: (n) the ability to provide value through some well-practiced application of knowledge within a given field of endeavor

SOAP
: (n) a messaging protocol built upon the HTTP protocol which seeks to essentially defeat the capabilities provided by HTTP in favor of a stilted back and forth of data using only a subset of HTTP message types

Software Development Framework
: (n) the collection of published guidelines used at Sun Microsystems in the 1990s and early 2000s for development of their software

software stack
: (n) the complete assembly of software comprising a product from the software accessing the raw data in the persistent store to the user or service interface.

solution space
: (n) the state of affairs in which the problem is not manifested because it has been resolved

specification
: (n) a solution-space document defining the surface features of the mechanism which resolves the problem

Standard Query Language
: (n) a declarative language used to design, configure, store data in and retrieve data from a relational database

state
: (n) potentially transient information describing a thing (e.g., the length of a list or the current floor of an elevator)

state of affairs
: (n) the way things actually are, regardless how they may appear to the observer

SQL
: see Standard Query Language

technical solution
(n) any mechanism which resolves a problem directly without consideration of the problem's origins or root cause

type
(n) a form defining the generic embodiment of an object

version
(n) a string of dot-separated numeric revisions of the form major.minor[.micro[.nano]] (e.g., 4.3.2.1) which are associated with an entity and which are used to indicate the compatibility of that entity with identically named entities having potentially different versions

Web Services Description Language
(n) an XML notational convention used to describe the interfaces offered by a server on the World Wide Web

workstation
(n) a computer configured to support technical work by a single specialist such as a circuit board designer or a software developer

WSDL
see Web Services Description Language

3: A Prestigious Failure

A thinker sees his own actions as experiments and questions – as attempts to find out something. Success and failure are for him answers above all.
                    Friedrich Nietzsche

The most prolific and rewarding portion of my career was the thirteen years I spent at a magnificent and prestigious failure. Sun Microsystems was a steady profitable company, growing quickly but cautiously and emphasizing innovation from 1982, its first year, until the dot-com bubble in the late 1990s. It developed technologies that have become fundamental to the functioning of modern computers and developed the building blocks for numerous network-related tools and protocols. Its emphasis on the notion that a computer was actually a cooperative collection of network-connected devices, established a philosophical foundation from which engineers in many venues could conceive of the modern mobile computing platform.

In the 1980s and '90s, when software architectures were less forgiving, Solaris was recognized as one of the most reliable operating systems in the world. The Solaris computer was turned on and could be forgotten, functioning with minimal maintenance for years. Patches were highly recommended; but within Sun, we often avoided installing patches which tended to only fix fairly minor problems. The up-time worst case scenario for a Solaris-based server was at a company that consistently applied all recommended patches every quarter. Such a system would be routinely rebooted four times per year.

Famine In the Bullpen

In my small quiet office with my Sun workstation on my desk, everything just seemed to work. It was a company teeming with expertise. The best engineers in the industry were a phone call away. From the inventors of public key cryptography, to the engineers who participated in the invention of Network File System (NFS) and key protocols still used in modern networking, when I had questions, I always received a polite and useful response – that was the culture. For my part, I took on problems in software distribution, expert systems and small versatile databases. I headed a team that built one of the first application servers; and enjoyed the camaraderie of people whose lives were wrapped up in the joy of addressing problems.

The tone of the company was whipped forward by its CEO, Scott McNealy, who spoke optimistically, deliberately and sometimes recklessly, defining, without nuance, our purpose and goals. He was brought into the founding by Andy Bechtolsheim and Vinod Khosla. They brought the technical expertise and McNealy brought the business skills. They had a vision of a computer that would serve the technical marketplace better than any other and, with the release of their first workstation, the rest of the industry was in catch-up mode.

I was hired in 1993 and shortly thereafter was flown to California for Sun's annual meeting. I was sitting in a large open-air amphitheater with my new colleagues. There was quiet conversation as we waited for the presentations to start. I remember hearing a loud growling to my left. I turned to see someone on a dirt bike driving down the concrete stairs. I watched as he chunkity chunked down to the aisle in front of the stage. I realized that I was hearing someone muttering loudly over the public address system as I watched the rider start up the center aisle, just barely controlling the motorcycle as he went. I heard, over the speakers, the palpitating UkuhUkuhUkuh of a body being jarred repeatedly as it took each unforgiving step. On the rear aisle, he drove to the rightmost stairway and started down, building up speed.

At the bottom, he moved directly to the stage stairs and climbed them confidently. Driving to the center of the stage and planting his foot on the floor, the rider dismounted. The motorcycle continued and

3: A Prestigious Failure

left its passenger behind as it sped off stage. The biker removed his helmet to reveal it was Scott McNealy. The crowd roared. This was the outrageous visionary driving our company and *we could not fail.*

There, in those uncomfortable rows of bench seats, were some of the brightest minds in the industry. I would spend thirteen years learning from them and I was elated at the prospect. McNealy's goal that year was to make the network easier and easier to access until we were able to make the newly forming Internet a basic part of every life. In a world without wikipedia.org or dictionary.com or netflix.com, we were preparing the way for those advances: a world where the network and the computer would be synonymous; where mobile computing would be a disciplined extension of the protocols we were already exploiting routinely. We would lead the way to a world where information was free and easily accessible; where communication would not be limited to those approved by a publishing house or media conglomerate; and where voice, video and data negotiated the same unobstructed highway as free citizens of the ether.

A rational person would naturally ask, at this point, "If Sun was so great, why did it go out of business?" That is a good question to which I hope to provide a clear, although necessarily summary, answer. Sun failed with a stable of brilliant engineers and wall-after-two-story-wall covered with U.S. patents. Its technical process, the Software Development Framework (SDF), was sound and promoted innovation from all employees. It was an environment wherein anyone could participate in the constructive activity of exposing a problem and proposing its solution. Solutions that seemed useful were sucked into the selective maw of the SDF where it would be reviewed and assigned to an engineering team for implementation, said implementation being reviewed at multiple phases and finally released into the wild.

There had been some problems with teams releasing software that was not entirely compatible with Solaris. Since the base operating system was the center of everything Sun did, this required correction; and, under the supervision of Sun's Chief Engineer, Rob Gingell, the SDF was born. The software at Sun was written to the standards set by the SDF, but also to the standards of the underlying culture which had been built up over ten years prior to my arrival.

In order to assure that all interfaces were compatible with Solaris, the SDF established the Architecture Review Committee (ARC), a group of six to twelve curmudgeonly engineers who would review each project to assure that its interfaces and behaviors were consistent with Solaris and Sun principles. As a result, every engineer became painfully aware of what interfaces they were changing, knowing full well that the ARC would be assuring consistency and demanding a reason for each change.

The Sun engineer spent plenty of time addressing bugs and basic improvements, but there was always that legitimate hope that the recently proposed project would be approved. With that, the tedium would abate while the engineer embarked on the development of a radically new approach to interval arithmetic, an improved update architecture, a new language that would revolutionize the software industry or whatever revelation that engineer had folded into the submitted functional spec. The tedium was always easier when a project was in the works.

The business side of the company may want a new product; but, the engineering side of the company (through the ARC) assured that the product was technically sound. Early on in my tenure, a conflict between the two was rarely won by the business side. They could have their product but it would be secure and sound. If that made it less convenient, that was not the ARC's problem. "Let Microsoft sell the pretty crap."

This continually running line of disciplined, architecturally sound and not-necessarily-pretty solutions (both hardware and software) rolled smoothly from the Sun production line yielding a steady stream of revenue. Universities, manufacturers and financial institutions counted on Sun innovation. Thanks to *cache-only-client*, a hardware failure at a trading desk could be remedied in a minute or two by simply replacing that computer with a blank one which would pick up where the broken one left off. The Sun *thin client* architecture made that swap

3: A Prestigious Failure

even faster. With NFS, a widely used program could be installed only once and shared in common by hundreds of users. Network Information System (NIS) allowed for a shared database of configuration values supporting rapid deployment of new desktop systems.

The Sun operating systems, SunOS and later Solaris (acquired from AT&T), combined with the ever-evolving Sun hardware resulting in Sun systems dominating the early Internet. Sun servers were famed for reliability and fault tolerance. The operating system policed the running programs looking for evidence of a stray and killing processes that misbehaved before they could interfere with the rest of the system.

This continued until the late 1990s when these innovative capabilities provided by Sun, IBM, HP and others revealed a new world of possibilities. In a rush to capitalize on this, entrepreneurs began to find funding and select servers to provide their new Internet content. They bought servers from IBM, HP and DEC, but mostly they bought them from Sun.

———•———

My colleagues recounted a speech they had heard from McNealy just prior to my hire in 1993. They recalled it as *The Parade of Bozos Speech*. In it McNealy entreated all hiring managers to avoid new college graduates. He reminded them that this was Sun and we would only hire experienced engineers. "Let IBM and HP hire the new kids," they recalled McNealy saying, "After they've trained them up on the basics, we'll hire them away and teach them how it's done."

This was the reason for the day-long interview sessions and the heated discussions around each interviewee to establish whether that engineer could advance our goals. It was the reason behind the Change Review Team (CRT), a member of which would review each software update prior to allowing it to be incorporated into Solaris. It was the reason for the ARC, for the focus on simple yet explicit documentation and the emphasis on solving problems as opposed to cranking out code.

I joined the company during a crucial pivot. In the 1980s, it had been selling servers and workstations to universities and technology-based corporations. The computer components were typically received by student volunteers or excited young enthusiasts in the IT department. Those folks would generally order pizzas and spend a nerd-fest night assembling and testing the computer. Unbeknownst to those customers, the computers had already been fully tested at Sun. For this to happen they had to be fully assembled at Sun; but Sun knew its customers. Knowing about the pizza parties, Sun would carefully disassemble the tested systems and ship them in pieces. In the beginning, the nerds at Sun had an intimate and innate understanding of the nerds to whom they were shipping their goods.

As the '80s began the transition to the '90s, Sun marketing had begun selling servers to new customers in the securities industry. Many of Sun's innovations, such as cache-only client and thin client were directed at this industry for which a minute of down time translated directly into tens of thousands of lost dollars. The sophisticated higher ups in the securities industry talked, at high-dollar soirées, with higher ups in the auto and chemical industries about their Sun equipment. Soon Sun was selling their equipment to people they didn't understand at all. Nobody wanted to have a pizza party. They wanted the server to arrive, be installed and just work. Sun was pivoting laboriously to accommodate these new demanding and unfamiliar technical integrators. The engineers at Sun were struggling to understand the requirements and the sales department was learning the new language of traditional business.

———— • ————

During one of the rough patches in this transition, I met with my manager, Barry Fish. We were originally talking about the next challenge for our team when one of the new financial client projects entered the conversation. I was concerned that it was unlikely to succeed. I told Barry that the project had an "engineering problem."

Barry's eyes were downcast and he had a half-smile creeping onto his thin angular face. "It's a management problem," he muttered.

3:   A Prestigious Failure

"No," I corrected. "The engineers on the team are talking about handling everything on the back end. That's their focus. The project requires much more UI experience."

Remaining still and bemused, Barry quietly repeated, "It's a management problem."

Confidently, I countered, "The engineers on the team are going to focus on the back-end because that's all they know. Without a really competent vision for the user's place in the product, it's doomed."

This time, the angular form looked directly at me and said, calmly but firmly, "It's a management problem."

Now I was puzzled. "What do you mean?"

He paused for effect and stated clearly, "It's *always* a management problem."

"But, the engineering team is wrong."

"A good manager would have selected the right team. It's always a management problem."

This wasn't the first revelation I'd had from Barry Fish. He was in the skilled cadre of middle managers who struggled to make the best of Sun's corporate direction: a direction governed by the puzzled pilots on the board of directors. The middle managers couldn't correct the problem, so they resigned themselves to smoothing the path to wherever we were going. Was Barry correct? Given good enough engineering resources, could poor enough management thwart success?

——— • ———

With the dot-com boom, Sun's previously rapid growth began to conform to the definition of *meteoric*. The demand for new servers brought more customers with more demands for more special features. In response, leadership steered the company smartly into the swelling tide and began buying up competitors and requisitioning new developers. The ARCs were beginning to lose arguments with the business side. The ban on new college graduates was forgotten and interviews, of necessity, were shortened to about an hour. We needed people coding up new features as quickly as possible and that meant not worrying too much about Sun's noble soul. Sun was shipping lots of stuff to lots of customers and that was all that mattered.

When the bubble burst, expensive Sun servers were dropped onto the resale market at a fraction of their original price. The Sun server was designed to run for years and sixty percent of the market Sun had grown rapidly to serve was now gone. Nonetheless, the computers they had shipped were still functional. The used computer market was now competing directly with Sun itself, offering perfectly fine, nearly-new Sun computers. Sun management was now struggling to address the repercussions of their headlong flight into the delusion of constant growth.

Sun had never had a layoff. This tradition was hard to push past, but a massive layoff was Sun's only hope. Instead, management came up with strange new visions for the company in the hopes that the bloated employee roster could be serviced. Strategies were giving way to desperate tactics as Sun tried a religious dedication to open-source, a foray into mass storage and a new fascination with tape drive robotics. It all seemed pretty pointless to the rank and file within the company. Respect for the charismatic leader began to flag and Jonathan Schwartz was installed as the new visionary, leading to a sudden flood of cynicism that assured significantly reduced enthusiasm and productivity.

It could be argued that Sun would have been insane to refuse new sales during the boom. Why, in 1999 Charles Kadlec, chief investment strategist for Seligman Advisors, wrote *Dow 100,000*[Kadlec_1999] wherein he suggested that everything was pretty good and was likely to just keep going up. Even so, such a sudden change in the environment should have probably suggested restraint, a restraint with which Sun leadership had recently become estranged.

During the crisis, upper management announced that Sun would stop advertising...

...

3:   A Prestigious Failure

There should be a bit of a pause here while you let that sink in. The decision was not widely communicated, but within Sun, many of us were informed. Sun leadership decided to *stop advertising*. In concert with that decision, the new director of sales and marketing gave a speech wherein he proudly explained that he was going to do "less with more." I was there, in the room, roughly twenty feet away from him as he was speaking. I saw his body language and his gestures. He was a good speaker and explained in great detail while pulling the threads together into a clearly observable whole. Even with all that, I had no idea how this was supposed to work. It sounded like Sun sales people would be traveling door to corporate door selling the Sun product from a sample case.

Shortly after this decision, I remember a television ad by a major competitor explaining that their computers were capable of predicting imminent failure of a disk drive allowing its replacement before degradation of performance. This was interesting because I had recently come out of a seminar with the Sun engineer who had developed the basic technology, a technology that had been recently divulged in *Scientific American*. He was able to make his algorithms work on Sun systems only because they had accelerometers and temperature sensors planted all over each system. There were enough sensors to be able to triangulate suspicious vibrations and heat sources down to a particular disk or group of disks. Our analysis of the latest hardware from the advertising competitor showed it to be particularly bereft of such sensors. Sun systems were nearly to the point that we could start general trials of a predictive failure product. It was not clear to us how that company, with its existing hardware, could do that.

During that same advertising hiatus, another competitor aired a commercial showing a nearly empty server room, the servers of which had been entirely replaced by a single server from that competitor. This was interesting because Sun had just released their new Niagara CPU, an innovative SPARC® chip that had largely eschewed data registers in favor of bit streams that were processed on the fly leading to a smaller silicon footprint and much greater throughput.

Famine In the Bullpen

A few years earlier, Sun had produced a server that passed all tests in California but failed intermittently at higher altitudes. The error was in the CPU cache and its sensitivity to cosmic rays. We had sold a large number of these servers to a large on-line auction house. After a year of trying to get the Sun systems to work in their far-above-sea-level data warehouse while Sun leadership offered excuses but no solution, the site replaced all of their Sun servers with servers from this competitor. The auction house openly swore off any more interaction with Sun.

A few years later Sun submitted for review a set of Niagara-based systems to that former customer who reluctantly tested them. Their assessment was surprising. Not only could they replace up to five of their current servers with one Niagara-based server; the sixty watts per CPU power dissipation (a roughly fifty percent improvement over competitive systems) would save millions of dollars in power and cooling costs. They replaced their servers with a smaller number of Sun systems despite the earlier offense, because every financial indicator compelled them to do so.

Meanwhile, that other competitor issued a commercial describing exactly the same scenario, but using their equipment. What was the reason for these commercials? While I am certain that both competitors were honestly representing their cutting-edge equipment, the timing may have been influenced by Sun's surprising decision. Could it be that part of their strategy had been to muddy the water for when Sun began advertising again? Doubtless, any attempt by Sun to present those features would now appear to be a pitiful game of catch-up.

So, was Sun top brass a bunch of incompetent showmen who could chart a course only across calm seas or were they brilliant strategists prosecuting a plan so clever that none of us were competent to carry it out? I cannot say. The company puffed up with the bubble and collapsed with it. Other companies, like Amazon and eBay also suffered, but managed to recover. Sun's damage was severe and the remaining Sun leadership was making decisions at each critical point to assure continued

3: A Prestigious Failure

failure. It struggled for nearly ten more years until it was finally acquired by Oracle.

———•———

I don't want to turn the notion that it's always a management problem into a catch-all excuse; but, by the late 1990s it had begun to appear that Sun top management could run the company successfully only as long as technological superiority minimized the effectiveness of the competition. When serious competition arose, it was from Sun itself and the combined forces of competitors whose servers were not overwhelming the resale market.

Since I will be making reference to Sun Microsystems throughout this work, it is important that the reader understand the justification for such comparisons. I have sought to provide evidence that the failure of Sun Microsystems should not impeach the value of its technological approach. I use Sun as an exemplar in many cases because I have never before worked at a company that demanded so much of me and repaid my efforts in so many ways. I was expected to produce value by solving problems, the solutions of which were not obvious; and, the provided technical methodology served that goal flawlessly.

I have not had that experience since.

4: Bound Fast

People, and that includes companies and clubs and anything made up of people, tend to make decisions based upon their belief system. They do this for two reasons:

one: thinking is hard

and two: error is punishable

A belief system may be a simple one provided by parents and a few influential teachers or it could be a messy complicated belief system developed by scraping together various droppings from ministers, disgruntled freemen and motivational speakers.

Once the belief system is established, most decisions are just rote recitations of the canon:

Q: Am I carrying a gun because I'm afraid?

A: Hell no, I'm carrying a gun because I'm exercising my rights under the second amendment.

Q: Is the planet warming at an alarming rate?

A: No, but scientists are getting rich trying to convince me it is.

Q: Is Bernie Sanders the ideal Presidential candidate?

A: Workers of the world unite!

The canon isn't always wrong. It's right often enough that belief systems remain extremely popular with the masses. They provide a quick answer in most circumstances and, since there are others holding the same or very similar beliefs, no one will tell you you're an idiot for believing it. At least not to your face.

4: Bound Fast

In the summer of 2009, I was enduring a phone interview with a representative of a Boulder, Colorado company specializing in Scrum support software. Scrum, a fairly rigid procedure for generating software in a manner most comforting to management, was being adopted by most software companies at the time. After forty-five minutes of answering questions about my background, the interviewer signaled the end using the standard invocation, "Do you have any questions for me?"

Finally I could ask what I'd been biting down on for the last half hour, "Is your company religious or pragmatic?"

There was a moment's pause followed by, "I don't understand."

I decided to ask a different but related question, "What is your company's plan for when Scrum goes out of fashion?"

This time the answer was immediate. "Scrum is the only way to do engineering."

With that, of course, she had answered both questions. The company was religious and it had no fall-back plan.

Like so many interviews, in my experience, it was clear that this would have been another dull job sweeping bytes through the standard corridor into the quirky little ante-room where the front-end coders would form them into the familiar dust bunnies so tolerated by the web customer. There would be no challenging problems, no engineering method, no documentation and no highly skilled teams reveling in victory when they accomplished something no one else could have.

That visceral sense of loss: that tingling, core-numbing disappointment that flows down the trunk of the body like a dousing of ice-cold beer, is a feeling for which I blame Sun Microsystems exclusively.

I have produced products or components in the fields of hydraulics, pneumatics, electronics and software; and while most of my colleagues are quick to note that software is unlike all other engineering disciplines; I have not been persuaded. The argument goes something like this:

> Software has no standard components and is subject to constant flux. It isn't possible to simply design a software product, you have to craft it. It's more like art than engineering. Engineering is predictable and procedural. Not true in software.

I still remember the small brightly lit break room in Colorado Springs, Colorado where this was explained to me by a highly skilled compiler developer. This exchange, taking place in 1994, was initiated after we had both attended a lecture on C++ (pronounced *see plus plus*), an Object Oriented (OO) language with which both of us had a passing acquaintance. One of the ideas presented by the instructor was that OO carried the seeds of a new kind of software development: one that was more akin to, say, electronics, since prefabricated objects could be figuratively pulled from a shelf and plugged into the software schematic.

The compiler developer's explanation struck me even then as fundamentally *religious*. Software people understand that word better than most. It is likely that the reader has been exposed to a technical software discussion where they have heard one engineer say something along the lines of, "The normalized database is rightly dead," to which the colleague at the other end of the table would respond with, "That's a religious statement." This is a correct and proper use of the term.

The word *religion* derives from the Greek word *religare*. The reader will notice two familiar fragments from English words. *Re* which is used to mean *again* or *strongly*; and *lig*, as in the word *ligature*, which refers to rope. It means *to be tied up tight, to be bound fast*. A religious statement is one that admits of no review. A person is religious about a belief from which even reason could not sway him.

In my friend's statement we see messages common to any religious view. For instance, despite having heard a reasonable proposal that software could be done better, he is bound to his long-held belief that software is special and cannot be practiced except by a gifted adept. He

4: Bound Fast

even defines the other religions as if he had experience of them, identifying them as inferior to the true way.

———•———

Perhaps software engineers are more prone to religious views than most. I don't know. What I do know is that religion, early in the Twenty First Century, pervades the industry. My Boulder interviewer worked in a primary citadel of the global institution often labeled *Agile*. The ceremony they offer is *Scrum*. Many agile concepts have been around for a long time. Sun Microsystems had been incorporating their test harnesses into some of their development workspaces since 1995 with developers writing their own initial tests. The development teams were fairly small. They communicated frequently. They developed software and tests using fairly minimal process. Since Sun demanded a functional specification prior to formal initiation of a project, tests could be written prior to development. Since all documentation was online (in a fashion), it was easy to adjust the specification with changing circumstances.

All of these were, and are, agile concepts, many of which were eventually documented by Kent Beck in his book *eXtreme Programming eXplained*[Beck_2000]. That book, published in the year 2000, could be read in one of two ways. Some took it to be a biblical account of revealed truth; a mystical tome; a gospel (good news) for those who were tired of analysis and specifications. It was a boon to those who just wanted to *get on with it*.

When I found out about the book, I bought a copy for each of the engineers on my team at Sun. When *we* read it, it seemed clear to us that eXtreme Programming (XP) was actually an open challenge to experiment with common wisdom. By taking its recommendations as a series of experiments, we undertook a scientific investigation.

Two heads are better than one, why not have two people write the program together? *Testing verifies quality*, why not write the tests first so you won't be influenced by what the programmer felt like doing? *Requirements change but documents don't*, why not minimize documentation and augment what remains with frequent short meetings?

Famine In the Bullpen

We found several of the concepts to be helpful and incorporated them into our practice. Since we were already testing in the XP way, we felt a certain justifiable pride in our prescience and went further with the use of VNC (a UNIX X Windows driver) to support on-demand collaborative programming even though the team was distributed across a wide geographic area. We found the reduced documentation to be unhelpful since we had so much experience with the short, explicit and easily changed online specification; but, our enthusiasm for Agile was sincere and backed by data and experiment. We were pragmatic, not religious.

———— • ————

Scrum, as a religious practice, was introduced to my world around 2004. Since Sun Microsystems had a well-defined process of its own, Scrum was slow to be accepted, although its advocates were vocal and I had to sit through a week of training. Until a problem is perceived, it is hard to find value in a solution. Scrum was presented as a disciplined way to develop software (something Sun was already doing). It was presented as *the only way to do engineering* (which made no sense considering our technical accomplishments). Industry stalwarts professed that Scrum's superiority was obvious. It would deliver high-quality software solving complex problems quickly and reliably. No more missed deadlines. No more useless documents. No more worrying if your product would be acceptable to the market. To the highly skilled senior engineers at Sun, these claims were not only nonsensical; they were insulting. They denied the actual facts of the entirely functional familiar world.

There is a multi-billion dollar industry touting Scrum as the paradigm shift that makes other paradigm shifts look like a selection of toothpaste. Since 2006, I've interviewed with a dozen companies and in that time, only one did not claim to use Scrum exclusively. This devotion is even more astounding when one reviews the Scrum claims against actual serious research.

A Scrum instructor will explain the precise step-by-step procedure that is Scrum: the two-week iterations, the lists of "stories" describing the product in pieces, the reduced (or typically eliminated) documenta-

4: Bound Fast

tion. The reasons for the procedures are not explained with reference to scientific data; but they are explained with *enthusiasm*. After that rigorous recitation of the canon, the Scrum instructor will start to confront the objections. The standard response in the two Scrum classes I've taken is that Scrum is just a framework and you'll have to adjust it to your needs. The instructor is saying that you can come up with exceptions to the process as needed and still call it Scrum. The problem is that it's impossible to develop a sensible exception to a nonsensical rule; so, companies either develop their own system or they follow Scrum like zealots. In either case, they sing the praises of Scrum and invite visitations by its many priests.

As one talks with Scrum enthusiasts, it becomes clear that they have very little experience with the complex engineering problem. Their backgrounds have been primarily dedicated to development of simple features or fairly straightforward projects that move data between a back end and a web page. I myself have seen Scrum work nicely for very specific kinds of software. It is true: for simple mundane software or bug fixing, Scrum works fine. With some serious tweaking, it can work for problems that require a little creativity but then, Rational Unified Process (RUP) works for that too. With Scrum, you can consistently add new features to an established product or integrate existing products into a new product; but that isn't the full scope of software engineering. In the 1990s I remember having exciting problems to solve. They were problems that no skilled engineer in the room had ever solved before. They were problems without precedent which could not be estimated because no one thought there was a practical solution.

I was at Sun Microsystem's Menlo Park campus in 1998, meeting my new team and bringing them up to speed on their new project. There were four engineers, our manager and her senior manager: a fellow with a clear idea in his head of what was to happen next. I summarized the problem to be solved as I understood it at the time. I then explained that two other groups of highly skilled engineers over the past three years had tried to solve this problem and failed. I explained their solutions, emphasizing how reasonable each one appeared, only to prove ineffective under trial.

What would we do differently? What other options were there? Clearly this problem was impossible, and yet, we must solve it. I took questions for about a half hour and we adjourned for a ten minute break. The senior manager pulled me into the hallway and sternly rebuked me, insisting that I stop saying this was impossible and instead reassure the developers that we had a solution. I remember staring at him, puzzled. I reminded him that everything I had said was based upon fact. This problem had been in the hands of other very good engineers for years and no one had a good solution in mind. I certainly didn't. All I had was a strategy and four engineers who love nothing more than an impossible problem.

The enthusiasm was clear as we dedicated the rest of the morning to exploring the nature and form of the issues to be addressed. The afternoon involved breaking out the specific unknowns and assigning research tasks. I would be talking to each of the developers every few days. As they worked and reported back, I summarized our findings in a common document and suggested ways that the new discoveries might fit together into a better understanding of the problem. We called frequent ad hoc meetings as each of us encountered complications and made new discoveries working together on aspects of our design document. As we spoke, we tried not to think about the solution, the goal was to understand the problem. It was glorious and fun.

Serious problems that yield a large number of side-effects and appear intractable on multiple levels present a particular problem for the rigid schedules of Scrum. The problem is that most companies assume Scrum is the only good option. It is the state religion. In a nation where there used to be little pockets of observers touting many belief systems, each adapted to its own needs; they are all supplanted by this common religion, a religion that only really works for simple problems. So who is developing the open-source software for the secure voting protocol of the future? Who is developing the control system for a global solar and wind network or automated teaching systems that learn from the stu-

4: Bound Fast

dent's responses and adjust methodology to optimize understanding and retention? What about music servers that select compositions based upon the topics of conversation in the room?

The problem isn't that these projects have no value. Indeed, some lucky few are working on them. There are real problems to be solved that would bring real value to the world; but, truly effective solutions to those problems are not well supported by the accepted methodology. It makes impossible problems appear impossible by virtue of the fact that they cannot be divided into predictable time-boxed operations. The impossible becomes measurably not-doable as opposed to merely a fantastic challenge.

The problem is religion in its most common guise: as a sanction against free thinking. When I was first exposed to IoC, I was cautioned that it wouldn't work unless "you give yourself to it fully." My mentor was being a little flippant, but, his advice turned days of reluctantly abandoning hard-earned skills into just a few hours of examining my conscience and accepting my new faith.

Ideas I had held for years about object-oriented methodology were tossed out and I accepted that Java is not a language, it is a growing complex of beliefs. Back then there was Java and JBoss and Spring and various fledgling frameworks with funny names. Had I watched this develop in the outside world, I wouldn't have been so surprised; but I was thrown into this world from the isolated confines of Sun Microsystems where our primary framework was Emacs and we saw Java as a basic OO language much like Python.

Within those walls, we built our Java software using *Make* and we configured it using a singleton and we instantiated our objects with both state and behaviors to serve as verifying emulations within the ontology defining our solution. We believed that by using what works, we couldn't go wrong; and, while this proved sufficient for our purposes, it did not prove sufficient in the job market outside.

Outside, we encountered the Java complex, consisting of Java plus a wide array of support tools which compensated for some of its basic deficiencies. When I use the term *Java complex*, I am often corrected and told that it is a *Java environment*. That would be true if the tools supporting Java were the same at all companies. Instead, the overall collection of options forms more of a complex with Java at the center surrounded by myBatis, JUnit, Spring, Tomcat, Jersey, Guice and others. From this wide complex of components, a company assembles its own unique Java *environment*.

Once assembled, the tools in that environment help to define how everything is to be done. Using MyBatis the developer maps a series of data manipulation operations to methods within the Data Access Object (DAO). Using Hibernate, the developer defines a data model and allows Hibernate to figure out most of the process. Likewise, Spring offers a wide variety of services from IoC to caching to database access. Each one provides benefits but, to some degree, you *must* believe.

It is not unusual to hear the term *Spring Magic* in a technical discussion.

"What's the format of that POST payload?"

"Not sure, it's Spring Magic."

"How do we invoke that local library?"

"Not sure. It's Spring Magic."

Now magic is fine as long as it's always doing what it's intended to. I become uneasy when the thing that's going wrong is somewhere deep inside that magic. My configuration is always to blame; but finding how my configuration broke the magic with the cryptic messaging provided is exasperating. The younger programmers don't have any trouble with it because they're used to it. They've never written an object to relational mapper. They've never written a massively parallel threaded program. They've never written a state machine. They think that debugging magic *must* be easier than doing those other things.

I have actually seen a comment in a problem description stating, "This should be implemented using threads. I think we need Akka." That was a skilled developer who recognized that this software was best implemented as a small number of parallel threads. Even though he was

4: Bound Fast

entirely bright enough to write that software, he had given up. He didn't even imagine that he could possibly write such a threaded program. He had been persuaded that he must wait for the threaded parallel sacramental he called "Akka." Now there's nothing wrong with Akka but it does much more than just threading. If all you need is a threaded program, you probably don't need Akka.

The magic is one of the ligatures that binds teams down, accepting that the unseen hand is more glorious in its power than anything they could do. Sometimes one may spend weeks in obeisance, trying to prove worthy of a boon, only to finally give in and accept that if FasterXML isn't going to serialize it the way you need it, then you probably don't need it serialized in that way.

"I suppose God didn't want me to get that job."

The first time I witnessed this, I felt sad. Now, I understand that this is just how we write software. The religion tells programmers what they can and can't do. Accepting their designated limitations, they don't even imagine that the problem could be actually solved entirely if they'd just write it themselves. This possibility is simply never approached.

While working at a newspaper publisher in 2009, we were deploying a content distribution service (CDS) from within a Spring container. This service was pulling its information from a database but the long term plan was to pull information from a competing CDS which was intended to eventually replace our current one. For reasons that do not bear recounting, it was necessary to switch the production server between the two sources dynamically without a restart. We were very serious about IoC, if you found yourself typing *new*, you were probably doing something wrong. One of our number was a Spring expert who took on the task of coercing Spring into letting us reconfigure without rebooting. It was suggested that we build in JMX, which would have supported this kind of reconfiguration but we would have had to refactor major portions of the service as ManagedObjects. It seemed much simpler to just get Spring's static configuration to flex a little for us and support a live change.

Famine In the Bullpen

I do not know if this was possible using Spring IoC. I'm not a Spring expert; but, our Spring expert couldn't figure out how to do it after a month, off and on, of trying. Finally, I made the executive decision to switch the service from Spring IoC to a simple dynamic configuration singleton. It took me an afternoon to write the singleton supporting dynamic reconfiguration without a restart of the server. My associates pulled out the IoC references that same afternoon and we deployed the new service the next week.

The service worked well without IoC. It worked so well that I suggested pulling IoC out of all of the services. The modified service was easier to debug, had fewer configuration files and was more logically organized. I called a meeting to discuss this only to find that the younger engineers, while enthusiastic about the first conversion, were hesitant to switch over completely. After that meeting I was taken out for coffee by one of our senior engineers, Erik Sahl. Wise man that he was, he educated me regarding why Spring IoC had to remain in the product. It should have been obvious to me, but I was too focused on my little triumph. It was simple; our developers needed Spring on their resumés and they would need to answer Spring questions in their next interviews. His argument was persuasive and, of course, we kept Spring IoC in the other services.

I can honestly state that I have never confronted a problem that Inversion of Control solved and I've twice encountered a problem that it made worse. True believers are shocked by this statement but it is a fact. As with any religious belief, actual experience cannot disprove it; actual data to the contrary will not persuade. Largely because these true believers have never configured a Java project using any other methodology, only IoC makes sense to them. They selectively accept all substantiating proof and discount evidence to the contrary.

———•———

These are not stupid people. These are committed serious people whose environment defines a canon of beliefs assumed to be true until they can be definitively disproved. I was sharing a table at a conference

4: Bound Fast

with a skilled engineering director and an IT professional responsible for a large Java development and test infrastructure. The director indicated that he needed an infrastructure that would support end-to-end tests by the developers on their desktop systems. He indicated that this was a complex software stack and that, as a result, the line between unit tests and integration tests was invariably blurred. The IT professional responded that "in the real world," the various layers of the stack were *mocked*, testing each individual component without the need to involve other layers of the stack.

I had spoken with him before and so I was familiar with his cadence. He spoke with such certainty that I – a non-believer – was tempted to accept his claim without question. His religious fervor presented a predictable world where verification of software components was a simple procedure that anyone dragged from a gutter on East Colfax could accomplish. In his head, and implicitly described, was a world where development was a step-by-step process, producing software that requests specific data and returns a processed result. His world was predetermined and utterly comprehensible. In it there were no problems, only solutions. The solutions were simple mappings from a particular complaint to a particular configuration of instructions that would resolve that complaint.

The world our IT expert described is a clean, white, ordered world. There is a faint scent of vanilla, but not real vanilla. It's a scent that reminds one of vanilla, but there's something missing. It's different. The full, rich essence of the world is reduced to a complex of frameworks and a series of instructions. Through the doctrine of FAQs and blogs, there is a manual for living. Like a biblical fundamentalist, the truth is known and unambiguous. Once read, it is not to be questioned; and the unquestioning dedication brings comfort and security.

In the world of the director at that table, and indeed, in the world of my experience, solving problems is not a formula. It is a messy tangle of data and consequences. The actual problem is not obvious and the discipline required to uncover the root cause, correct it and then verify the results is a deeply personal process. I warned my associates at the newspaper publisher against designing solutions for *something*. We instead sought to design for *anything*. Designing for anything is a little harder than designing for something; but, once the enterprise is complete, the solution is beautiful. It isn't accounting. The engineer doesn't feel a glowing satisfaction when the columns balance. The engineer looks for a much more complex beauty: a beauty encompassing the simple cause and the complex side-effects and the intricate Celtic knots that bind them. The glorious simplicity of the unifying function that resolves all of the twisted tendrils into the sweet simple line between real problem and real solution carries a symmetry and wonder that leaves the engineer transfixed.

It is that joy that drives the engineer to take on the challenges presented by the real world. Without it, engineering becomes a tedious recitation of the standard canon. The engineer becomes the disillusioned priest reciting the mass day after day; the passion of Christ decaying to the rhythmic repetition of the rites; faith falling to mere security in the calming sonorous reminiscence that makes the real world go away.

But the real world is fascinating. The real world has real problems that must be addressed and the engineer craves that challenge. Simple religion is a pitiful substitute for a real vocation.

5: Feature Factory

It is possible that customers are truly impressed every time their Android upgrades an app to the latest version. It is possible that there are true fans of each new Firefox release, gleefully testing each security correction and striving to fully use every new capability. It is possible that after weeks getting used to a particular iPhone interface, the user grows tired of the mundane reliability and yearns to adapt to a different interface, thanking all that is holy when Apple upgrades them and modifies the behavior of select buttons in subtle ways. It may be that every time a flash player needs to be upgraded, a loyal user rejoices at the opportunity. It is possible that people who get used to a particular procedure or process and become comfortable with it are true anomalies.

We are all restless. We want red licorice, continuous kick boxing and frequent application updates. On the other hand, when you buy a new stove top for your kitchen, it does its job without upgrade for decades. One could argue that a stove top is very simple and performs such a simple function that it cannot disappoint. Its being a stove top has lowered your expectations and that's why you don't immediately want to see the new rev.

A car is more complex and serves a more advanced function. Modern cars get regular software updates but the fenders aren't updated. The steering isn't updated. It looks the same. Why aren't automobile owners demanding a new look every few months? An expensive car brings with it serious expectations, why don't special Lotus mechanics show up every few weeks with cooler and cooler quarter panels? Replacing the steering wheel with a joy stick? Swapping the six forward speeds for seven?

Famine In the Bullpen

Could it be that frequent software updates are not provided at the insistence of the customer? Are we shipping frequent updates for some other reason? Maybe what was delivered last wasn't very good or maybe we ship frequent updates because it's part of the belief system. If your company is uniformly set up to deliver features then you'll be delivering features.

Every company has to maintain its existing products and that means providing corrections and new features. Every engineer, regardless their seniority, has had to spend time cranking out some requested capability. The job is fairly predictable and usually does not demand the full capabilities of the people involved. Companies establish departments to handle these routine requests. We could call these *feature factories*. Every manufacturer has a feature factory where simple features are constructed and delivered in a predictable fashion. The people who work at the feature factory don't need to be the best and brightest. Reasonably smart folks can build out features just fine.

Generally, the feature factory is a part of the company, but it doesn't comprise the whole of the manufacturing resource. At Tesla, existing models are improved and fancy new capabilities are pulled together to sell to existing owners. The onboard software is routinely corrected and updated; but, that isn't all. New battery technologies are under development. Research into hazard detection algorithms and improved manufacturing techniques are ongoing concerns. Those departments are not responsible for turning out simple predictable consumer items, they are undertaking tasks which were considered impossible or impractical only a few years ago.

Experienced engineers with big ideas are sometimes committed to healthy stints in the feature factory. Before you can develop the power saving toaster that heats the bread using LED lasers, you have to participate on the team responsible for extending an existing toaster's lever by two tenths of an inch. Before you can build your stereo amplifier that filters its output to optimize for the acoustics of the environment, you have to increase its output power by five watts. Before you can develop your online music program that schedules tunes based upon overheard

5: Feature Factory

conversations in the room, you have to move the pause button to the lower right corner and color it blue.

Different departments within any company use methodologies that are designed to accommodate the tasks at hand. If you find that your new toaster doesn't comply with UL standards due to insufficient insulation between the power cord and the metal frame, you pull together a team to change the wire routing accordingly and the problem is solved. If you want to design a battery-operated toaster for campers, your approach is very different. You will call upon your most experienced engineer and have her pull together a team committed to devising a revolutionary new concept in toasters.

In the world of software, the standard methodology is Scrum. It is praised by most software companies in the U.S. and goes by the general moniker of *Agile*. There is no doubt that agility is always good; so the question becomes, how much agility do we gain from Agile?

———•———

Every Scrum company in my experience uses a completely different methodology. My most effective exposure to Scrum was under the tutelage of Brooke Schwerdt, an Agile Master who understood where and when to apply a strictly canonical version of Scrum. She drove the Scrum process with precision until she encountered a case where Scrum did not apply well. At that point, she opened up options for creativity, returning to Scrum when appropriate. Under Brooke, I participated in a smoothly running Agile machine that turned out reliable results without having to crowbar every problem into a Scrum frame. After that experience, I have never returned to a functional Agile shop.

For this reason, I suspect it is unlikely that anyone who is reading this has had any of the same Scrum experiences I describe. My formal understanding of Scrum derives from the two classes I have taken, as well as in my practical education under Ms. Schwerdt for whom Agile ran more smoothly than I have seen anywhere else. My ten years of experience with Scrum have formed a spectrum ranging from productive efficiency to plodding confusion. I have seen it played out by the book and I have seen it used as an excuse for repeated bad behavior. While my experience is with Scrum as it appears in the wild, I will try to present it here as described by the Scrum Master teaching Scrum from the book. I will try to present my assessment both accurately and generously.

A canonical Scrum shop organizes its workers into teams that take on tasks identified in a backlog of task definitions called *stories* using a rigid procedure. There are three job titles: Scrum Master, Product Owner and developer. Any Scrum Master can take on the job of any other Scrum Master and any developer can take on the job of any other developer. Only the Product Owner is expected to be a specialist in a particular subject.

The Product Owner is expected to commune with the customer on a regular basis. The Product Owner is expected to develop the larger vision of the solution, presenting it to the Scrum teams as a backlog of prioritized stories and to shuttle the customer to the development site every few weeks to review and comment on the team progress through a set of demonstrations. These comments may result in new or modified stories which the teams will tackle later.

Every developer is expected to write the software and test it. Technically, there should be no testers because every developer is expected to also test. This, we are told, results in higher product quality. Every Scrum shop in my experience, though, has had quality assurance personnel who test the product, but that test cycle invariably interferes with the expected scheduling.

All work takes place on an *iteration* (period of work) of typically two weeks. At the beginning, the team meets to plan their two-week *sprint*. Each story is assigned a particular number of *story points* arranged as a Fibonacci sequence up to (the decidedly non-Fibonacci) *twenty*. A story of three points may be accomplished in a few days. One of thirteen points may take a developer a full two weeks to complete. At twenty, we're into *epic* territory and no one wants that. For that reason, twenty point stories end up at the bottom of the *backlog*, the list of stories to deal with later, unwanted and out of sight. Some groups are diligent in

5: Feature Factory

returning to epics and breaking them into actionable stories, most in my experience, do not. It is important to note that epics which are intended to yield ground-breaking innovation may require extraordinary creativity and disciplined preparation. These may be impossible to break into effective two-week sprints.

The Product Owner provides the collection of stories to be addressed in this sprint. Each story is defined using the following precise form: *As a <blank> I want to <blank> so that I can <blank>*. It should be clear that Scrum presumes that every solution to every problem can be defined by filling in three blanks: someone wants something and the developer provides it. The notion that a problem may be complicated is addressed using an instrument referred to as a *spike*. With a spike, some developer is given an opportunity to figure out how to solve the problem.

Spikes are commonly *time-boxed*. That means that if it can't be figured out in a fixed amount of time, it's abandoned. This is a small parcel of enlightenment in an otherwise dull democratization of mediocrity. To admit that some problems do not have obvious solutions is good, but it fails to grasp the creative process which may require multiple iterations to even get to the point that the problem can be described. Once described, various spikes may be required to get to the point that the intended solution is obviously ill-conceived. At that point, a *new* spike may be required to reassess what the problem actually is; or, more likely, the research will simply stop.

———•———

This notion of time boxing shows up all over the Industry, even in shops that do not claim true dedication to Scrum. When I was interviewed for a position at a major Internet retailer, I was told that if the problem couldn't be solved in twenty-four hours, it was ignored. That development team was constantly under pressure to deliver something. Solving a particular problem was less important than delivering *something*, for God's sake.

The ongoing constant panic eased its way into the interviewer's every statement. As he spoke, the anxiety painted its acrid film onto every jittery word as his nervous backward glances became audible over the phone. We spoke at length about the distress and fear and commiserated over what tactics might prove victorious over the inexorable pain of the departmental task list.

Finally, he admitted the shameful secret that would undo the interview. He said, "You know, we write everything in Perl. Are you OK with Perl?"

I provided a well-practiced response: "I refuse to take seriously any language for which a string of punctuation marks constitutes a valid command."

That, of course, was the welcome end of my prospects with that company. My spouse had been an independent vendor with them for years and had told me of the independent vendor's nickname for their developers. They called them "the hamsters and gerbils" since no matter what they did, it never seemed to get anywhere.

Now I understood why.

While this particular department may represent an extreme example, the general concept is preserved in the view that if it can't be addressed in a predictable (and short) time period, it isn't worth fixing.

———•———

Scrum instructors tell their students that the best way to organize developers is in an open-plan office where they can talk to each other whenever they need to. The research and studies I have found that support this claim tend to begin with phrases like, "Knowing full well that Scrum is the only way to develop software..." and so should be treated like the promotional literature they are. The alternative view, however, is supported by research such as a 2009 study[Tuomaala_2009] published in *Ergonomics* which concludes:

> *The results suggest that the open-plan office is not recommended for professional workers.*

5: Feature Factory

A 2013 study from the University of Sydney[Kim_2013] is pretty clear:

> [...] *our results categorically contradict the industry-accepted wisdom that open-plan layout enhances communication between colleagues and improves occupants' overall work environmental satisfaction.*

In addition, a 2015 12-month longitudinal study[Bergström_2015] published in *Work* shows perceived decreases in productivity when creative workers are moved from private offices to an open-plan office. These suggest that creative professionals, like engineers, are most productive in offices with doors that can be closed allowing them to concentrate in silence and which open into a common area where they can talk with peers and explore ideas.

This is further confirmed by the *Coding War Games* conducted by Tom DeMarco and Timothy Lister of The Atlantic Systems Guild. It is referenced throughout their fascinating study of methodology called *Peopleware*[DeMarco_1999] beginning on page 44. The description of that study is a good and lengthy read but it seems to have been inspired by a somewhat more digestible informal study conducted at Cornell University in the 1960s. I will present the description of that study and then reinforce it with a personal anecdote. The Cornell study is recounted by DeMarco and Lister on page 78 of *Peopleware*. It was a review of a commonly used solution developers currently apply to the bullpen problem – they listen to music. It was not audited and was apparently just to satisfy someone's curiosity, nonetheless, it provides a fair summary of the more disciplined Coding War Games conclusions.

The researchers assembled a number of computer science students and divided them into two groups based upon whether or not they liked to listen to music while they worked. They gave each participant a problem to solve using Fortran and sent half of each of the two groups to solve that problem in a silent room (so roughly half preferred silence and the rest preferred music). The other half of the two groups was sent to a room with headphones where they would be required to listen to their favorite music while solving the problem.

Famine In the Bullpen

The speed and accuracy of the results were equivalent for both groups in both rooms, but that wasn't the whole story. DeMarco and Lister conclude as follows :

> *The Cornell experiment [...] contained a hidden wild card. The specification required that an output data stream be formed through a series of manipulations on numbers in the input data stream. For example, participants had to shift each number two digits to the left and then divide by one hundred and so on, perhaps completing a dozen operations in total. Although the specification never said it, the net effect of all the operations was that each output number was necessarily equal to its input number. Some people realized this and others did not. Of those who figured it out, the overwhelming majority came from the quiet room.*

I believe that story because I've experienced it. As a senior staff engineer at Sun Microsystems, I sat in my private office with my large whiteboard. The lighting was very dim and I listened to jazz from KUVO. At least a half dozen times I remember this experience. Confronted with a complex problem, I would be scribbling on my whiteboard, drawing diagrams, talking loudly to myself and puzzling over what could possibly constitute a clear understanding of the problem at hand.

After multiple scribbles followed by erasures, I would become aware of an ache. It was not clear where I was aching but it was an ache. I would find myself staring at the whiteboard completely flummoxed with what I had deposited there. Unconsciously, I would turn off the music. Suddenly the ache would disappear. I would return to scribbling and drawing and presently, an understanding would arise with astounding clarity. I would stare with satisfaction at my result and turn on the radio. I did this several times before I finally spotted the pattern. Music is processed by the right hemisphere of the brain, the same one we use for creativity.

This is not a new understanding. Sir Edward G. E. Bulwer-Lytton in his 1834 book *The Last Days of Pompeii* wrote of the folly of trying to concentrate while listening to music. Glaucus explains,

5: Feature Factory

> *"[...] pleasure and study are not elements to be thus mixed together [...]. It was but the other day that I paid a visit to Pliny: he was sitting in his summer house writing, while an unfortunate slave played on the tibia. His nephew [...] was reading Thucidides' description of the plague, and nodding his conceited little head in time to the music, while his lips were repeating all the loathsome details of that terrible delineation. The puppy saw nothing incongruous in learning at the same time a ditty of love and a description of the plague."*

Listening to music, you can follow the simple procedure, but it's hard to be creative. Despite that, companies all over the U.S. are putting engineers at picnic benches blocking out the surrounding noise with music because they believe that it is contiguous to virtue.

———•———

Eighteenth Century philosopher Jeremy Bentham spent nearly twenty years developing the concept he called the Panopticon. It was an innovative form of imprisonment which placed the prisoners in cells surrounding an observation tower. The cells were constantly lit sufficiently to assure that the activities of each prisoner could be observed from the tower at any time. The guards in the tower were obscured in such a way that their actions could not be observed by the prisoners. This meant that no prisoner would be able to determine if he was being observed at any given time. It was possible he was being observed constantly. Maybe there was no observer at all. He had no way of knowing.

This was considered a very humane and progressive approach to incarceration. Bentham was a brilliant polymath. Philosopher, utilitarian, abolitionist and humanitarian, his intent, with this invention, was to train these criminals to self-observe and self-regulate in reaction to the possibility that any inappropriate act may be surveilled. The external observation would eventually be internalized causing the malefactory mind to mutate into a self-conscious well-ordered mind. In other words, the persistent external conscience would irradiate and nurture a new self-sustaining internal conscience.

Despite Bentham's prestige, he never managed to build his Panopticon. Modern corporate prisons borrow some of his concepts but not enough to verify its effectiveness. While Bentham's goal was benign and his concept revolutionary, it is likely that rather than produce a personal conscience in the prisoners, the intense sensation of always being watched would instead manifest as severe neurosis.

In the modern workplace, though, we have produced a grubby simulacrum of the Panopticon. We call it the *open-plan office* where employees are arrayed at picnic tables, always exposed, always possibly under observation. Unlike in a collection of private offices, before the accountant searches the web for the meaning of a word he suspects he should already know, he will look about in hopes he is not being observed. Before the developer looks at the Java API to review the methods on an object with which she should already be familiar, she will check for any hope of privacy. More likely, each will proceed without verification and hope the spell checker or IDE will enlighten them.

The modern Panopticon is intended to provide the same benefits as Bentham's: to assure proper behavior among all participants as a result of potential constant scrutiny. Like Bentham's Panopticon, it tends, instead, to induce a cautious overly-reflective behavior which inhibits risky creative thinking. To launch into an experimental Python program to test an advanced concept would be spotted and questioned by any technical manager looking over the developer's shoulder. "What are you supposed to be working on?" would be the question to which the answer would reveal the developer's iniquity.

At Sun Microsystems, this statement was often overheard, "Every engineer at Sun is working on two projects, the one his boss knows about and the one his boss doesn't." The one the boss didn't know about was often the one that provided a new vision for a long-murky project or proved out a faster way to compile iterations.

This, of course, was basic to the culture. When the engineer revealed the private project, there was general rejoicing. My notebook computer was full of new projects at various levels of development, implementing various concepts that I would introduce to the Sun ecosystem from time to time. I was so used to the notion that these would become Sun projects that I kept them in an encrypted partition with Sun copyrights. When Sun laid me off, I had to make sure I had scrubbed all the projects I had transferred to Sun and globally change the remaining copyright entries.

The culture followed the principles laid out by our U.S. founders. Secrecy is not, in itself, vile. Indeed, it is necessary for free people to keep secrets. Libertarians may plan their march in secret without inviting suggestions from local Socialists. When an engineer thinks she has a good idea but isn't sure yet, her exploration of that possibility is rightly kept secret until the concept has matured to the level of a supportable proposal. People must feel free to theorize with abandon and disciplined whimsy without the interference of outside observers questioning each crazy creative turn.

The open-plan office bans secrets and drives all inmates to a constant, consistent norm. This is the reason for the cynical contrivance called the *innovation sprint*. The inmates need a creative outlet that doesn't disrupt the strictures of the sprint. The problem with the innovation sprint, of course, is its implicit identification of innovation as a necessary threat that must be isolated within a protective zone. Like human excretion, yes it has to happen but there's a time and a place for it and we don't talk about it after the deed is done. This is not the attitude corporations show toward obedience, loyalty or greed, although each of those is more easily carried too far than is innovation.

———— • ————

Scrum instructors tell their students to minimize documentation because complex concepts are best conveyed face-to-face verbally. They reference poorly designed experiments to support this claim. Actual serious studies[Garousi_2015] and successful engineering projects indicate that complex concepts are best conveyed in well-structured documents. That's why the architect produced a drawing of the house before pouring the floor. It's why you wrote down the recipe for your Mother's coffee cake. It's why people write books. Despite this, modern companies across the U.S. are eschewing the printed word and returning to an oral tradition.

This tradition is predicated upon the belief that the team is most successful when they solve problems as a group, talking things through and making decisions together. This is why it is rare to find a Scrum shop with *technical leads* because the team is assumed to be a confederacy of equals: the new kid who loves Hibernate holding equal sway with the veteran developer whose experience argues for MyBatis in this situation.

There are certain aspects of Scrum that exploit the group effectively. For example, one way to assign the appropriate points to a story (establishing its level of difficulty) is by using *planning poker*. Recall that each story is assigned a ranking, indicative of the presumed difficulty in the form of *story points*: an integer from the Fibonacci Sequence between 1 and 20 inclusive. In planning poker, each developer holds a hand of cards (like playing cards). Each card has one of the extended Fibonacci Sequence on it (i.e., 1, 2, 3, 5, 8, 13, 20).

The procedure is usually to discuss the thing to be done and then each developer selects the card that corresponds to their assessment of the difficulty. Each developer puts their card face down on the table. On signal, all developers at the same time turn their cards face up. The reason for this, the Scrum folks will tell you, is to keep the participants from influencing each other until they've committed to a number. This is a wise precaution to keep the more alpha developers from intimidating the introverted developers.

The highest number and the lowest number require explanation. Each of those developers must make a case for their assessment of the difficulty and in the end the developers come to an agreement about the story points to be assigned. This and other mechanisms for arriving at consensus are common forms within the Scrum process.

The closest thing the Scrum team has to a technical lead is the Product Owner. While *not* a technical lead, the Product Owner is ex-

5: Feature Factory

pected to be technical enough to communicate with the developers. The Product Owner sets the vision for the product feature to be produced. If the developers are unable to settle on a technical approach, they may call in the Product Owner to arbitrate requiring at least enough technical expertise to be able to distinguish which technical approach will best yield the desired result.

Usually the task at hand is fairly trivial: a particular piece of data needs to be shuttled to the web browser and put in a particular place in the presentation. Such a problem requires little if any discussion around implementation methodology; but, for the rare complicated problem for which the Product Owner is only capable of providing a general gloss, technical discussion may be required. It is this technical discussion that betrays the claim that there is no technical lead. As a general rule, the more alpha developer will assume the position of lead whether he is technically competent or not.

In this circumstance, there is convincing evidence that the team simply plays no role in the process. Instead the most bold of the team members identifies an implementation and the rest go along. This is clearly not the intended result. In fact neuroscientist Gregory S. Berns, of Emory University, conducted a study[Berns_2005] in 2005 wherein volunteers were called upon to play a game that required concentration. When working alone, the players gave the wrong answer only 13.8 percent of the time. When playing with a group that provided wrong answers, that same player gave the wrong answer 41 percent of the time. The group is a very poor substitute for a single skilled individual concentrating on the problem and proposing a solution. Once the solution is documented, the group returns to critique the solution and correct it as needed. In that case, the individual critics are not responsible for the initial innovation and may more comfortably and constructively identify issues.

So how is it that Scrum Masters support this kind of group design activity when they have already demonstrated an understanding of deleterious group effects in the clever process of planning poker? If there is any reason why I have not thrown up my hands and abandoned the industry entirely, it is because I can easily assume the role of lead in most Scrum teams. If this system could not be "played," I would have gone mad by now.

Early in the Twenty-First Century, I was made responsible for moving an Internet server from a NoSQL back-end called Cloudant to a SQL back-end called MySQL. The Cloudant repository had no meaningful structure and, of course, there was no documentation explaining what data was being stored in it or for what reason. Based upon repeated patterns within the massive data set, it was eventually possible to figure out the rough data model and with the help of numerous competent reviewers to finally propose a normalized database schema to hold the Cloudant-based data.

I wrote several documents and published them on the wiki explaining the nature of the original problem; a data requirements document explaining why each piece of data was retained and how it was to be used; a mapping between the data in the Cloudant and MySQL repositories and finally a migration plan explaining how the data would be migrated on the live system without interrupting normal operations.

Half way through the project, while writing the data access layer for the MySQL implementation, a new team member was added. This new developer was also used to running teams as the alpha developer. Upon arrival, he made it clear that we would have to shut down the servers while migrating the Cloudant data to the MySQL repository. He quickly proposed an implementation to support that disruptive process.

As I listened to his explanation, I became doubtful of my plan, which did not require any interruption in services. I did not speak as he explained the software he would implement to support that shutdown and, after the meeting, I began carefully reassessing my method. What had I missed that he clearly understood? How did he know an interruption in service would be required?

The migration plan explained exactly how this would be done without service interruption. I took two days to satisfy myself that there

5: Feature Factory

was no flaw in my approach and I, an admittedly alpha participant, finally mustered the guts to challenge his plan.

He expressed worry that there was no clear way to accomplish this since the two databases were so different. He indicated that he had some experience migrating databases and this was more complicated than the others he'd attempted. I pointed him to the documents, including the MySQL schema, the data mapping and the migration document. The next day, he expressed his deep concern that the only way to do this would be to freeze the two databases and perform the migration which may require hours of down time. I reminded him that the plan did not require down time and he began to question the plan more specifically.

"How do you deal with the scenario wherein you've migrated one record to MySQL and then the Cloudant record is updated?"

I was able to respond, "That is scenario #5 in the migration document. It's mitigated by dual-write mode."

"Well what about if you're in dual-write and you try to update a record in MySQL that hasn't been migrated yet?"

"That's handled by copy-on-fail as described in scenario #12 in the migration document."

"What if one server in the cluster fails and the other members of the cluster keep writing to the corrupt database?"

"That's why we have the override_status table in the MySQL schema. The migration document explains how it's used."

Then it became clear what the problem was. "What's this migration document you keep talking about?"

Having provided him a pointer to the document four times, he had not read it. It wasn't because he was lazy or because he couldn't read or because he was a poor developer. On the contrary, he was well-educated and skilled. He could list numerous impressive accomplishments and was widely recognized as a software architect. I suspect there were three problems:

1. He had never worked on a project with a detailed plan. He had only worked on projects where the developers talked through what they were going to do and then did it.
2. Having worked only in Scrum shops, he had never even considered taking on a complex project of this sort, because it doesn't break easily into two-week iterations.
3. As alpha tech lead on all of his projects, he had never had to argue a complex design that he couldn't hold comfortably in his head.

What struck me most deeply was how he could even imagine taking on such a task without a documented plan? In a world where documentation is taboo, so is the ability to analyze the complex problem. In a world where analysis is taboo, so is problem solving. In a world where problem solving is taboo, so is engineering.

———•———

The Scrum instructor will emphasize that Scrum engages constantly with the customer. The customer is involved in the development of the solution because the customer observes and critiques the bi-weekly demonstrations of the product. The problem is that the customer doesn't know what the problem is; much less the solution.

I observed this at Sun when a customer couldn't explain what was bothering him; but was absolutely sure that if we just finished development on his little Perl script, everything would be OK. I sat down with the customer and started asking questions. While enthusiasm for the Perl script would occasionally resurface, we talked about the problem they were experiencing. We thought back to the first time the difficulties arose. What were those difficulties? Was it a sharp pain or a dull pain? What was happening when you noticed the pain? When we were done, it was obvious to both of us that the Perl script wouldn't actually address the problem. Customers (and consumers generally) are not aware of what they want. Philip Graves' thorough assessment, *Consumer.ology*[Graves_2010], provides extensive research and insight into this issue. The problem is complex because the customer's perception of the

5: Feature Factory

problem is muddied by past experience and their personal beliefs regarding what is and is not possible.

Despite solid data to the contrary, companies invite the customer in to simply observe and correct, relieving the engineer of the entire problem of figuring out what the problem is anyway. Without an understanding of the problem, one can honestly state that there *is no* problem, just a set of instructions from the customer with which we will comply.

Have faith in the process and the tedious reward will be yours.

———•———

I once attended a telephone meeting conducted by a Director of Engineering. She dialed up the customer, a syndicate responsible for collecting and republishing designated portions of her company's data content. The interfaces had been confirmed and this was to be a meeting to finalize the deal before opening the data valve.

At a lull in the discussion the VP asked a question that startled all senior engineers in the room. "What else do you want?"

There was a long pause as all of the engineers waited, hoping for a simple acknowledgment that all was well. Instead, the customer came back with, "Well, if you're asking, it would be great to be able to filter the content by keywords." This was beyond scope and should have resulted in a quick correction that we were interested in desires that were consistent with the agreement. Instead she simply said, "Anything else?"

As a result of what the VP started, we ended up redesigning the entire interface to support a contract that no one had ever signed. If asked what they want, every customer will, without fail, clarify that they want *everything*.

This is why the customer plays a deleterious role in the Agile process. When brought in for regular consultation, the customer must be constantly reminded of the problem being solved. That is the problem we are addressing *now*. We are not addressing every problem the customer can pose. It took several meetings to get to the point that the customer understood what the problem was in the first place. With that milestone accomplished, frequent invitations to add what else they want is simply an attractive nuisance begging for a long march and a failed project. Even worse, it demands ever more disjoint features bolted to the sides of the original well-conceived solution.

———•———

The folks who invented and actively promote Scrum, despite their belief that face to face discussion is more effective than documentation, seem to produce quite a few reference documents. A web search will also reveal a large number of books explaining how to do Scrum. All of this despite the fact that almost every company that uses Scrum initially hired a Scrum instructor to teach a class on Scrum. The instructor used face-to-face word-of-mouth to explain Scrum. One wonders why that wasn't sufficient.

Among the key Scrum documents is *The Agile Principles* which deserves a quick review. These principles comprise the main body of a document often referred to as *The Manifesto for Agile Software Development* or *The Agile Manifesto*. It has spawned numerous agile methodologies including Scrum; and while that document moderates these principles in reasonably constructive ways, in Scrum shops, the interpretation is invariably skewed in the direction of minimalistic and ad hoc approaches.

Different agile methodologies interpret these principles differently. I will not be reviewing those other interpretations here because the focus of this chapter is Scrum and the other methodologies, briefly enumerated in Chapter 6, are almost unknown in the industry.

The Agile Principles

1. *Our highest priority is to satisfy the customer through early and continuous delivery of valuable software.*
2. *Deliver working software frequently, from a couple of weeks to a couple of months, with a preference to the shorter timescale.*
3. *Welcome changing requirements, even late in development. Agile processes harness change for the customer's competitive advantage.*
4. *Business people and developers must work together daily throughout*

5: Feature Factory

the project.
5. *Build projects around motivated individuals. Give them the environment and support they need, and trust them to get the job done.*
6. *The most efficient and effective method of conveying information to and within a development team is face-to-face conversation.*
7. *Working software is the primary measure of progress.*
8. *Agile processes promote sustainable development. The sponsors, developers, and users should be able to maintain a constant pace indefinitely.*
9. *Continuous attention to technical excellence and good design enhances agility.*
10. *Simplicity--the art of maximizing the amount of work not done--is essential.*
11. *The best architectures, requirements, and designs emerge from self-organizing teams.*
12. *At regular intervals, the team reflects on how to become more effective, then tunes and adjusts its behavior accordingly.*

Clearly, this is at least one of the motivations for the frequent delivery of features. You will notice that some of the principles are fairly benign common sense statements about management such as #4, #5, #9 and #12. Some are motivational statements such as #2, #8 and #10. Finally, the rest are claims that tend to approach what we could call "principles."

Principles #1 and #3 explain the importance of delivering frequently, implying that this will lead to customer satisfaction. It is not clear how this satisfies the customer. It would seem that whatever is delivered to the customer is inadequate to their needs since otherwise, the next delivery would not be necessary.

Principle #6 explains that face-to-face discussion is preferred over documentation, within a Scrum team. This means that one of two things must be true. Either the discussion within a Scrum team is totally different from all other kinds of technical communication or Principle #6 is essentially a violation of Principle #6.

Within a Scrum team the most common communication is about understanding what the feature is and deciding how to implement it. In a Scrum class, the primary communication is about what Scrum is and how to implement it. Either these two forms of communication are fundamentally different or this principle should have been communicated to the users of Scrum by the instructor who trained them; and then communicated verbally to all new employees as they join the teams. If Principle #6 is valid, why would anyone need to document this?

Principle #7 identifies working software as a key metric for success. This is fine; but, what seems to be missing is an assessment of whether or not the software actually solves a problem. Software can easily work (do what it's supposed to do and pass all of the tests) and not solve the customer's actual problem. So this seems a barren basis for measuring progress. It may also explain why each new update is bigger and slower rather than smaller and faster. It's hard to demo smaller and faster.

Finally, the promotion of self-organizing teams (#11) is a fine idea. The problem is that you can't start a self-organizing team. You can't really even promote it. A team either self-organizes or someone else has to organize it. If the team self-organizes, then there is the claim that the best architectures, requirements and designs (all understood through face-to-face discussion) will arise. This may be true. I cannot find any scientific studies to support it.

These are the principles behind Scrum. A well-managed department within a company producing features or bug fixes could easily choose Scrum as their methodology. It works fine for that sort of thing. If an entire company fully embraces Scrum for all operations, it has defined itself as a feature factory. The Scrum interpretation of *The Agile Principles* imposes this definition.

If this is your company's goal, then it needs to be clear about what it will and will not do. It will deliver new features to customers on a regular basis. It may produce new products, but only if the products are built out from existing components. It will not develop the next great thing. It will not dedicate time or money to research that will lead to truly unique products. It will not explore solutions to larger problems

5: Feature Factory

that belie the obvious solution and are not even recognized by future customers who are used to the status quo.

You may suggest that Google is the perfect example of a truly innovative Scrum organization, but Google has not accepted Scrum as their only methodology. Google produces all sorts of interesting technologies, some successful, some not. Some built up from *existing* technologies and others based upon new innovation. Some developed within Google; many acquired from third parties. Not all of those use Scrum. The Go team is agile but not Scrum[5]. The Google driverless car was conceived well outside the Scrum methodology[6] and beyond that, companies deploy all manner of different methodologies and still call most of them "Scrum."

So we've looked at how Scrum works within companies and its basic principles. I have tried to demonstrate that those principles tend to drive a focus on mundane features as opposed to innovative solutions to problems. This is not intended to discredit Scrum. It is one of many methodologies and it, like all of them, works well for certain things. The problem I have sought to expose is the one that arises when a company turns exclusively to Scrum. At that point, the company and its employees comprise the simple clockwork. Features are conveyed through the mechanism utterly unsullied by creativity.

If the company's purpose is to ship features, it will be in fine shape with Scrum. If its purpose is to solve problems, it should be agile but it should not tie itself to a single methodology; and no one should believe the claim that Agile *is* Scrum as if there were no other agile options.

---

5   https://groups.google.com/forum/#!forum/golang-nuts
6   http://www.ted.com/talks/sebastian_thrun_google_s_driverless_car

6: What Is Rigorous...

To know the pine, go to the pine. To know the bamboo, go to the bamboo.

Matsuo Basho

My good friend and former manager, Barry Fish, once said, "First-class people hire first-class people. Second-class people hire third-class people."[7] That explains why substandard management tends to grow until determined first-class management clears it out. The problem that second-class management has in abundance is fear. Fear that they will be shown up by the next new hire; fear that forces they don't understand will overtake them and thwart their plans; fear that their subordinates are doing something horrible that they are not smart enough to grasp.

This is a problem with any substandard manager but it is worst when the manager is supervising highly technical people. Technical people have a language that is confusing and abstract. It is almost a *foreign* language: "You don't need to implement a concretion, just declare an interceptor for that interface in the application context and pass it to an appropriate factory."

I remember, at the age of seventeen, standing next to a man who was repairing an early Multibus computer. I picked up an integrated

---

[7] The actual origin of this quotation is not certain. Barry attributed it to Carroll Smith, well-known race car driver, engineer and author. Others attribute it to Manfred Kets de Vries or Peter Drucker, both authorities on leadership development. Whoever originated it, its recitation illuminates any discussion regarding employment practice.

6: What Is Rigorous...

circuit from the table and looked at it. The repairman calmly turned to me and said, "That's NMOS" (pronounced *enmoss*).

I responded with a grunt to which he more slowly and distinctly repeated, "That's NMOS."

I said, "Oh. Yes." to which he now said firmly, "Put it down!"

He understood that NMOS is very sensitive to static electricity and that I was not properly grounded. I did not understand that, and so his statement did not convey to me what it would to another person who was skilled in electronics repair.

To a manager who is not comfortable with trust and who is not skilled at distinguishing between competence and bluster, every conversation with the engineer must carry horrifying risk. "When he said, 'that's NMOS,' what did he actually mean? Did I misunderstand? Is the project at risk and I just don't know it?"

Everyone has had this problem. When you needed a plumber and your friend recommended her cousin, Buster Pipes, you hired the guy. It took twice as long as you expected and the tub still leaked a little. From that experience you took positive action. You subscribed to a web page that rates local repair people and you decided that from now on you would talk to the repairman a little bit over the phone before you would have him start the job. You sought advice from various FAQs and you learned a couple of telling questions and the expected answers so you could determine whether this is a serious plumber. You are now prepared to define and prosecute your next plumbing project.

You have just resolved one of the problems that managers encounter on a regular basis as they cycle in new people and strive to get the best performance out of them. You have done it the way a first-class manager would do it. The way you solved the problem was difficult. You had to apply yourself and expand your understanding of the field in order to improve your ability to assess plumbers. A second-class manager would be hard pressed to apply himself in that way. It would be far easier to restrict the problem by not using the faucets too much and bathing infrequently in order to put off the possibility that a seal will wear out.

Famine In the Bullpen

In the same way, if the manager can assure that the technical people are following a limited and easily tracked procedure, she can shackle her management problem with process. Scrum is one such process, but not the only one. There are several other formal methods and countless methods that companies just made up from a little history and analysis. Not all such processes limit the scope of the engineering endeavor to the same degree, some actually enhance it. Various processes have been in play ever since the first large company started developing software. It would have been entirely contrary to the culture or management inclination of IBM to start their first-ever software project by telling Bob to, 'Go figure it out and let me know when you're done.' They developed a process.

•

I have been required to attend two one week Scrum training sessions. Near the end of each one, some experienced developer said something to this effect: "I'm not persuaded that this will work," to which the Scrum Master teaching the class responded, "What're ya gonna use? Waterfall?"

I'm not sure why that ridiculous retort always quieted the room. In each case, almost none of the attendees had ever used the Waterfall method, which is generally reserved to companies working with large authoritarian institutions. The reason no one responded was probably because none of them had ever worked at a company that could assign a name to their process – it was just the way things were done.

To the inexperienced developer, their first thought was probably, 'Was I using Waterfall (whatever that is) at my last company?' To the more seasoned, the statement probably delivered a stun from which the moments required to recover would not admit of a timely response. I know that explained *my* silence the first time. The second time I heard that exact phrase, I responded, but not effectively. The question forces a frame which itself is nonsensical and while Waterfall was the only other formal method with which I had had experience, it was at a defense contractor which used it primarily to assure a wide distribution of

6: What Is Rigorous...

blame in case anything went wrong. It was obvious to me that the method was highly restrictive and would not apply anywhere else.

So far I have focused on Scrum because it is, by far, the most popular formal method in U.S. industry. As surprising as it may be to Scrum instructors, Scrum and Waterfall are not the only formal methods. Indeed, recently a new, even more restrictive method called Scaled Agile Framework (SAFe®) tries to layer on top of Scrum but instead largely redesigns it to conform to the structure of more traditional methods. It encourages planning by quarter with defined outcomes, while Scrum claims that you can't predict much past a month. It forces a strict metric for the story point while Scrum counts on the story point being of unspecified size, customized to each team.

On the plus side, it does acknowledge a key fact that most people would recognize from their own experience: the workers know what is going on much better than management does. Management promotes the fawning sycophant whom the workers know is an imbecile. Management selects the new database because the salesman was so convincing even though the ideal selection wouldn't have required as much sales perseverance. Management chooses a direction for the company that is not supported by the company's existing skill set and is inconsistent with market sensibilities.

Unfortunately, the direction in the SAFe shop can still be set by upper management having very little consultation with the workers. The only thing the lower level employees do is figure out how to accomplish the goals set by the same confused management that used to set goals before Scrum put much of that responsibility in the hands of the Product Owners. I was once in a SAFe planning session wherein a Director literally thanked the assembled employees for doing his job for him.

To be fair, there is a sort of genius to SAFe. It takes advantage of a principle called *affinity fraud*. It's the same technique in use when we hear someone say, "Sell fifty subscriptions and you can be a Junior Golden Acolyte," or "Become one of the thousands of discerning investors taking advantage of this loophole." The method persuades the mark that he holds a similar station to others he fears may be his superiors. People will work like demons to prove they are the equal of their "betters," and this form of fraud persuades an entire work force that they must work to prove they can measure up to this very public directorial challenge. The quarterly planning sessions typically begin with a C-level executive declaring to the assembled workers, "I'm the guy in charge but you're the real power behind this company." It gives management all of the advantages of a worker-owned coop without requiring the surrender of any control. Those employees feel "empowered" and important when they are, in fact, the unwitting tools of a likely detached and confused long-term vision. SAFe gives the team members the delusion of control while they are actually highly constrained by the goals, schedules and deadlines set by top management.

There are companies that use SAFe as an innocent excuse to get everyone together once per quarter to talk things through, but that is not the actual intent behind it. SAFe is a formal method which presumes that Scrum can be scaled to the full enterprise as long as the basic principles of Scrum are generally expunged[8]. It also presumes that this hollowed-out Scrum can be used everywhere in the company for all types of tasks. Unfortunately, the hollowed-out Scrum does an even poorer job on complicated tasks than real Scrum. It suffers all the deficiencies of Scrum plus it adds rigid deadlines and demands impossible predictions of future behavior. Despite the formality and the emphasis on planning, SAFe still doesn't work for all technical projects.

The iterative approach used by Scrum, SAFe, Adaptive Software Development (ASD) or eXtreme Programing (XP) presumes that the initial delivery won't be the final product. The delivered product may well include known bugs to be addressed in the next iteration. This is fine for your mp3 app; but would not be acceptable for the software controlling a manned rocket – the second iteration will not restore the deceased astronauts.

---

8   This is another example of a case where a company is doing something very different from Scrum and yet they readily call it "Scrum."

6: What Is Rigorous...

Within a company, it is not inconceivable that one department may deliver a trivial app while another delivers critical banking software tied to rigid and complex regulations. It would be silly for such a company to designate exactly the same process for those two departments. While a process like Alistair Cockburn's *Crystal* is specifically designed to adapt to both highly critical and simpler more casual projects, the polar dimensions supported by Crystal are nonetheless rather different approaches. Two teams, using Crystal, and fulfilling very different requirements may find that one will not recognize that the other is also using Crystal. Cockburn, a seasoned software consultant, developed the method to support his successful consulting firm so he wouldn't have to tailor a new process to each of his diverse projects.

A fascinating comparison of formal methods may be found in Barry Boehm and Richard Turner's book *Balancing Agility and Discipline*[Boehm_2004]. In it they contrast and compare thirteen different formal methods. It is an easy read and well worth the acquisition. My reading of the book left me feeling that they had struggled so hard to be fair that they had missed some key contrasts between the approaches. Their excess of niceness, however, arises in their descriptions, not in their methodology, which is well-conceived, or in their data, which is gathered with discipline and clearly organized.

Each of the formal methods is assessed along several different dimensions including the criticality of the result (do lives depend on it?), the maturity of the personnel, the size of the team and others. In the end they present the conclusions they've derived from their study and one of the conclusions is that developers should look beyond formal methods altogether; arguing that, in some cases, the rigor of the formal method may damp the creativity needed to accomplish truly useful results.

French mathematician and early member of Bourbaki[9], Jean Dieudonné, once said "What is rigorous is meaningless." As a mathema-

---

9 Known under the pseudonym *Nicolas Bourbaki*, this was a group of (mostly French) mathematicians who sought to formalize mathematics by grounding it in set theory. Publishing numerous very abstract and rigorous books and treatises, they advanced concepts and terminologies that are still in use today.

tician, he must use rigor in order to assure the accuracy of his claims; but the process of reaching those results requires musing, soaring imagination and the application of experience and knowledge to the characterization of the phenomena being assessed. The whole thing must not be rigor. There must be room for disciplined whimsy.

——————— • ———————

What is clear about each of these formal methods is that the primary goal is to provide management with data. It can be argued that without data, management cannot plan, and that is a fair assertion. Methods that provide sufficient data for planning make sense on a number of levels, but if the data is used to assure that the plan is timid, the effort is wasted.

Clearly some approaches take this into account. For example, both Dynamic System Development Method (DSDM) and Lean Development (LD) incorporate risk assessment into the process. The team may establish a fair estimate of risk against benefits and management may make decisions based upon those criteria. In such cases, the numbers are presented and rational choices are made and the company advances step by well-informed step.

Given this, the question arises: how does management plan for the spectacular? How did management plan for the Apple iPod? How did management plan for the Toyota Prius, a groundbreaking hybrid automobile? How did management plan for the Espresso Book Machine®, a device that can build a perfect-bound book before your very eyes? How is it that there are managers willing to invest time and effort into first-time projects without precedent? Projects for which there are no data, no history and no prior experience? Aren't these the projects that extract the most value from the potential of the creative employee?

When circumstances call out for a solution to a problem, it is rare that the problem may be easily resolved. Problems that may be easily resolved have already been resolved. To resolve a real problem requires an approach that is daring and extraordinary. Such an approach rarely has precedent. If it had precedent, someone would already have applied that precedent and there would be no problem. Generating software features based upon the customer's guarded requests is easily planned and delivered. Solving the problem that *automobile on-board software must be connected and upgradable but also invulnerable to hackers* is not easily planned. The corporate goal may be profit; but the goal of the individuals running the company is to remain employed. When innovation succeeds, the company may profit. When it falls short, profit and jobs are at risk. Unless the corporate culture embraces innovation, no one will take that risk.

——— • ———

When limiting processes are applied throughout a company, the creative pressure has to be released somehow. One of the more comical relief valves is the aforementioned innovation sprint. Any Scrum company that sponsors a periodic innovation sprint has forfeited the right to innovate. It has demonstrated a failure to comprehend innovation as a concept; and, it has repudiated the commonsense notion that innovation is fundamental to engineering, competition and progress. It has advanced the claim that innovation is an exchange commodity that may be inserted into any product as a component. This furthers the common goal of modern Agile to comfort management by assuring them that they are not dependent on exceptional people, but only on a mechanism that may stamp out any part they want, be it feature, fix or innovation. These are all simple selections and management need only turn the dial.

Innovation needs to be built in to the entire culture of the company. It has to be possible for anyone in the company to identify a problem and propose a solution. Such proposals need to be reviewed regularly; and, if deemed worthy, engineers eager for a challenge need to be marshaled to the impossible cause.

Given a serious problem, an engineer may need to dwell on it for a while. She may be on another job while the rumination begins. In the quiet moments, she may return to the problem, making occasional notes on her whiteboard as a plan begins to emerge. A few weeks into it, as her current project winds down, she begins to put full time into the problem. There were four possible approaches in the beginning, but over time she has winnowed that down to two.

With two reasonable possibilities, she calls in a few sharp colleagues and discusses her conclusions. After that discussion, she's up to three possible solutions. She talks through the issues with her manager and redoubles her efforts. A week later, she sees where the three solutions come together. There's a revelation. The three solutions all have a common root. There's really only one solution. The elation kicks in. This is what the engineer craves like a drug. There is tearful joy in bringing to ground the inaccessible understanding. Now it's obvious and now she can actually start formulating a proposal that she can present to the council for architectural review.

Here we see a solution that is disciplined. Her training has provided the underlying skills to take on such a problem. Her history has tempered those skills into a reliable process which usually yields a solution. As with all problem-solving, some of it happens consciously and some unconsciously. There is no simple mapping. If there were, we would not need engineers.

That process is terrifying to all but the most skilled managers. What if the engineer can't come up with a solution? What if a different engineer could, but I chose the wrong one? What if, even after all that thinking, the proposed solution is wrong? Far better to allocate a short space of time for innovation. Turn it on, count out the days and then turn it off. If nothing pans out, you didn't lose much. You may then remind yourself that nothing here requires special skill or defines a true challenge. Thus you may talk about great challenge and worthy adversity without ever being personally concerned about actually confronting risk. This juvenilizes all workers, but especially those who may provide genuine value through innovation.

While developers are the grist for these processes, the decision to use them is invariably from management. Management latches on to a particular formal method because it provides something that management wants.

7: Common Knowledge

> *The fact that an opinion has been widely held is no evidence whatever that it is not utterly absurd.*
>
> Bertrand Russell

The software development culture is driven by principles. The first principles I encountered were the OO principles enumerated in *Object Oriented Software Construction*[Meyer_1997] by Bertrand Meyer. The Single Choice Principle: *There must be one and only one way to perform any operation.* The Open-Closed Principle: *A class must be open to extension and closed to modification.* Stepping away from OO, some may be aware of the Rule of Three: *You can do it and then do the same thing in another place, but when you start on the third copy, you need to consolidate the algorithm into a shared procedure*; or the somewhat more obscure Law of Demeter: *Your service may talk to its neighbors. It may not talk to its neighbors' neighbors.*

Different principles apply depending upon the language, the methodology and the problem to be solved. In the OO world, Meyer's principles hold sway. In procedural programming or the class of languages called *declarative*, different rules make sense. When writing in C, your function may cause a printer to begin printing (it has a *side-effect*). In Haskell, your function is an actual *function*: it maps across sets. You *could* try to write a function that had a side-effect *but don't!* The principles of the functional language and the principles of functional methodology dictate against that without the use of an isolating monad.

Famine In the Bullpen

Principles serve as repositories of knowledge built up over years of trial and error. Why do we observe the Uniform Access Principle? Because, when variables within an object are exposed, opportunistic programmers will acquire them directly, abrogating the object's superior understanding of the variable's semantics such that, when the mechanism for generating the variable changes, those opportunistic programmers will be reading faulty data.

Of late, I've been running into very popular principles that are not borne out by the evidence. We can include some of the Scrum principles which have already been discussed; but beyond that are ancillary principles that seem to crop up in various Agile shops, including the avoidance of documentation; the strict distinction between unit and integration tests and the refusal to address the whole problem.

For that reason, I'd like to spend a few pages talking about common knowledge and how it has morphed into a sort of ad hoc set of bad principles that developers simply assume to be true.

———— • ————

In 2010, I was being interviewed by a fellow of German extraction in Boulder who worked at a company responsible for processing high volume data streams. His company was doing this using Java, even though a better choice would probably have been to use a lightweight language with a minimum of scaffolding like Erlang or C. He and I walked to a nearby coffee shop where we sipped lattés and conversed in a relaxed fashion. He asked good questions and told entertaining stories. In the course of the conversation I asked about their philosophy regarding documentation. At this, my congenial interviewer turned to face me directly. His countenance became stern and he spoke with Teutonic authority. "Our philosophy is 'No!'" In his thick German accent he emphasized their creed. "Ve haf no documentation. None! Ve ah very proud of zis."

I was a bit startled by his sudden fervor, but I pressed on. "So," I responded, "you must provide that information as comments in your code."

"No!" he retorted, "No comments. None! Ve ah very proud of zis."

7: Common Knowledge

'Well,' I thought, 'this is clearly not a match.' Our interview ended shortly after that with a friendly handshake and a mutual understanding that this pleasant conversation would not result in a hire.

This view is very common. I am persuaded that good software engineers have been convinced to follow this approach by programmers who can't spell. The philosophy only makes sense if the product of the developer is so simple and so degenerate that all procedure is contiguous to intent. This is obviously true in the most trivial case such as:

```
public String getText() {
    return text;
}
```

Of course a comment would be irrelevant here. It would be required only by a developer who had suffered a recent brain injury. But take a look at this tested and fully functional method and figure out why it's doing this:

```
AB_SQUARED = EARTH_EQUATORIAL_RADIUS *
        EARTH_POLAR_RADIUS

def get_m_of_phi_miles(phi):
    a_cos_phi = EARTH_EQUATORIAL_RADIUS * math.cos(phi)
    a_cos_phi_squared = a_cos_phi * a_cos_phi

    b_sin_phi = EARTH_POLAR_RADIUS * math.sin(phi)
    b_sin_phi_squared = b_sin_phi * b_sin_phi

    denominator = math.pow((a_cos_phi_squared +
            b_sin_phi_squared), 1.5)

    return (AB_SQUARED / denominator)
```

The variable names, of course, give the whole thing away; but if you were not familiar with *Vincenty's direct method*, this would need some explaining. As an old man, I often forget the exact formulation so even I, in my own code for my own personal use, insist upon a comment:

```
##
# Return the Meridional Radius of Curvature (in miles)
# at the provided latitude in radians.
#
# @param phi (float) latitude in radians
# @return float apparent radius in miles
```

It is possible that this would not be needed by my German interviewer. Undoubtedly the mathematical application of the MRC is not something that would escape him; but, for ordinary people like me, a comment is required. I used this exact method (written in Java) in software written for a publishing firm (for reasons which will become clear in the next chapter). I provided this comment so that the next developer to come along would understand not *what* it was doing but *why* it was doing it. The comment for the method that invoked this method completed the picture, explaining even why Vincenty was chosen over the Google or the FCC algorithm.

I once reviewed a change to a Ruby program wherein two instructions, originally arranged as two lines in the more common fashion were concatenated with a semicolon in an uncommon fashion. When asked why the change had been made, the developer responded that, for some reason, the separate lines confused the deployment framework. I suggested that a comment to that effect would save a future programmer inadvertently correcting the unconventional style. The developer was so devout a *noncommentarian* that he simply responded that the next person to change it would figure out the problem when it wouldn't deploy. Yes, better to waste a few hours of a developer's time than to add a dozen words of explanation to a quirky codebase.

The only possible explanation I can imagine for this religious fascination with no comments is that no one in the industry is doing anything interesting. Interesting software is certainly simple and concise but the procedure (what you can glean from the software) does not unambiguously reveal the intent (what is in the developer's heart). If someone were called upon to refactor the above code without comments, how would they do it? Is it yielding the required data in the most efficient possible way? It's obvious what is being returned, but why?

7: Common Knowledge

What is $(a\cos(\varphi)^2 + b\sin(\varphi)^2)^{1.5}$ supposed to express? The notion that code requires no comments and that software designs require no documentation implies that what software developers do is fundamentally trivial. If it is trivial, what value is it bringing to the community? Why isn't it being done by machines?

This is most often traced back to a well-executed book by Robert C. Martin called *Clean Code*[Martin_2009]. Martin advocates not adding comments where they provide no value; but a serious reading of his thesis doesn't lead to the utter rejection of comments. It could be imagined that a developer could write code so precisely that its intention is always clear; but, honestly, the purpose of code is to communicate instructions to a machine, not to a human. To construct code that formed a semblance of readable sentences explaining not only the *what* but the *why* would be a glorious feat worthy of praise; but no one does this. Why?

Computer languages conform to simple grammars, the most common being the *context-free grammar*. A context-free grammar can be parsed using any number of simple tools based on a *BNF specification*. Specifications for such languages as C, Python and SQL are readily available on the web and may be used to produce a functional interpreter or compiler. Such grammars are well suited to the task of defining procedures and are therefore ideal for communicating with machines intended to perform tasks.

Context-free grammars convey the *what* but they are simply not capable of consistently communicating the *why*. For that task we use *generative grammars*. The generative grammar is not easily parsed and is even harder to specify. Indeed, a nearly adequate specification for such a grammar may require a few hundred pages. On the plus side, using one, we may convey the what, the how, the why and the deeper meaning of any procedure. This is possible only because of the innate power of the generative grammar.

Languages conforming to a generative grammar, such as Italian, Mandarin and Swahili, evolved specifically for the purpose of conveying meaning between human beings. While the only adequate parser for such languages remains the human brain, there are plenty of those to go around and nearly every developer is equipped with one. We are advised to use the right tool for the job and the merit of this recommendation is recapitulated with each successfully executed engine repair, home project and web page. If this is not a canard, if there really is merit in using the tool best suited to the task at hand then we are wise to use a simple grammar to communicate with the computer and a generative grammar to communicate with humans.

———— • ————

My first exposure to JUnit was rather disappointing. It became clear that, unlike the previous test harness in my experience, it had no built-in ability to test over the network. In a world where the computer and the network are so tightly conjoined, how far can you get without involving the network in your test?

When I folded a simple socket interface to localhost into my test, so that I could verify my code's response to a network request, I was quickly reprimanded by my technical supervisor, "This is a unit test. You can't use a network interface." When I asked how I could exercise the network interface without a network, he told me that I should *mock* the network which means, of course, that I actually don't know for sure how this would respond to an actual network. That, apparently, was the job of a separate integration test to be written in Selenium.

Over time I've worked at companies that mock more or less than others; but, for all of them a strict distinction is made between unit tests and integration tests. Unit tests test one thing only, while integration tests test two or more things in concert. Since software interacts with software, this distinction is immediately suspect. Whatever piece of software you wrote is using various libraries and calling various other procedures and isolating those is more complicated than anyone wants to take on. The notion that you can test only one isolated piece of software is a delusion.

A test is always better for testing the actual thing rather than a simulation of the actual thing in a simulation of its actual environment. As

7: Common Knowledge

they say in aerospace, "Test it like you fly it.[10]" For this reason, I was used to organizing my tests in prescribed order so that they would first test the lowest level interfaces to the underlying repository or remote service; then test the business logic that used those interfaces; and then, the services that used the business logic. In each case, using the tested lower layer as a part of the test itself. When I reached the topmost interface, I was simulating the actual real world environment.

Those who distinguish strictly between unit and integration tests would advocate the use of mock objects to emulate each of the other layers so that the test would be *pure* and the other layer wouldn't introduce anomalies. To that, the most reasonable response seems to be:

1. If the tested layer introduces an anomaly, you didn't test it very well.
2. If the other layer's behavior changes and you don't remember to modify your mock, you've missed something important.

The more you mock, the less you grok. If you know the low level functions work, why wouldn't you include them in the test at the next level? Why, if the network and computer are inextricably entwined, wouldn't network tests be fundamental parts of your testing strategy and why would you have to use multiple different test harnesses to test your whole product?

After hearing that the JUnit folks decried the use of test suites, preaching that all tests should be able to run in any order without any grouping mechanism, I struck upon a theory. I think the modern strict distinction between unit and integration test was asserted because, since JUnit only supports unit tests, it was important to establish this common knowledge so no one would start asking why JUnit didn't do this obviously necessary thing.

There are reasonable classifications to be applied to tests and reasonable reasons for applying them. If we want to run just the tests that verify the functions top to bottom so that we have a very quick sanity

---

10 I was reminded of this by my old friend Sherry Winkleblack with whom I worked at Martin Marietta.

check for the product, we may put that into a *sanity suite*. We may want to run all of the important tests but leave out all of the tests that fail on corner cases not considered essential; we may put those into the *acceptance suite*. We may identify tests that take more than two minutes to run and sequester them into a nightly test suite that we may call the *slow suite*.

It is a good idea to distinguish certain tests that require an outside network for, for example, stress testing or to distinguish tests that modify data in a destructive manner and, therefore, may not be run against production systems. These are all test classifications that make sense. Any one of them may be testing one software element or a stack of elements and it is difficult to understand why, as long as any test failure clearly identifies what went wrong, we care about which it was.

———•———

One key principle of modern Agile is to do what has been requested but no more. To do more would be to satisfy a request which was not made. This has been formalized as YAGNI (Ya Ain't Gonna Need It). This is another way of saying that we don't pay attention to the larger problem, we just fiddle about with the symptoms – one symptom at a time.

When I worked at a defense contractor, we were called upon to design a remote actor for the Space Shuttle: a tethered machine with anthropomorphic arms that would allow an operator inside the shuttle to manipulate space-based assemblies outside of the shuttle. NASA had contracted with us and had proposed much of the general design as a set of trade studies. The remote was to have three arms. The bottom arm was primarily for stabilizing a work piece but the top two arms were very like human arms having a shoulder, elbow and wrist as well as a grasping hand.

An internal study had suggested the use of what was known as a *ball hand controller* which consisted of a ball, upon which the astronaut's hand would rest, with a cluster of buttons. The astronaut would move the end of the six foot arm by holding down a button and moving the

7: Common Knowledge

ball in an appropriate direction. Applying pressure to different buttons, he would indicate if the end was to move up and down, forward and back or side to side. It did not seem intuitive to me. For example, it provided very little control over where the elbow was situated. If the elbow was obstructing movement, special adjustments would be required.

A little investigation revealed that our company had developed two very useful technologies that would contribute to an improved level of control. Specifically, there was an exoskeleton suit that could be slipped on allowing the transmission of the user's shoulder, elbow and wrist joint angles. There was also a glove that would deliver the user's hand position. It seemed obvious to me that since the robot arm was configured like a human arm this would be a much better way to control the remote end effectors. The user would unlock and activate the device which would bring its two upper arms slowly to the position of the user's arms. From there on, the user would simply move in a natural fashion and by moving his own arms would assemble the complicated piping that defined the remote's original task.

When I approached the director with this proposal he listened quietly until I was done. He could have argued that my proposal was inferior to the ball hand controller, but that issue wasn't even in play. It had nothing to do with his understanding of the problem. Instead, he leaned forward over his desk and clasped his hands together. "Julian," he stated flatly, "*Meet* the requirements. *Never* exceed them."

That was a principle from aerospace that assured the government would get only what it asked for and not necessarily something that would work. Both options paid the same; but, the latter would cost more and require a long-term commitment. I now find that same principle applied in the commercial software industry, as we play the same game with the customer. "Oh, you wanted to be able to delete the file, too? I'm sorry, that wasn't what the story said. We'll fix that in the next iteration."

YAGNI is an unfortunate response to an inability to comprehend *form*. In philosophical discourse, form can take on several roughly similar meanings. Wittgenstein's understanding is closest to ours. He writes

"The form is the possibility of the structure." To understand the form is to understand that the problem is not a thing but a dynamic. It is a part of a sequence of events in space-time. Understanding it in this way, we may grasp the possibility of assessing the events that led to the problem and the events that may propagate naturally from the problem. In the context of the form, the problem is not and cannot be isolated. The dynamic reveals not only the root cause but all of the side-effects surrounding the root cause. Understanding those side-effects reveals the likely next problem to be raised and the nature of a solution that may address the current and future related problems.

The engineer takes on the task of mastering the form of the problem meaning that the solution doesn't just deal with the immediate impression, but the problem's entire footprint. To take each little reported issue as an independent thing-to-fix, the developer is not required to understand the problem as a whole. He can spend the rest of the quarter coding up fixes to all of the little problems that get reported after that first fix fails to address the entire problem.

When I encountered this at a large publishing firm, I insisted that the engineering team *solve the class, not the problem*. We understood that whatever problem is reported, it isn't the problem, it is a side-effect of a problem which is a member of a class of problems which, when analyzed, will reveal a root cause. It is that class of problems that must be addressed by correcting the root cause. More often than not, after we had provided the feature requested by Marketing, they would return with an easily-predicted next demand (easily-predicted because we understood the form of the problem). Our response to that demand was a simple change to an anticipated configuration value.

I took to occasionally saying, "If the next request from the customer requires more than a configuration change, the first request was not satisfied." To understand the problem is to master its form. A mastery of the form identifies an array of related problems, and their relationships to this problem may be defined with mathematical precision.

7: Common Knowledge

It is not true that these tidbits of common knowledge are part of the software culture because years of engineering experience have clearly proved their wisdom. They are part of a larger belief that management must be placated with the delusion of certainty. This promotes both bad engineering and bad management. It promotes an excess of time gathering statistics of limited value and planning behaviors which provide no benefit beyond comforting higher ups and giving customers the feeling that their participation is valued.

What is the root of management's fear? Why is it crucial to coddle management in such overt ways?

8: Fast Follower

The Sun Microsystems culture was unforgiving as regards error. Some companies provide for an embarrassing token such as a dunce cap or a statuette made of coconuts for the programmer who breaks the build. At Sun, the concept was not even to be considered. The Solaris build did not break and anyone who wanted to challenge that claim was brought to book with the quiet certainty of the mad zealot. Yes, the build did occasionally fail; but, it was not discussed among polite company.

Fairly early in my thirteen year career at Sun, I made a modification to the cpio utility. The next morning at one o'clock I was roused from quiet slumber and informed that my change had broken the build. There was no anger or recrimination; it was simply assumed (and this was made clear without an exchange of words to this effect) that this problem would go away within the next fifteen minutes. I logged on immediately, corrected my error and checked in the change. I was politely thanked and reminded that this does not happen and we would not speak of it again.

Working amid some of the brightest minds in the industry was a grueling and rewarding education that has twisted my perception of the engineering discipline ever since. The SDF provided for formal architecture review and required that each project be defined using a functional specification. Code reviews were required before check-in and when Solaris was in beta, two or more code reviews could be required.

No software could be checked in to Solaris without the approval of a member of the CRT who served as the final gate into the holy sanctuary that was Solaris. For each such check-in, the CRT member would

8: Fast Follower

open the gate, allowing the software in, and then close it immediately behind. The Solaris build did not break. The Solaris tests did not fail. Solaris was the most stable commercial operating system in the world. Everyone at Sun knew that and everyone was committed to assuring the continued blessings of this delicately maintained market-wide perception.

While the purpose of the SDF was to assure primarily that Solaris was guarded from error, all other projects within Sun were guided by its protocols. Every new or changed public interface was to be reviewed by the ARC which would assess the functional specification, discuss, recommend and ultimately approve or reject.

One might view this as a burdensome and highly restrictive environment but ARC review required only ten or twenty minutes. Most obvious changes were handled through an accelerated *fast-track* which was addressed outside of a formal meeting. Most importantly, everyone at Sun was expected to propose new projects through what was called a *one pager*. It was a half page explaining the problem and another half page proposing the solution. At that early stage, before the network was universally the computer, problems abounded and I was fortunate enough to find myself taking a regular diet of intractable problems.

In time, I found myself typically addressing problems that other departments had failed to solve. It was exhilarating to pull together a team of competent engineers, present the insoluble problem and ultimately discover that the problem wasn't the problem after all; it was a side-effect. Over and over, the problem would be revealed as a huge clumsy canard which obscured a simple comprehensible root cause which was the actual problem to be addressed.

This cycle was repeated throughout my tenure at Sun. It became commonplace to listen politely as the problem was explained, knowing full well that this was not the problem and that our first job would be to discover what the problem actually was. Once that was done, to apply our skill and creativity to devising a solution that would address not just the side-effect that had been presented to us but also the other side-effects that no one even knew were related.

———•———

I have been writing software in Java since early 1995 shortly after James Gosling dropped by our offices to tell us about this cool little language he was developing. Within a month I was writing a test harness in Java for one of the first actual Java projects.

While enthusiasm for Java grew, my teams remained fairly isolated from the frenzy. We were addressing specific problems using established methodology and were not finding that approach inadequate to the task. We would hear talk of the Tomcat app server and of the upcoming WAR file and the SOAP protocol, but our development and deployment method was entirely satisfactory. Our software was working and delivering the required services. It was easy to maintain, test and extend and it was ARC-approved. Seeing no problem, we were not in a mood to fix anything. This was standard software development using a new language. We would change that approach when the standard method showed signs of wear.

My relationship with Sun ended in 2006. No longer a Senior Staff Engineer with an innovation powerhouse, I found myself working for a newspaper publisher in Denver as a mid-level Java programmer. There I was confronted, for the first time, with what had actually happened world-wide in the Java community. I first encountered what would become the modern *Java Complex*. I was first exposed to JBoss and Inversion of Control and Maven. I was first introduced to the concept of a container and I had to learn the confusing new language of Java in the wild.

For the first time in my career, I was seeing the mind-numbing simplicity of software development. There was no serious discussion of problems to be solved, because for every problem there was a simple framework that fixed it.

I spent two years engaged in the tedious job of plugging other peoples' software together to form a sloppy assembly that we would call a

8: Fast Follower

solution. What I had done at Sun with 50 lines of ksh, I was now doing with an over-built framework having only an FAQ for reference. The young people around me were perfectly happy with this approach, they knew of no other. In the third year, I became back-end lead architect and was responsible for much of the company's software strategy.

Even as a lead architect, there was little I could do to turn the job interesting simply because top management was terrified of ideas. I was told repeatedly that we were a *fast follower*. We let the competitor take the risks and then we copied what they had done.

That too, of course, was a delusion. Without real technical innovation, we couldn't copy what an innovative competitor had done; but, the problem was bigger than that. No similar media companies were taking risks, either. They were *all* fast followers, waiting for some timid outlier to take a risk and succeed so they could copy and follow. It never happened. Tedious day followed on dragging tedious day until some kid at one of the affiliated newspapers had an idea: why don't we put a map on our newspaper websites showing pins where news stories took place? The reader could select a pin and read the story about what had happened there.

While some of us imagined that we could ask the reporters to provide coordinates for their articles, we were told that reporters were too busy. They would never take the time to do that. Don't worry, though; there was no risk here. We would use a mapping company experienced in reading English language text and geolocating points of interest. It was amazing, someone had been creative and the company was actually going to try something new.

A few days later, with the price quote from the mapping company in hand, we were going to give up. The price tag was simply too high.

We were very fortunate to have a technical manager, Erin McDermott, who understood the potential of our team and a Scrum Master, Brooke Schwerdt, who was prepared to be flexible in support of innovation. Erin pulled me aside one morning to inform me of this failed corporate venture and asked if we could just write something to do that. That is to say, she wanted to verify that this team could write software to read an English language newspaper article, determine if it identified a meaningful location and then determine the longitude and latitude of that location or locations for pinning on a map.

Well, this was the first challenge I'd had in five years, so, of course, I assured her that there would be no problem doing that. I talked through a plan with Brooke and brought two other engineers, Joe Henry and Jason Rist, into the project. We delivered the software in about nine weeks. At peak, it was reading nearly 400 articles per day and assigning locations as appropriate. Two newspapers were designated as guinea pigs and their web sites sported maps with pins indicating the store that was robbed, the location of the meeting and where the tornado touched down.

After release I was called into the office of the president of the company. He was nervous. He leaned back in his voluminous deeply-padded chair and told me he was worried. I asked him what the problem was and he said, "Look at those maps. They make for easy access to the stories that affect you. It gets us closer to personalized news."

"Yes. I think it's a good approach."

"Here's the problem," he leaned forward with a look of puzzlement tinged with fear. "How do we maintain it?"

I was uncertain of the context but I responded, "It's all automated. We monitor the feed of articles and geolocate each one as it passes through. The data comes from free sources and it's fully documented. I don't think there's a problem."

"What do we do when you leave?"

I remember my face going somewhat slack. Human communication moves smoothly because the brain is good at predicting what is about to be said. My brain missed this one entirely. There was an awkward pause. I recovered momentarily and responded as would have been expected. "The architecture is fully documented. Any engineer could understand it, maintain it and extend it."

8: Fast Follower

"Yeah," he responded firmly, "but how do we find an engineer?"

---•---

This, then, finally clarified why we were a fast follower. Management was terrified of engineering as a concept. They didn't even recognize the half-dozen skilled engineers in their own software group. Innovation was a responsibility they did not want to undertake. If an employee could come up with an idea that would distinguish them from their competition, they would suddenly have to bear the burden of actually competing.

Of course management cannot accept that there are real problems because if there were problems then someone would have to solve those problems. Who would we find to do that? Why, it would have to be someone skilled at understanding and solving problems, and who would that be? The manager understands that he couldn't do that. I mean he's tried and it's never worked out. What manner of man are you that can conjure up fire without flint or tinder?[11] Where would they even look for a necromancer of that ilk?

Oh no, far better to simply not have problems – only bugs and enhancements. Slow and steady wins the race.

After this discussion I began wondering what had changed. When I was designing high accuracy pressure gauges for the chemical industry, competition was a constant nagging concern. Every decision was driven by what our competition might do next. We dealt with competitors trying to get employees to copy our drawings and to pass on floppy disks containing our source code. We were painfully aware of our competition.

Even at Sun, we were routinely reviewing what our competition was doing and adjusting our goals based upon our ever-changing understanding of their direction. There was genuine concern that Microsoft or Intel would figure out the next solution to any one of the assembled big problems. We were driven to take risks because we knew our competitors would, and our competitors were driven in the same way.

---

11   From *Monty Python and the Holy Grail*.

Famine In the Bullpen

It wasn't just this publisher that had an aversion to risk. I haven't encountered a competitive company in ten years. The interviews are all about the skilled use of specific frameworks or incessant questions about how much I love technology. I'm rarely asked how I solve problems and that's about the only thing I do well.

---•---

This isn't limited to technology-fringe industries like newspaper publishers. Microsoft has been a fast follower for years. They purchased 86-DOS from Seattle Computer Products which borrowed and disguised features of CP/M and UNIX to yield MS-DOS. While it developed Microsoft Windows in 1981, it followed the pioneering work of Steve Wozniak in 1977 on the Apple II, the first consumer color computer with a rudimentary windowing system. We've all watched as Apple popularizes a new idea and the next year we have a Microsoft variant. The Windows Phone followed the iPhone. The Windows Tablet followed the iPad, but they didn't just copy Apple. C# was, I believe[12], a direct reaction to the popularity of Sun's Java.

Apple too has settled into a fast follower mode. A cold impartial assessment reveals that the iPod is a Sony Walkman without tapes, a fairly linear step taking advantage of Thomson's mp3 format and Intel's Flash memory. The iPhone is a well-marketed iPAQ[13] running a proprietary operating system. Of late we see simple features added on to existing products or new products, like the Apple Watch which puts an iPhone on a wrist band; or Apple TV which puts a stripped down Mini-Mac behind an HDTV. Each a very natural progression from an existing product, just like we would expect from any feature factory.

---

12 There is evidence that something like C# was in the works prior to Java, but the public release followed Java and was so similar to Java in so many ways that independent development is very hard to believe. Neither I nor anyone I knew believed there was no connection. .NET may have been an improvement, however, over the Java Complex.

13 Back when Compaq was an innovator, this was one of the coolest ideas of the year 2000. The iPAQ palmtop computer was a significant refinement of the IBM Simon which came out in 1994. It could even run Linux. Later they added a phone.

8: Fast Follower

I'm not going to ask where my flying car is (that's a lost cause), but why is the Tsiolkovsky rocket equation[14] still determining what we can take into space? Why are we reformulating and re-patenting existing cancer drugs rather than putting serious research into cancer cures? Why is our federal government subsidizing oil and coal and leaving a handful of private companies to limp along developing renewable energy sources? We are all caught up in this mentality: "Let's put our money into the stuff we understand and stay away from the risky unknown stuff."

This is why, when you proposed that brilliant new product to your boss, he was unenthusiastic. It's because, as a modern manager, he thinks differently about new products. You were thinking, "This is an excellent product and I want to build it." Your boss was thinking, "That's an excellent product. Some kid is probably working on it now. We'll keep an eye out and buy that kid's company." He was thinking that, because he has learned that engineering is risky and only stupid people expend money on the unknown. There are stupid kids working on good ideas all the time, the ones that succeed will join the big company that didn't want to risk the R&D money that the stupid kid did.

This is why, in every really interesting make-or-buy decision in your experience, buy has always won. Buy is always management's preferred approach. Sun Microsystems was prospering during the time when this timidity was beginning to take root. While Sun was better than most at valuing its own proprietary technologies, it too was mostly buying as it neared its end. It bought its way into the storage industry with both disk and tape media and it bought its way into the office software industry. None of that helped it survive. Indeed, several of the disk storage gambits yielded the kind of amateur fragility one would expect from a modern start-up mentality. Many months of work, correcting the deficiencies of the purchased design, resulted in the realization that the original concept was simply ill-conceived and that the purchase would need to be written off as a loss.

---

14 The rocket has to carry a payload but it also has to carry enough fuel to carry the payload and enough fuel to carry the required fuel. In other words, a lot of fuel is wasted just delivering the fuel.

Famine In the Bullpen

Despite these expensive lessons, most companies will continue to put their money into gas stations and avoid robotic battery replacement stations that can top up an electric vehicle in 90 seconds. It means that only the most paltry funds will trickle into plant-based plastics and solvents. It means no one is even considering lining the Federal highways with solar cells, pouring power into the grid and boosting any electric cars appropriately equipped to accept the power. It also means that, lacking a real need for smart people, secondary education and universities will continue to beg for funds in a world where human beings are only required to follow process and pull the correct levers.

9: Unless God Builds the House…

You just got a new job. Your computer is on your desk and all you need to do is set it up. It's running Linux but it doesn't have your favorite IDE. It doesn't have any of the frameworks you need to build your new employer's product and access to the workspace is really complicated compared to your last job. Upon reflection, you recall it was complicated at your last job too until you'd done it for a month or so.

Now your job is to go to the new developer wiki page and follow the step-by-step instructions. Since it's a wiki, it's only part right. Most of it works, but it isn't until two days later that you realize you mis-installed a key component. Of course, it called out a version and that version was no longer available so you went with the latest. Now you find out that it isn't compatible with another component. So, now what do you do? Do you call all over this new company looking for someone with an old version or do you refactor your entire installation to try to pull together a compatible set that still builds your company's product?

You ask around. No one has installed this stuff for a few months and so no one can really help you. It can take a day or two to finally figure it out and that seems to be no problem for your colleagues. They spent days setting up their system and are happy to give you plenty of time.

When you're done and your system is fully functional, you can do your job. Was this a useful exercise? By installing all of the tools and frameworks, did you gain new insight into the product you are about to build? To have the system ready to use would have been extremely helpful and you could have focused on the new feature to be addressed right away.

Nonetheless, a problem remains, your system is not configured identically to the build system. You won't notice it right away, but eventually, the tests will pass on your system and they'll fail on the build system. You'll spend a few days figuring out a solution to that problem and no one at the company will think that's strange.

This is the way it was done at four of the last five companies where I worked and the one case where I didn't need to build out my environment didn't require me to *have* an environment. Even though all of them specified a Linux or Unix workstation, not one of them provided a fully constructed and tested build environment as an NFS distribution. Any one of the companies could have constructed a Common Build Environment (CBE) containing all of the required tools. The IT department could maintain it and keep it up to date as required. It could have been automounted by my workstation as soon as I powered it up. Why didn't they do that?

Is NFS too slow? Well, it's slower than the local disk but NFS also does a very good job of caching. If that isn't good enough, why not have it mount NFS over FS-Cache? I have direct experience of that strategy working very well, even when the filesystems being mounted are a thousand miles away. All access was local until a tool was upgraded at which point I would have to wait a few seconds while the local cache was refreshed. The advantage was that I was productive on my first day at the company.

None of the technologies I've described cost money. They are open-source and building out a CBE is no more difficult than installing all of the various tools to a workstation. What about the fact that a lot of companies provide a notebook computer rather than a desktop computer? How does NFS deal with me working on the bus? Well, some variations on cache filesystem copy the whole file so that it can function in disconnected mode, but let's pretend that isn't practical. Why not just periodically copy the remote CBE. The command is simple:

9: Unless God Builds the House...

```
rsync -auv —delete /usr/dist/CBE/ /usr/local/CBE
```

Now the CBE is truly local. See to it that /usr/dist/CBE/bin precedes /usr/local/CBE/bin in your PATH variable, and you're using the latest when connected at work and you're using your latest *copy* when on the bus.

This solution is not ingenious. It's a fairly conventional application of twenty-year-old technologies and it saves your company days if not weeks of lost time for each new employee. Beyond that, IT can verify that the CBE is functionally identical to the operating environment of the production systems. That way, if the tests pass on your local system, you know they'll pass on the build system and they will perform correctly on production. That spares you even more wasted time.

For that matter it is trivial, using DHCP or some other network information system, to automount a *different* CBE for each of your company's products. If you need to build the old version of a product, your workstation could easily automount the older CBE with the older compilers and then forget all about it when you've checked in your change.

Am I missing something? Why is it not this easy? Why is it better to have each developer's build environment constructed from scratch?

In 2016, while sitting in a bar in Nederland, Colorado, I overheard a conversation between a high tech start-up entrepreneur and a salesman. They were both sitting at the bar, the entrepreneur explaining how difficult it was to keep all of his workstations synchronized to the same tool set. The salesman reassured him that the technology to address that had been developed by his company. He offered to sell the entrepreneur a system that would make the software he required available from a central place so that when the tools on that central server were upgraded, they were made immediately available to all workstations. The entrepreneur expressed amazement that it could be so simple and the salesman drank up the praise as he described precisely the mechanism we had used twenty years earlier: a mechanism using simple (now open-source) protocols and a few definitions in a NIS map.

Imagine, at your place of business, needing a new web server for an internal application. What is required for that? Well, you'll have to file a ticket. With what division? Is it IT or is it Data Services? Once you figure that out, you'll file the ticket and wait, hoping you filled everything out correctly.

The process in the guts of the system is engaged and the sprockets begin driving the cam that will nudge out the web server to which you will be attached. It takes a while. It isn't because there isn't the equipment to satisfy your request. Any existing piece of modern hardware can be pieced out with a new VM and that VM configured to satisfy your needs. It usually isn't a matter of everyone working on other things of higher priority, it's a matter of remembering how it's done and then doing it again. Sometimes the method is written down and someone needs to dig it up, often on a wiki. The junior IT guy did a search, found a page and only after reading it through realized that it was out of date (they don't use that type of Dell anymore).

Finally he finds the right page and slogs through the step-by-step instructions. When the new web server is ready, he marks the ticket closed, you are notified and there's your web server. Maybe the designated user and password work. Maybe they don't. You'll negotiate back and forth for a while and finally the next day, you're back in business. This was resource distribution in 2016.

All of this despite the fact that spinning up a new VM under the control of a simple script should take thirty seconds. Strategies abound: Docker, VMWare, VirtualBox. Dedicating a few hours to building out and testing the script, someone in IT should be able to automate delivery of a web server to anyone who needs it.

Back in the old days before virtualization was so common, when you had to literally install a new operating system to a bare metal computer, this was easier than it tends to be now. In 2002, I needed a server:

9: Unless God Builds the House...

a SPARCStation 10 running Solaris 2.4. I walked into Brad's office and asked if he could find me one. He turned to his keyboard and typed for about five seconds. He turned back to me and said, "Done."

Brad Keiser was one of Sun's lab managers. He had written a simple script to locate a compatible system in his lab, and call upon a JumpStart specification to install the desired Solaris release. In the end, when the installation was done, the server would email me its host name and root access. I didn't need to file a ticket because it was just too simple.

I have seen that process nowhere else. It's always a ticket, a bunch of explanation and a day or more; not a twenty minute wait for the email from my new server delivered by a set of now open-source tools controlled by a simple internally-written program.

———•———

When you check in your software, it probably goes to a build server which, within minutes of your checkin, begins a build of the product with your new code. Once the build is complete, the automated tests will be run and the results will be posted for review. If the tests fail, your next job is to figure out what is different between your computer and the test machine.

Your IT guy will go on and on about how cool this build system is. If something fails, he'll tell you to try again and often that works. If the system isn't quite doing what you need, you may ask the IT guy if he can make that adjustment. It may be simple; but, in all likelihood, you can't have it because the build and test framework is an agglomeration of paid-for and open-source software he's put together from scratch. Not only is he proud of it, he doesn't completely understand how it works.

What he knows is that he's never seen anything as slick as this tool which monitors the source code control system and shuttles the software to the appropriate system for the build. It coordinates that system with the test system, runs the tests and then posts the results on the web where everyone can see it. It might even send you more annoying emails explaining every shift of your software through its twisted gut.

Famine In the Bullpen

The Solaris build was controlled by a rather esoteric program the name of which I never knew. We typically just referred to "turning the crank." For smaller projects within Sun, a smaller, simpler build system was used. It used the Sun proprietary source code control system, CodeManager, to determine when each modification was checked-in (referred to as a *putback*). For most of my projects, the IT person wrote a simple shell script that would then watch a timer and start the build. When the build was completed, it would initiate the test by simply invoking make test. The test harness was simple, written internally, and wrote out its results as HTML to a specified file system where it became visible over the internal web.

All projects, like Solaris, specified and built a CBE which would be mounted by each build system upon demand. That meant that the developer's system was configured in a manner that was functionally identical to the build system and to any system that would be running the software. For that reason, it was very rare that the build and test systems would provide results different from the developer's workstation. Nonetheless, after each putback, the build system would build and test and publish results and logs. All done with maybe 100 lines of ksh.

In fact, I do the same thing myself. When I was collaborating with others on a Python program, we deployed a rented server on the Internet with our Mercurial repository. It also served as our build and test server. It, like our Sun systems, built and tested with each checkin. It published test results and logs to a simple web page for review by my associates and me. Now that I'm working on my own, my home build server – a Thinkpad T60 – does exactly the same thing. It is done using sixty-five lines of bash.

———•———

In the modern world, all of these convenient automated processes are available; but only in the form of fairly complex frameworks. Unless a framework can be found, the process will not be attempted. No self-respecting IT worker would even imagine writing sixty lines of bash to control their build and test system. As the Vulgate proclaims in Psalm

9: Unless God Builds the House...

126: "Unless God builds the house, the worker's labor is in vain." Unless a recognized manufacturer of frameworks provides a solution, that problem is insoluble.

The frameworks make things easy but they also force a common mediocre approach: the framework makes you as creative as the kid who wrote the framework. While working at that publishing house, we provided a consistent view of the database using a series of DDL and DML files under Subversion source code control. With each build, Maven would apply the latest DDLs and then DMLs in order. The system worked well and required only a few lines in the pom.xml.

At a later company, updating the database was a nightmare. A ticket was filed and a Database Administrator (DBA) would verify the provided SQL and apply it. If the software was tied to the database change, the deployment of the software would be manually synchronized with the DBA by literally calling him on the phone and assuring that you each hit *return* at about the same time. I was a contractor at that place and, as a contractor, I fully endorsed whatever process was identified by the client. It was desperately frustrating; but, my job was to cooperate. There were lots of smart engineers there and I kept waiting for one of them to add those few lines of code to the pom.xml. It never happened.

Instead, a framework was found. An enthusiastic new developer found it and figured out how to fold it into the workspace. He introduced an additional, rather involved procedure, wherein SQL had to be embedded in XML. Merging was nearly impossible and the tedious process became a nemesis to everyone who had to modify a schema or add data to a table.

There are much easier ways to use this common framework, but a few lines of XML is even easier. The point is that while anyone could have introduced that change to the pom.xml, they would have had to justify it. They would have had to defend their solution to others. They would have had to take responsibility for improving the process.

By proposing an existing tool, this developer was only responsible for *finding* the solution, not for solving the problem. The solution was,

Famine In the Bullpen

of course, acceptable because it was a *standard framework*. Other companies were using it too. The people who developed it sponsor an annual conference, for God's sake. It went well beyond what was required, but it was certain to solve the problem. If it didn't work, the blame would fall on the framework. If it worked, the kudos would fall to the proposing developer.

As a result of this very clumsy application of the framework, everyone had to work even harder to update the database. It quickly became a massive burden; but once incorporated, it was almost impossible to extract. After many tense discussions, I resolved to follow the procedure, as ridiculous as it was. As a contractor, I did what I was told. Being as I was more likely to be dismissed than a regular employee, it would be discourteous for me to interfere in the natural progress of the company. I did my job and watched.

In a discussion with the developer who had proposed this solution, I was asked what I thought of it. I had actually thought about that for a while and in my internal dialogs I had already said this to myself a few times. As a result, I came off as more polished than I actually am. I responded, "I have fairly low expectations for anything developed by a kid in his grandparents' basement hopped up on Jolt Cola and NECCO® Wafers."

I was unprepared for the reaction. The advocate's face lit up. His eyes snapped wide and he exclaimed, "You've met him?"

"Who?" I asked.

"The guy who wrote the framework," he effused, "I met him at a conference. He looked like he was nineteen."

"No, I haven't met him."

As I turned away, I thought how much this exchange had explained.

———•———

This isn't a new phenomenon. In the 1960s, everyone knew that *nobody has ever been fired for selecting IBM*. Everyone knew of someone who had recommended an innovative new computer from DEC only to

9: Unless God Builds the House...

find that it didn't do something that the old IBM used to do. They were demoted or fired and resolved never to step out of that comforting IBM box again.

Even though only a tenth of the facilities provided by the Jenkins framework are typically used, you cannot fail if you choose Jenkins. Even though almost no one knows how to write a pom.xml without copying it from another pom.xml, you cannot fail if you use Maven. Even though threading is fairly simple in Java, you cannot fail if you hold off your threaded program until you have Akka.

In so doing, the software developer is clearly identified as a simple *tool user*. Bringing on a new developer is cheaper because everyone knows how to use the tools. No one has to learn the clever build system Richard Whatsisname developed before he left the company. No one has to learn how to modify the innovative high speed compiler that fellow named Gil developed (and then didn't explain to anyone) before *we* started using it and *he* quit. The tools are industry standard and so is the developer. The developer becomes as interchangeable as the levers he pulls.

Unless God builds the house, whatever you're trying to do will be degraded and derided. How dare you figure out a better way to do that! How will we explain it to the new people? We use readily available frameworks. What God has provided is always sufficient.

10: A Failed Experiment

Software projects are undergirded by languages. Any given project may make use of numerous languages and each language provides specific facilities which address particular aspects of the problem. There are two general families of language: imperative and declarative. Imperative languages follow the familiar scheme used by the first language most students ever learn: they define a step-by-step procedure. Using the language, the developer identifies the first step, then the second step, then the third step and so on until all of the steps add up to the desired result. Declarative languages strive to avoid the procedure in favor of identifying a goal and a process from which the step-by-step procedure (required by most microprocessors) is automatically generated. Both families include gray areas and in many cases, we may look at a particular language and be uncertain of its provenance.

Every developer has to work with languages from the two families. In most cases, if you need to translate an XML file into a different schema or convention, you will use the declarative language called XSL. If you need to inspect and clean a directory on a Linux system at a particular time each week, you may write an imperative procedural bash script initiated by a cron job. Developing a safety-critical system responsible for monitoring sensors in a power plant and identifying potential safety risks, you may want to use an easily verified declarative functional language like Haskell which isolates side-effects, like external device reads, from the internal understanding of state. The point is that the language is chosen to suit the job in the same way that any tool is chosen – or at least, it should be.

10: A Failed Experiment

The decision should be based on what language best supports the goal, but there are a lot of other factors that must play into the final decision. I worked for a company that had chosen to implement their solution in Ruby, a perfectly respectable object-influenced language, but they ended up later porting everything to Java because Ruby programmers were rare and expensive. I later saw a company switch from Clojure to Java for the same reason. Whatever brilliant language you choose, you still have to find someone who will develop software using it.

This may apply even more to the engineer who specifies the language. A good engineer can certainly identify the pros and cons of a language within the context of a particular problem but in order to actually use it, that engineer needs to be comfortable with the principles of that language, and part of that comfort level is driven by the engineer's brain. While it was clear to me, in discussing the high-speed data collection algorithm with my German-speaking interviewer, that he would be best to write his solution in Erlang, a simple and fast declarative language, or C, a simple and fast imperative language, I myself would lean toward C simply because I don't tend to think in declarative terms. When up against a wall, I write decent declarative code but I have to bend a few internal concepts until they hurt. I'm just an imperative sort of fellow.

I began my career designing electronic circuits for a company in Oklahoma City. I started with an understanding of what was required. I broke that up into the component functionalities that would support the goal: low-noise amplifier, differentiator, timer, analog-to-digital converter. I would review, reconsider and rearrange until I had designed the simplest possible configuration that would satisfy the requirements. I would then build out a prototype to demonstrate the proper functioning of my design. Each integrated circuit was documented thoroughly by the manufacturer, specifying exact voltage and current thresholds and precise timing as well as impedances that could be used to calculate the shape of leading and trailing edges and the construction of circuit board traces that would introduce minimal signal distortion.

I became so accustomed to trusting the documentation that in one critical case, I designed and ordered the circuit boards before the key analog-to-digital converter chip had been fabricated. When the first chips finally arrived, no changes were required. It performed exactly as specified.

When I moved from designing circuits to writing software, I was disappointed by its mushy, undisciplined nature. I was writing in C and I was finding myself thinking in terms of procedures and data rather than in terms of the more familiar *things*. I described my solution using a Warnier/Orr diagram, a sort of flow chart, when I *wanted* to describe it in terms of things and what they did as I had in designing electronic circuits. Unfortunately, that wasn't how C, as I had learned it, worked.

The other problem was documentation. The way software functions are documented, it is nearly impossible to know what the software will do without actually writing some code and testing it. That, of course, didn't tell me what the function was *supposed* to do. If I use a function in my design and then the original author comes back and corrects it so that it now behaves as he originally intended, my software is broken. This is the key problem with those who claim that documentation is not required because you can just read the code. The code, no matter how well written, cannot reveal, with certainty, the author's intent.

Having developed solutions using both software and hardware, I appreciate the keen similarities between a well-conceived hardware solution and a well-conceived software solution. In developing an electronic circuit, I would write the functional specification explaining its interfaces and behaviors. I would then produce schematics, timing diagrams, circuit board designs and then specify the test protocols. For a software solution, I write a functional specification followed by flow charts and state diagrams and then specify the test protocols, often accompanied by initial functional tests.

10: A Failed Experiment

The two approaches are not that different except that it is easier to skip key steps and just hack out a software solution. When it becomes easy to fabricate an integrated circuit or a circuit board on a desktop system, we'll start hacking those out as well, at which point the usefulness and reliability of hardware will be as tenuous as that of software. Hardware warranties will be as uncommon as modern software warranties and every purchase will be at the buyer's unsupported risk.

The functional specification may remain agnostic regarding whether the solution is implemented in hardware or software. A well-designed functional specification for a television would not need to identify whether the video generated was produced by a specialized CMOS circuit or a microprocessor running micro-code. There are a number of products we use commonly such as telephones (meaning the telephone portion of a smart phone, of course), automobiles and musical instruments whose functional specifications, for the most part, remain unchanged and yet, the functioning of each has moved from a collection of specialized valves or integrated circuits to a standard microprocessor running specialized software. The surface features (the interfaces) remain unchanged but the implementations have moved radically in the direction of software dominance: a dominance so pervasive that it is now possible to "hack" an automobile while it is in motion.

This trend is neither bad nor good. Software is certainly easier to modify and, possibly, improve while specialized hardware uses less power and, due to its specialization, is inherently more secure. Real problems may be solved using either or both approaches. I enjoyed solving problems using electronic circuits because I found the result easier to comprehend than my C solutions. To understand my software solution, I had to run through a number of transformations in my head. *The bus is providing an integer and I'm reading the integer and calling a function that will return a mapping to a functor that may be invoked to, etc...* In the hardware world, it wasn't a batch of functions, any of which may do something, it was specialized integrated circuits that did specific things. I understand the similarity, I just have to confess that I naturally think in terms of things that do stuff.

―――― • ――――

After a 1994 class in C++ at the Sun Microsystems Colorado Springs campus, I was intrigued by the instructor's claim that software engineering could be like electronics engineering. I knew how similar the integrated circuit was to the modules I had been writing in C for the Solaris platform. It struck me as perfectly reasonable that software could be so structured as to allow off-the-shelf components that could be pieced together to form more complex components and finally a product.

I had just finished writing a state machine similar in so many ways to the state machine I had constructed on a circuit board five years earlier. The only thing preventing me from stocking and reusing my software state machine in any other piece of software was the lack of a common context. What is the agreed-upon method for defining the interface? How would it transfer to a different platform where the compiler would take liberties with its types and adjust it in incompatible ways? How would I explain to other users how to apply it and how would I allow for those who wanted to augment it?

I began looking into OO. I found the seminal text *Object Oriented Software Construction*[Meyer_1997] and began to take its principles to heart. There are those who claim that OO methodology (OOM) may be used in any language, but anyone who has tried to apply object principles using the language C, realizes that it is a struggle. A laudable struggle; but, a struggle.

I found that my attempts to write object-oriented software in C++ did not fare much better than attempts using C. Lots of windows had to be up at the same time and development environments were either primitive or expensive. There were also ongoing arguments regarding incompatible C++ libraries. There was a fledgling open-source Eiffel that was good enough for experimentation but not much more. I continued to focus on writing fairly conventional procedural software at work and reading what I could about object methodology at home.

10: A Failed Experiment

When James Gosling explained his cool new language to our Colorado Springs team, he described it as a way to deliver web content to fledgling browsers (some of us were still running Mosaic). Despite this early underestimation of its ultimate potential, many of us were very excited that we might have access to a simple competent OO language in the Solaris suite.

Gosling's explanation of the Java language was full of complaints about C++. It seemed to be largely an attempt to step beyond that language. Java allows a class to extend only one parent because multiple inheritance in C++ had proved exasperating for Gosling. It required minimal help from an IDE (most of us were using Emacs) because the C++ IDEs had proved cumbersome. It was bytecode-driven so we wouldn't have to recompile it on each platform. No one in that first year was prepared to argue that Java was not significantly easier to use than C++.

As that year wore on and more and more of our Java work was running on the back end, some of us began to question why C++ was the language of comparison. It was rather like taking on the challenge of improving the 1965 Volkswagen Beetle. Yes, a lot of things could be improved. The windshield washer is powered by the spare tire, why not use a dedicated pressurized tank? The engine is air cooled and overheats if the fins get oily or dirty. Why not wrap it in a water jacket and pump the water to a radiator to keep it clean and cool? Yes, you can build on the VW Bug theme and improve it; but, wouldn't you be better off to improve upon the 1993 Mercedes 500E? Now that would be a challenge: to start with an excellent car and make it a superlative car – to start with an excellent language and develop a superlative language. It would not be the first time this had been done with software[15].

Of course, Java was already exposed and it was concluded that without marketing, superlative doesn't amount to much. With enough marketing momentum, though, a language that improves upon C++ has become the most popular programming language in the world and that has to be praised as a victory of some sort.

---
15 See Sather, a language designed as an improvement upon Eiffel.

Famine In the Bullpen

In casual conversation many Java developers will claim that they are object-oriented programmers. That term carries forward from Gosling and the Java team at Sun. They too held to the notion that Java was an object-oriented language. They believed this because it supports the notational conventions common to object-oriented languages in that a data structure may be constructed from a template and the data manipulated using accessors ("getters") and mutators ("setters"). Unfortunately, this notational convention is not sufficient to define a language as object-oriented.

While early Java programmers worked to develop object domains using the language, it was soon discovered that such domains were deficient in a number of important ways. For example, unless your objects were trivial in the extreme, the single inheritance restriction of Java made it nearly impossible to develop a domain that adequately emulated the problem space. It became necessary to expose the inner data structures of objects so that various Java programs could inspect their contents and make decisions about their disposition. The need to serialize stateful Java objects drove the need to assure that those objects had no behaviors and included no other complicated objects, since behaviors and composition confused early tools for serialization. In time, a real attempt to emulate the problem space was abandoned. Objects were segregated into two distinct kinds: objects with state but no behaviors (generally known as *beans*) and objects with behaviors but no state (sometimes called *machines*) constructing what is commonly referred to as an *anemic domain model*. Note that, in the interest of clarity, for the remainder of this book I will use *bean* only to mean a Java object with state but no behaviors (definition #2 in Chapter 2) and *machine* to mean a stateless Java object.

With the introduction of the Enterprise Java Bean (EJB), a number of problems arose which played a role in the development of frame-

10: A Failed Experiment

works supporting Inversion of Control[16]. IoC generally dictates a *procedural methodology*. This procedural methodology is easily recognized by a comparison to the language C. In C, collections of data, known as *structs*, are transferred between library procedures which act upon those structs. The procedures modify the structs in various ways and deliver either new structs or side-effects, such as visual displays, or reports embodied on a printer. In Java, collections of data, known as beans, are transferred between methods in injected machines which act upon those beans. The machines modify the beans and deliver either new beans or side-effects. This pattern is driven, in part, by the fact that IoC only injects stateless objects.

C has a long and deservedly respected history. It was developed by Dennis Ritchie in the early 1970s at Bell Labs in a rebellious attempt to get something done in a stilted and highly restrictive software environment. It is the language in which I had to prove myself in order to acquire my position at Sun Microsystems. It is the language in which SunOS, Solaris and Linux are largely written. It is very close to the *bare metal*, even allowing the programmer to request that a particular variable be stored in a register of the Central Processing Unit (CPU or processor).

To get closer to the CPU than C would require that the programmer write their software in *assembly language*. The problem with assembly language is that it is peculiar to one and only one particular processor architecture. That means that if you want to run your program on the newer processor or a processor possessing a different architecture, you would have to largely rewrite your software. You would have tremendous control over what the processor was going to do for you right down to assigning a particular pair of variables to particular registers and optimizing your barrel shifter for multiplying large floating point variables; but, it would only run on one processor architecture.

---

16   Inversion of Control frameworks only inject machines and often instantiate them only once using a Singleton pattern, passing the same machine to all requesters. The Spring framework specifically refers to these as *beans*, not machines. It can be argued, based upon the earliest conception of the Java Bean, that the bean has state but no behaviors (it is not injectable). Some see this as unfortunate since there are crucial differences between beans and machines.

Famine In the Bullpen

At the time of C's greatest popularity, there were a large number of processors all competing for a growing market. Each offered specific advantages and applied well to certain kinds of problems. The Motorola 6805 and the MOS Technologies 6502 were well designed for embedded applications. Sun's SPARC processor was superb for large enterprise applications. The Z8000 from Zilog also competed in that space and some people even liked the Intel Pentium® platform.

This meant that if you wanted to write your software only once, you had to give up some control. The C language allowed an entirely reasonable amount of control while abstracting the specifics of the hardware platform. You could still write your own barrel shifter; but, there were plenty of C compilers out there with fantastic math libraries. You couldn't put a variable into a specific hardware register, but you could ask the compiler to do that with fair confidence that it would comply. As a result, software written in C for the Motorola 68020 could be easily recompiled for the Intel 8085 and, in most cases, it would simply work. This is why *Write once, run anywhere*, a Java slogan, was received unenthusiastically by C programmers who could, for the most part, make the same claim[17].

C is an imperative procedural language and has a distinguished pedigree. Despite this, all C programmers have, from time to time, recognized that they were working harder than they needed to in order to accomplish certain common tasks. With Java, many of those tasks became much easier until the introduction of the EJB, which moved the Java developer back to the imperative procedural world. Java was still easier to use by many measures, but when OOM was largely abandoned, so was much of Java's genuine edge.

———•———

While occupied as a contractor at Digital Globe, I engaged in a philosophical discussion with Cliff and Anton, two highly skilled senior Java developers. Cliff described a problem he was addressing wherein

---

17 Of course the slogan *Compile once, run anywhere* would have applied to Java but not to C. I suppose that seemed too technical.

10: A Failed Experiment

data in a particular bean had to be exposed to numerous other machines, some of which were written by other teams. He noted that he needed to expose an interface that would protect the bean from inappropriate data. Knowing this might get a rise out of one of them I mischievously said, "Well, I know this is taboo, but you could use object-oriented methodology," to which Anton responded quickly and confidently, "OO was a failed experiment."

I was impressed and a little embarrassed. They were both fully aware that they were using procedural methodology and Anton knew why. I thought all Java developers believed themselves to be OO programmers but I was clearly wrong. I would have to spend some time thinking about Anton's definitive proclamation.

While Anton was called upon to write software in Java, his preference was clear in every line of software he wrote. He never modified a Java bean; instead he would always instantiate a new bean with modified attributes exactly as if all Java objects were immutable. He would write his methods to always return a valid object upon which methods may be called and string them together in long chains as if he were writing in a language that supported functional composition. Yes, Anton preferred functional languages but was stuck with Java.

With the news of each new Java release I hear the Java fans talking about how much more declarative it will be. The Lords of Java continue to express their confusion over what their language is by folding declarative-like constructs into the language as if adding lambda functions and simplifying the passing of method pointers can morph a language with methods into a language with functions. You can't be functional with methods because methods have side-effects, and functions don't. You can't add a few relations and queries and claim you have a logic language. The point is that you have to breed a lot of Chihuahuas into a Great Dane to produce an issue that will fit through a cat door. Even then, it's still a mongrel.

———— • ————

The first programming language to experiment with object-oriented concepts was Simula, developed at the Norwegian Computing Center in Oslo. As the name implies, it was intended to support simulations. Simulations are typically performed with reference to real things like people and assembly robots and cars (what we might call *objects*). In the late 1970s, Alan Kay of Xerox took it a step further by theorizing that the idea of an object could be well applied to more abstract software concepts which could play a role in a domain of things rather than processes. His language, Smalltalk, became a central tool for experimentation into various principles including OO, message passing, chaining and dynamic closures. Used primarily in academic environments, it was the inspiration for numerous other languages including Dylan, Objective-C and variants on Lisp.

OO is still quite popular in Europe, where many large companies write their enterprise software using Eiffel. It is also possible to implement a real OO project using C++ or Python, so OO may be more common than it appears. Nonetheless, for the most part, Java has become the language of choice, and so Anton's claim seems to be supported by observation. I wonder if this could be due to the problems developers were having with C++. I worked very little with the language, but Gosling's complaint was not the first I'd heard on the subject.

The problem arises from the way most developers were first introduced to C++. The languages of choice, prior to C++, were COBOL, C, Fortran or some variation on BASIC[18]. None of those languages are object-oriented and without understanding the principles behind OO, it is very easy to get off on the wrong foot. For example, if the developer starts out thinking in terms of data and procedures, she will very naturally use the multiple inheritance capability within C++ to merge data structures. This common error leads to complaints such as the *diamond problem*, touted by critics of multiple inheritance, and the *fragile base class problem*, touted by critics of OO generally. When using objects as data structures, as in the languages with which the programmers were originally familiar, the hiding of the data made no sense. Getting at the

---

18 Seriously, BASIC was used all over. There was Visual Basic, Business Basic, Benton Harbor Basic, Cromemco Extended Basic and many others. All of this despite the fact that BASIC is an abbreviation for Beginners All-purpose Symbolic Instruction Code.

10: A Failed Experiment

underlying data is more complicated than simply reading and writing an element of a data structure. To make anything happen you had to write the template, instantiate it whenever you needed it and then destroy it when you were done with it. If the developer wasn't well acquainted with the reasoning behind these operations, the whole ordeal seemed pointless.

I'm discussing languages and their uses in a book about innovation because, in an innovative culture, we choose the tool that suits the correction of the problem. Before going deeper into the culture of innovation, I would like to provide my reader with some examples that may offer the basis for this kind of decision-making. In the culture of the mundane, we choose the tool that is easiest to hand and fits our existing process. Currently that tool is the Java Complex. Companies use it whether appropriate or not because Java programmers are relatively cheap and numerous. Further, the task of analyzing the problem in order to figure out exactly which tool is right for the job, is a lost art. Of course you'll use Java. Everyone else does.

If I were a language guy, I could expound upon the specific features of numerous languages, but I'm not. I know drips and drabs about a few declarative languages like Erlang, Haskell and XSL although I've written quite a few parsers using Lex, Yacc and ANTLR. I have been schooled, by engineers that I greatly respect, regarding the specific advantages of various declarative languages for resolving particular problems and I have great respect for the engineers who use those languages.

What I know is object-oriented methodology. There are other ways to understand the world[19]. There are other ways to model a solution but one entirely reasonable way to do it is using objects. I've developed simple OO projects using Java and more robust and interesting projects using Python. The fact that the industry largely abandoned OO is a

---

19 Alfred North Whitehead in his 1925 book *Science and the Modern World* suggested that our growing understanding of particle physics implied that we would be better to understand reality in terms of events rather than objects. Such an understanding would better apprehend the dynamic nature of the world and would represent a radical and perhaps enlightening shift in the most basic mechanisms of comprehension.

side-effect of this lack of interest in developing solutions to problems. While I cannot provide the reader with an authoritative assessment of how to choose the correct language tool for any problem, I can provide some insight into OO and how a disciplined application of its principles applies to stable and reliable solutions that are easily extended and adapted to changing situations.

It is important to understand that while a competent OO language is a tremendous aid when developing an OO solution, it is not required. We may argue over this language or that being superior in this regard; but even C can be used to implement a fair OO solution. If I were implementing an OO solution in, for example, Java, I would probably ignore inheritance altogether and simulate multiple inheritance as best I could using composition. I would prefer a well-disciplined tool like Eiffel except for the fact that it is an expensive language with a few performance issues. I liked Sather quite a bit, but no one else did. I have generally settled quite happily for Python. I have to forgive it for its scripting language pedigree, but once I've done that, we are reconciled.

Python is not the ideal OO language. Its implementation of multiple inheritance is only partial and while it is type-aware, it doesn't enforce types in formal arguments. It also doesn't support method overloading. I make frequent use of all of those capabilities and so I have to include my own additional code to provide suitable emulations of them. Despite those few additional lines of code, Python works fine. It is important to understand that the language may be useful, but methodology is not bound to the language.

In describing the application of OOM, I will also explain why it tends to be incompatible with the feature factory except for when the project reaches *maintenance mode*. I will try to demonstrate that OO provides an improved product over the long term and that it is readily compatible with an agile but definitely non-scrummy development methodology. With a more flexible development schedule, true advantages may be demonstrated; but, caution must be exercised: such a process inevitably carries the threat of engineering.

11: Playing With Paradigms

Every good regulator of a system must be a model of that system.

Ross Ashby

To consider the differences between the various common imperative paradigms, we'll review a specific problem. Let's imagine that we are writing software to control three elevators. We will, in shameless summary, compare a solution in C, Java and an OO language like Python or Eiffel.

The elevators are actual things: this makes the explanation a little clearer, but we should remember that anything we comprehend is likely to be a thing: a document, a list, a picture. There are very few concepts in software that do not correspond to something we understand from our physical world. That means that there are a number of different approaches we could use for this demonstration, but an elevator is a very obvious physical thing. We'll avoid nuances and gray area by writing software for something that is seriously physical.

We begin by thinking through what the elevator must do. This is required for a procedural program but it is also required for any engineered solution. A full specification would occupy several pages but, for our purposes, we can summarize it satisfactorily in this form:

1. The elevator system is comprised of three elevators, the three elevator shafts, a set of floor buttons in each elevator and request buttons on each floor next to the elevators indicating

whether the user wants to go up or down with the exception of the top floor which will only accommodate down and the bottom floor which will only accommodate up.

2. Each elevator is comprised of an electrically actuated door, a mechanism for raising and lowering the elevator enclosure, a button panel (floor buttons) identifying target floors and sensors identifying the current floor and the state of the doors.

3. The doors are to be closed when the elevator has been stationary on a floor for at least ten seconds.

4. Each elevator will have a home floor: a floor to which it should gravitate if it has been stationary for at least two minutes.

5. The home floor for the left-most elevator will be top floor minus 30% of the total floors. For the center elevator it will be the top-most floor minus 70% of the total floors. For the right-most elevator, floor 1.

6. When a request button is pressed, a strategy will be executed to determine which elevator may be best scheduled to service that floor. Based upon the strategy, the designated elevator will be scheduled to move to the designated floor.

7. When an elevator arrives at a floor in response to a floor button, it will open its door for ten seconds, adding four seconds every time a passenger crosses the threshold, closing it if a floor button is selected or if the time has elapsed.

8. The elevator system will routinely send status to and respond to requests from the building manager's industry standard Monoid® building maintenance system.

This, of course, doesn't describe a real elevator system, but it should suffice for purposes of demonstration. We'll take it a step further and note that this software is designed to manage any number of different kinds of elevator system; and, in this case, we're managing three Floorthought Model 10 elevators covering a ten story building. Floorthought elevator systems communicate with their controller software using a proprietary HTTP protocol. That means that the software

11: Playing With Paradigms

has to be HTTP-aware and it has to understand the proprietary message semantics.

---•---

A C implementation will designate data structures (structs) identifying the data describing each elevator's current state as well as the state of communication channels and of the overall system (e.g., the up button on the fourth floor). Each struct may be subdivided as appropriate to further the project. For example the left_elevator_struct may include a **short which will identify the ordered list of floors to be visited. We would think through what computations will be required using those data to be able to carry out the required behaviors. The elevators will be managed by the main program, initiated at power up, which will loop over the system looking for changes in state such as a button being pressed or a moving elevator tripping a sensor to indicate that it is arriving at a designated floor.

That program will invoke library functions in response to state changes. For example, when the center elevator has tripped the sensor indicating that it has arrived at its target floor, the main program will detect that in its loop and a library function will be invoked which will spawn a thread that will take on the task of slowing the elevator and opening the door. It will indicate, in that elevator's struct, at which time the doors were opened so that the main program will be able to time them out and invoke a function to close the doors after the designated period.

When the *down* button on the third floor is pressed, the system struct will be updated and, when the main program detects it, a function will be invoked with the identity of the button. The function will consult the struct for each elevator in order to determine which one is best positioned to move to that floor. The struct will include the current direction the elevator is moving, its next floor, the various floors at which it is currently expected to stop, that sort of thing. An algorithm will determine which elevator will be assigned to the floor and that elevator's floor list will be updated accordingly.

Famine In the Bullpen

This continues with the main program looping, looking at the state of each button and the data in each elevator's struct and invoking functions based upon that data. The amount of threading is optional based upon the problem. Certainly there could be three persistent threads, one for each elevator, each managing one of the elevator data structures. The main program could indicate new floors to each thread using semaphores. Alternatively, we could use threads only for dealing with long running processes that need to be monitored like slowing the elevator at a floor or closing the doors.

For communicating with the elevator and the request buttons on each floor, a Floorthought protocol library will provide functions which return requested data or issue commands. For example, the light behind a request button indicating that it has been pressed and acknowledged will be turned on using the Floorthought protocol library function:

```
void illuminate_button_light(enum button_id)
```

This library may be used to populate the appropriate elevator struct with current elevator state.

A Monoid library will be provided for communication with the Monoid building management executive. The executive may request elevator status or may initiate a diagnostic by setting appropriate bits in a struct the main program monitors. Seeing those bits set, the main program will respond by invoking an appropriate library function in exactly the same way as it would if a floor button were pressed by a passenger.

The C algorithms are essentially standalone. If an algorithm functions incorrectly and adds the non-existent twelfth floor to an elevator's target floor list, the elevator will fail by commanding the lift motor to go beyond its programmed limit. In C, the algorithm doesn't typically get double-checked by anything else.

Threads, in C, introduce risks in that they share a common memory space and data locking is somewhat ad hoc. Any rogue thread may write bad data to any spot in that memory space. For that reason, a certain

11: Playing With Paradigms

amount of experience is required before one undertakes to thread a C program.

The other complication accompanying a C implementation is memory management. In order to store any non-primitive value, such as a string or a struct, memory must be explicitly allocated and then, when no longer needed, freed. Failure to do this consistently leads to the *memory leak* by which a program may demand more and more memory until it is exhausted forcing the operating system to kill the process. When threads are combined with sloppy memory management, the threat is compounded, leading to memory leaks that are very difficult to correct.

As you can see, the C program consists of a main program which monitors the state of the system and makes decisions based upon data stored in structs. Based upon changes in that data, it invokes functions which cause actions to take place, the result of which is changes to the data in the structs. The actual objects, the elevators, are represented as a collection of data. The program reacts to that data and modifies it as needed. The text of the program provides little understanding of the actual physical operations taking place in the real world. This is not a serious fault since the developer is thinking in terms of specific step-by-step procedures that cause appropriate states to arise. The fact that a servo motor starts over there or a light illuminates over here is interesting but is not fundamentally expressed in the code.

———— • ————

Using Java, our approach is similar. Instead of structs, the Java programmer will create three beans[20], one for each elevator, and place them into an associative array. Each bean will be built based upon a template called a *class* typically named for the thing being monitored: in this case the *Elevator* class. Each bean will be named to identify each of the three elevators: elevatorLeft, elevatorCenter and elevatorRight. The main program, from our C example, may be called ElevatorManager. The El-

---

20 Most developers refer to most Java objects as "beans" but we will stick with our established convention here: beans are stateful, machines are stateless.

evatorManager is a machine very similar to a C library function. Like a C library function, it doesn't remember data; instead, it uses the current data found within each bean. Back before threading was commonplace in C, there were library functions that remembered their last state. This was fine as long as there was only one thread of control. When threading became popular, *re-entrant* versions of those functions were quickly provided for *thread-safe* operation. "Thread-safe" essentially means that the library function doesn't retain state.

Each bean will be paired with a machine: we'll call it an Elevator-Controller. For instance the left elevator's controller will be instantiated as elevatorLeftController. It will be the *behaviors* part of the Elevator. The ElevatorManager will receive events (a Java-supported message passing protocol) generated in response to the request buttons then consult each of the elevator beans to determine which is the best candidate to receive the request. Each elevator controller will monitor the floor buttons and respond to events from the sensors so as to update each elevator with its current state so that ElevatorManager will be able to work from current data. As above, the ElevatorControllers may be in separate threads. They may each maintain their elevator bean and may become active with each event issued by the monitored sensors and buttons.

The Elevator bean may be further specialized. It may be associated with a ButtonPanel bean which holds the data about the state of the floor buttons in the elevator. It may be associated with a Door bean which holds the door state. Each bean may be associated with a corresponding Controller, as described above, a Verifier, to assure that the bean is holding valid data, a DAO, which might persist the state of the bean for retrieval after a power outage, or a Data Transfer Object (DTO) used to deliver only changed state over a serial interface.

Unlike C, Java manages memory using a *garbage collector*. That means that except for certain uncommon cases, the programmer doesn't need to worry about allocating or freeing memory. Java also simplifies threading to a fair degree with thread-aware and thread-spanning objects like ThreadGroup and Future. Java is easier to use than

11: Playing With Paradigms

C in this regard, but the basic approach remains procedural. Stateless actors make decisions about and with collections of data which they may manipulate as needed to convey the important states to other actors which send signals that actuate relays and motors in the real world.

Java uses inheritance to help organize the data of the beans and the behaviors of the machines. For example, in order to assure that the ElevatorManager can communicate with the elevator system, it may inherit a parent class called FloorthoughtNode which provides the various proprietary protocols and the corresponding HTTP client and server. In order to provide these facilities, FloorthoughtNode may in turn inherit a parent called FloorthoughtProtocol, a parent which may provide the details of the proprietary message formats, or it may instead inherit a parent called Http which would provide it with an understanding of the industry standard HTTP protocol complete with the server and client. It cannot inherit both, so one of them may be incorporated through inheritance while the other will be incorporated through some other means like an included object or a *mixin*. The fact that they cannot both be incorporated through inheritance leads to a very stilted use of inheritance generally driving the exposure of bean internal state, further defining the bean as a simple data structure.

In the same way, communication with Monoid would be provided by a class that understands the Monoid protocol. The behaviors of that class might be incorporated into ElevatorManager through inheritance but will probably be injected into the ElevatorManager through the IoC mechanism. The methods of the MonoidProtocol would be invoked directly as needed and the MonoidProtocol object would notify the ElevatorManager that a diagnostic or elevator status was required using an event which would be delivered and addressed asynchronously.

As with C, we are focused on the operations to be performed, despite the fact that we can name our data structures after the objects to which they correspond. Instead of directly reading our data from a struct in an allocated swath of memory, we use an accessor associated with the bean; but there is no functional difference between that and reading a struct. A faulty ElevatorManager may still write faulty data to the elevator bean without consulting the corresponding Verifier. The controllers and the manager are monitoring the data in the beans, making decisions based upon changes in that data and reacting to those changes by modifying the data in those beans.

———•———

Now, imagine we are going to address this issue using object-oriented methodology. We will define types which will not merely hold data but will instead emulate the various things that we will be controlling. We will certainly have an Elevator, but in our case, the Elevator object is a functional and self-verifying emulation of a physical elevator. The software that emulates the physical elevator is connected intimately to its corresponding physical elevator by inheriting FloorthoughtNode and directly invoking the FloorThought protocols. There isn't a stateless controller communicating with a collection of data. The controller, the verifier and the data are combined into the emulation itself. The elevatorLeft object *is* the elevator. Any attempt by external software to instruct the elevator to do something inappropriate will result in an error response. The elevator, since it is a self-verifying emulation, is never in an invalid state.

There will probably be an ElevatorManager, but its relationship to the elevators will be very different. The request buttons will send their state to the ElevatorManager which is responsible for helping the three elevators coordinate the process of picking up people on the various floors. The ElevatorManager will inherit its ability to communicate with the elevator system by inheriting FloorthoughtManager. By inheriting it, we acknowledge that the ElevatorManager is itself a FloorthoughtManager, a statement that is true since it is in fact a device that manages the operations of a Floorthought elevator system. By so doing the ElevatorManager is capable of doing everything required to act as a Floorthought elevator manager.

In an object-oriented model, each object has *both* state *and* behaviors. They also may *inherit* both state and behaviors. There is certainly the occasional object with only state or only behaviors. There's nothing

11: Playing With Paradigms

wrong with that per sé, as long as the object is doing what an object must: emulating the thing it represents.

The Elevator also inherits FloorthoughtElevator which includes all of the data and behaviors needed to communicate with a FloorthoughtManager. As with any inheritance, this is valid only because our Elevator *truly is* a Floorthought elevator. Were it not, that is were we inheriting just to join data sets, we would encounter extensive intractable difficulties in the future. This class would *become* a fragile base class and would be more likely to encounter the diamond problem in ways that could not be easily addressed. Since this is OO, the full complement of capabilities are provided to the Elevator and ElevatorManager objects by their parents.

We apply The Information Expert Principle to these objects meaning that the object with the data is the only expert in the manipulation of that data. For this reason, the ElevatorManager, when it receives an event indicating that someone selected the down button on the sixth floor, doesn't ask the Elevators for their data and then calculate which elevator should get the order. Instead, it tells all three elevators about the sixth floor request and asks each to return how quickly it will be able to get to the sixth floor to service the request. The ElevatorManager will simply provide the new floor request to the Elevator that provided the best response time. If the ElevatorManager suggests the twelfth floor to the Elevators, they will all respond with an error, since none of them are capable of going there. If one of them actually were capable of reaching a newly constructed twelfth floor, it would be the only one to return an estimate, and ElevatorManager would naturally always pick that elevator for that floor.

Since the Elevator is the expert in what an elevator is and how it works, when it receives the new floor request, it will take responsibility for placing it in the optimum spot in its ordered list of floors to visit. By letting the expert handle what needs to be handled, the software is greatly simplified. For example, elevatorLeft knows that its home floor is seven and it will automatically home there when it has no other requests. Its compatriot, elevatorRight, homes at the first floor and will automatically home there when there are no other requests. ElevatorManager doesn't know where elevatorLeft is at any given time because it's none of its business. In the same way, the elevators know nothing about what the other elevators are doing and have no way of communicating with the other elevators for the same reason.

This, to be clear, is why I am partial to OOM. Each Elevator is a tangible component which serves as vicar for the actual physical elevator. The ElevatorManager will send a new floor to elevatorLeft and elevatorLeft will take on all attendant responsibilities. When elevatorLeft decides to open its doors, the elevatorLeft object will issue the instruction to the physical elevator using its FloorthoughtNode behaviors. The ElevatorManager is the expert in dealing with an elevator system. While its FloorthoughtManager parent gives it all the tools it needs to manage a set of Floorthought elevators, the custom software in the ElevatorManager provides the specific behaviors that optimize these elevators for this building. For example, if there is a convention on the third floor leading to more frequent third floor requests, the elevator manager will recalculate the home floors and propose them to the elevators. At that point, the elevators are again individually responsible for tending toward the new home floors clustered around the third floor until the convention is over and the original home floors may be resumed.

The approach is still imperative, but the step-by-step procedures are assigned to experts in the field. The procedures are used to build out the expertise to be expressed by each object. We impose the Single Choice Principle assuring that there is one and only one way to do anything. For example, since the Elevator is responsible for scheduling its floors, there is literally no way for the ElevatorManager to order an elevator to a particular floor. If you feel the need to do that, then you haven't thought through your elevator design very well.

The Uniform Access Principle sees to it that each elevator's internal process for providing data or causing a side-effect is not visible to the outside world. When the elevator is asked how long it will take to get to the third floor, the data provided may be a running calculation main-

11: Playing With Paradigms

tained at all times for all floors, or it may be calculated upon request. How it's done is irrelevant. The requester gets an answer and that is all the requester may know.

Writing software using OOM, also greatly reduces the need for additional frameworks in favor of abstract classes which impart required capabilities to objects. There is no need for serialization tools like Jettison or FasterXML because the object will provide its own well-conceived serial representation by inheriting a serializing parent. The need to use XSLT to convert across various XML formats will be eliminated since the object defined by the original XML format will accept the XML record as a formal argument to its constructor. The object that uses the other format will be instantiated using the first object and then will return its preferred format using a method like getXML(). The objects do not expose their internal state so, in an OO solution, serializers would not be able to access the information required to generate a serial representation anyway. Also, since very few objects even bother to expose their internal state, there is no need for tools that generate or otherwise provide the tedious getter/setter boilerplate which pointlessly exposes the entirety of each bean's inner data.

In our modern software culture, the language drives an understanding of the process which drives an entire industry producing frameworks that reinforce the process and the understanding of the language. The standard trope is that the frameworks do the simple stuff so that you, the programmer, can innovate. Unfortunately, the framework handling the "simple stuff," has to demand specific formats and techniques which limit the programmer's options. While you may want to reconfigure an object without stopping and restarting your product, if you've injected that data into the object using IoC, you'll soon realize that to do that, you'll need to convert the object to a Managed Bean (or Mbean) and implement JMX. That will distract you for weeks largely because you'll think of all the other objects you want to be able to reconfigure and you'll turn all of them into Mbeans because what if this happens again? You don't want to go through this every time you realize that an object needs live reconfiguration.

In a well-designed OO project, you would take an afternoon to modify your configuration singleton to support a synchronized reload. This is easy to do because it's your code. In the contemporary world of standardized processes, your entire approach has been stifled by the demands of specific frameworks – frameworks designed to solve specific problems, while likely exacerbating other problems; all the time limiting your actual ability to innovate.

———— • ————

There are legitimate complaints about OOM. They include the fact that the close relationship between data and behaviors, may defeat common caching schemes. To those with a functional bent, the issue may be that the object is an unnatural tool for understanding something that is always basically a set of operations. Rather than a hierarchy of child and parent classes, the program is best defined as a composition of operations. Concerns around performance are common because instantiating an object involves the time-consuming task of allocating memory. This was an ongoing issue in early Java wherein some advised instantiating objects as rarely as possible in order to improve performance. IoC frameworks take this to its logical conclusion by instantiating each object only once as a singleton and sharing it among all objects that require it.

Some argue that objects don't actually emulate anything. The objects, for example, are not actual objects, they just represent objects. Beyond that, they do things that objects don't, such as verify their content. If you want to write software, you need data. Objects hide data, making calculations difficult. The concepts are abstract but objects aren't abstract, they're real things: they're unambiguous. They're real and the software is not. The concept of objects in software is simply nonsensical, but then physical objects are also nonsensical. That's the real problem.

12: The World as Object and Representation

A father sits with his young daughter on his lap. She has just unwrapped the chocolate bunny he has given her. She holds it up and asks, "What's this, Daddy?"

"That," the attentive father responds, "is a rabbit."

She bites off the rabbit's ears and presents it again asking, "What is it now?"

Cleverly, the father answers, "Now it's a chipmunk."

The young girl now bites off the tail and asks, "What is it now?"

"Now it's a gibbon."

The young girl now takes a bite out of the back of the former bunny and asks again.

At this point, of course, the clever father is at a loss. He can think of no name for the fragment of chocolate being shown him. In each other case, there was a clear transformation from an object he recognized to another object he recognized. Now, there is no connection to a known object and he feels compelled to confess that it isn't anything.

Our intrepid parent is worthy of praise for taking the game as far as he has but his last claim is incorrect. It *is something*, it just doesn't represent a recognizable object. When a thing in the real world threatens us or proves useful to us, we identify it as an object. When a thing in the real world annoys us or is pleasurable for us, we identify it as an object. When a thing forms a component of a thing we've identified as an object, and we suspect we may need to deal with that component at some point, we identify it as an object.

We identify things as objects only when we believe we will need to call them out and manipulate them, or avoid manipulating them in the future. By this I mean that we don't identify everything as an object. Objects are things we care about, and so there is no object designation for the portion of a wall four feet from the rightmost edge. It isn't important to us. There is no designation for the middle portion of the ulna bone.

We describe a coffee cup three quarters full of hot cider by its attributes not by a distinct name. Most people are wholly unaware that the furrow between the human nose and lip became an object when some show-off medical researcher designated it *the nasolabial trough* for reasons that are not clear to anyone.

The object, once named, is no longer a complete thing. It is a schematic representation of a complete thing. All of the things we look at congeal into artificial constructs. These constructs are not representations of the actual world. They are abbreviations that simplify our thinking.

We don't say: "He cut the tree in half." We say: "He cut down the tree." A tree is a large organism involving roughly equal proportions of branches and root and yet, when we cut through the trunk, we claim that the tree is *down*, not that the tree is *bisected*. The world is a hodge podge of things that the community has generally agreed are to be things. These conveniences fit into our perception of a world of things the nature of which comprise our implicit agreement with our fellow beings. In a very sparse object domain, we may describe complex things by applying attributes to primitive objects. We may have to indicate that a friend should meet us under the multiplicity of green rounded planes suspended over the flat multiplicity of small green elongated roughly triangular planes that project north and east from the raised concrete area. In a richly-populated domain we can say "Meet me under the lime tree at the south west corner of Miller's Field."

12: The World as Object and Representation

We have all agreed that "tree" identifies the visible portion of the organism, even though a biologist would understand it to project both above and below the ground. We refer to being "under" the tree indicating that, in some cases, the tree is the part above your head. Partly through language and partly through teaching, we learn these idiomatic conventions for treating arbitrary partitions of reality. You work in a building, not in a sequestered area comprising one of many openings in a solid structure. We have accepted these words and we construct an artificial, and often inaccurate, view of the world based upon these generic forms.

How often do we say: "It's smaller than I thought it would be," or "He doesn't look like he sounded over the phone," or "I thought you'd bring a car, not a motorcycle." The human mind has a terrible time dealing with *nothing*. Given a sparse description of a person, we will invariably construct a complete image of that person in our minds. The image doesn't include black areas where the undescribed eyes would be, nor are there transparent portions for the undefined chest area. We construct an entire person, filling in those portions that we do not know by grafting on generic portions in order to fill in the blanks.

We do not do this consciously, our brains do this for us. The brain, exposed to example after example, constructs a schema for each of these generally accepted things. The brain objectifies and iconifies the things of our world. This is why an image of a square with an upside down "V" on top of it is quickly understood as the object "house." An upright rectangle with a small circle half way up its left side is quickly recognized as a "door." Even though houses and doors don't actually look like this, we understand both the object and the icon because we have come to common mutual agreement.

There was no class at which we were all in attendance that informed us of these things, we all picked them up as a part of our incorporation into this society. A person who doesn't adhere to these conventions would have difficulty communicating with the average person. He may readily comprehend the individual pieces without requiring that those components comprise a thing recognizable by other people. When other people identify an automobile, this person may not be sure if the designation is referring to the wheels or the chrome fixtures or the system comprised of machine and road. In a sense, this person is ignorant of the preconceptions that simplify our communication; but, at the same time, is free of the artificial constructs that limit our perception of reality.

Rather than looking at an ornate bar, labeling it as a "bar" and looking away; this person would have to take in the entire scene. No abbreviation. Instead he would see each of the liquor bottles backlit in blue through the frosted glass. He would assess the black marble counter top and the mahogany cabinetry sweeping up smoothly from the floor and breaking into ridges that wrap like fingers to a few inches from the marble forming a spill guard all along the length of the drinking area.

He would not be able to summarize it and dismiss it. He would have to assess the entire thing at which point he may well conclude that it is consistent with what might be called a "bar."

To be fair, all objects are corruptions of reality. We construct, with our minds, a world of objects so that we, with our limited perceptual machinery, may nonetheless comprehend the world. We move easily within this domain because we have objectified it. We see a moving mass supported by four wheels and we call it a "car." We see a moving roughly tubular furry thing having four legs and big eyes at the front of a small head and we call it a "cat." We see a cloth structure encompassing the top of a human head and we call it a "hat." The convenient names that we have assigned to these things do not improve our understanding of them, they excuse our ignorance of them. They are a mere gloss of the actual world.

Our objects, however, are driven by necessity. You may fill in the blanks when your friend describes her father, but when you meet him, all of the necessary parts will be present. While your guess at the size of his chest or your guess that his hair is gray may prove incorrect, the basic schema of *male human being* remains intact.

12: The World as Object and Representation

Listening to a philosophy podcast called *The Partially Examined Life*[21], I heard a modern philosopher railing against those who question the nature of reality. He said that he was sitting at his desk and looking at a chair across the room. The thing on the other side of the room, he said, was obviously a chair. He didn't need any further tests to verify that the chair was actual and real and a part of his reality. He was indignant on this point but he was missing an important part of the problem.

He knows it is a chair because of history. In fact, without history, we cannot actually know anything. If this philosopher were seeing the chair on the other side of his office for the first time, he would be wise to wonder, especially considering the context, if this were a real chair or a light plastic façade, blow molded to look like a chair only from one angle. To verify that, even our reality-based philosopher would get up and walk around the chair to assure that it looks like a chair from all angles. He may pick it up to verify that it is not a hollow 3D model and he may try to sit in it to assure that it will support his weight. He now has a history with the chair. Without that history, he cannot know if this is really a chair. Indeed, without history, *nothing* is certain.

We see the thing and we remember that we saw the thing under those circumstances. We then see it again and again and we form, in our mind, a reliable model only because we see and remember. Consider carefully that your own consciousness would have nothing upon which to stand without history. You yourself are defined by your history. If you had come into existence with all of your faculties intact and no history, from what would you resolve your self? Who are you? What are your capabilities?

The answer is that without something to define a past, there is no future and, in a sense, your *now* is barren and entirely empty. It does not actually exist because there is no context within which to define it. Without that, questions like "Who am I?" and "What is my purpose?" don't even come to mind.

---

21 An excellent podcast. Hear it while it lasts at http://partiallyexaminedlife.com.

Famine In the Bullpen

An object has a purpose and a history. It pulls together pieces (components) in the service of that purpose. Even a trivial object like a ribbon may serve as a tie for hair or may serve to delineate a restricted area. Despite its being artificial, it represents a distinct unit which may be distinguished from other objects. Even when we are at a loss to decide if two objects are actually components of a single object, their "objectness" allows us to grasp them (or it) and hold the decision regarding their composition until later, confident that the things we saw earlier will remain at least identifiable until our deliberations are complete.

———•———

In short all objects are artificial constructs. We use objects to clarify our understanding of the world we see. We define them arbitrarily depending upon what we want to do with them. All objects are simply tools and we can use them as we require.

If we approach our object domain in the way that we approach a C data model, we are lost. They are completely different things. An object built up from a C-style data model is, almost by definition, anemic; and yet, this is exactly what is typically done in building out a Java domain. The developer establishes data structures to hold the states of the various things that need to be addressed. He places that data into beans that he names after the things of interest. Then he writes procedures that he puts into various machines to manipulate that data. As long as he doesn't find himself believing that these objects can actually be treated like objects, he's OK.

Lots of excellent software has been written in C using this exact approach. Structured programming guidelines drive the process and the resulting software may accomplish exactly what it is supposed to by expertly manipulating data; but, there is a completely different way of understanding a solution that merits review.

The problem with OOM is the process required to construct a stable object domain. At its base, the process is philosophical. While data analysis is common to all software development, it is *epistemology* that drives an object domain. Epistemology is the study of knowledge:

12: The World as Object and Representation

what it is, how you get it, how you know that you know it. When applied to the whole world of experience, epistemology is a complicated and intractable field. When applied to an engineering problem, it is much more manageable. The reason I feel comfortable introducing this philosophical term to the engineering domain is the fact that an epistemology typically produces an *ontology*: a collection of objects that must exist in such a domain given the structure of what we know. After determining what can be known and what must be known, we establish the list of necessary objects. We describe the objects that will serve as experts in the understanding and processing of this data. We develop an ontology. This ontology is the object domain. It is not a data model.

The objects that define the ontology need to be understood as parts of a comprehensible whole. In philosophy, ontology asks questions like:

1. What can exist?
2. What is meant by existence?
3. What purpose do the existing things serve?

In general, software ontologies ask primarily the first and last questions. By understanding what must be known and what can be known, we devise the objects by which we may derive what is required. Our objects are the tools by which the required knowledge is processed and the required behaviors are manifested.

Each object will be responsible for one critical well-defined area of expertise. It will have all of the data required to perform its function and its behaviors will use that data to provide processed results (e.g., longitude and latitude or a derivative) and meaningful side-effects (e.g., printing a report or closing elevator doors). It is as clever as the engineer needs it to be, retaining historical data and learning from past errors or collaborating with other objects to leverage their expertise. In each case, the object is necessary to the epistemology. Its functioning is defined by it.

In the earlier example, the Elevator was defined based upon what an elevator *is*. We designed it to manifest all behaviors necessary to an elevator *and nothing else*. In order to be an elevator, it must have a way to get in and out (the door) it must have a way for the passenger to select a floor (the floor buttons). It must have a means for rising and descending in a controlled manner (the motor and pulley or the hydraulic cylinder). We don't define exactly what kind of door mechanism or exactly what method is used for selecting floors. Those are each defined as abstract objects incorporated into the Elevator. They too are defined based on what is necessary to satisfy their function and nothing else. Are the floor buttons physical buttons or are they displayed on a touch pad? We don't care. The ButtonPanel abstract object figures all that out and simply returns the one thing that it needs to return: a floor number.

If we start worrying about the specifics of this particular elevator, we will build attributes into the base class that are not necessary to all elevators and our base class will become too specialized to serve its purpose. Let's imagine that FloorThought decides to add an ice cream dispenser to one of its elevators. That would not be added to the Elevator class because it is not common to all elevators. Instead the engineers will observe the Open-Closed Principle and build a new class called DeluxeIceCreamElevator. It will inherit Elevator which will provide all canonical elevator behaviors, but any elevator of type DeluxeIceCreamElevator, will also include an ice cream dispenser and associated software interfaces.

Let's say that the ice cream theme inspires marketing people at FloorThought to propose a variety of elevator "flavors" with mix-and-match entertainment features such as soft drink dispenser, ongoing cable news, and red licorice extruders, each with appropriate software management in the form of buttons, sensors and diagnostics. In this case, the software team, knowing what their marketing team is likely to do (that is to say, they understand the *form* of the problem), will establish each of these as abstract types to be inherited by a largely empty elevator object. So, if we are managing an elevator with soft drink and red licorice, we instantiate a softDrinkRedLicoriceElevator which inherits Elevator, SoftDrinkProvider and RedLicoriceProvider. It would

12: The World as Object and Representation

get almost all of its behaviors from its parents and provide only minimal additional capabilities.

———•———

If the various elevator objects had been organized based upon the data that was required, their structure might be very different. We may create structs or beans with data about the elevator only; but our focus on data means that other arrangements are also reasonable. I've seen this kind of data organized as a single associative array of parameters and their values. Sometimes the data is organized based upon what particular library needs to consume it. Indeed, this approach is common for network protocols like RPC, the data the requester requires is bundled into a struct regardless what various entities it comes from: some from an elevator, some from a request button, perhaps.

The data may be organized based upon what data is local and what is delivered from remote sources. It may be organized as static data and data that changes frequently, to simplify access as a block. The data is just data and is not part of an ontology. For that reason, developers moving from procedural approaches to OOM, tend to include unnecessary data in their classes. When that happens, most of the OO advantages disappear.

When the objects in the model are assembled as necessary objects and not as data sets, OO becomes far less problematic. The Fragile Base Class Problem is addressed by the fact that your base class is constructed only from those components that are strictly necessary to the concrete thing it represents. We will never add a trash compactor to our Elevator – it is not necessary. We will never add a list of contacts to our Telephone (they may work together but the contact list is not a necessary function for communicating over a cell tower). We will never eliminate the start() method from our Stopwatch. We distinguish between what is necessary and what is not.

If we need a special Stopwatch that starts timing upon instantiation, we will devise an instantStartStopwatch which inherits Stopwatch, invokes a private __start() method upon initialization and overrides start()

with a method that does nothing. If we need a bank of Stopwatches, we will construct it from a Collection of Stopwatches along with behaviors to start or stop them in designated groups.

We construct the objects of our ontology based strictly on their necessary attributes. Such an object is probably applicable to many different similar object domains; and thereby, we begin to realize the possibility of reusing objects that have been written ahead and shelved for future use. Each one responsible for a competent emulation of the concrete object it represents.

———————•———————

Constructing such an object domain is not amenable to the feature factory mindset. If the goal is to develop an actual solution, it may take a week or two just to fully understand the problem. Once it is understood, the solution may require another week or two. With the solution conceived, it will need to be documented so that others may review it. The understanding of the information available and derivable within the solution-space and the necessary ontology that services it needs to be explained well enough that reviewers can actually understand it and identify its deficiencies.

Once that is reviewed, the object domain needs to be built out sufficiently that interactions between those objects may be put into play. So far, nothing that can be demonstrated to a customer has been produced; but, the engineers on the team have made significant progress. Once a sufficient number of objects have been implemented and tested, actual product features will be demonstrable. Will they be demonstrated to the customer? Would the customer understand what the initial primitive interactions mean? Maybe, but it must be understood that demonstrating a piece of a well-conceived OO solution, may be as meaningful to the customer as demonstrating the impeller design for a well-conceived vacuum cleaner.

To accelerate the OO design so as to allow a quick demonstration will force a premature object model which will invariably fail to qualify as an ontology. Such an object model will be subject to all of the prob-

12: The World as Object and Representation

lems we associate with the *failed experiment*. Our types will not define useful objects and our base classes will be fragile and methods will be sloppily named leading to frequent encounters with the diamond problem.

If, on the other hand, we use currently popular procedural methodology, the problem appears to go away. We throw together a quick demo and accept that those data structures may get frozen into the design for a while until we refactor. We will use inheritance sparingly, if at all. We will build easily modified data structures and apply them with full awareness that we may need to use our IDE to change that structure and everything that touches it. We keep our interfaces internal for the most part. We assign revisions[22] to our public interfaces so that we can change them with a minimum of difficulty. This all looks agile; but it is actually a careless application of methodology.

Any engineering process should be agile. There should be no more documentation than is needed. There should be no unnecessary components. There should be no irrelevant tests. There is no requirement imposed by agility that denies us the resources to comprehend the form of the problem and address it fully. There is nothing in agility that denies us full and effective documentation and time for reflection and confidence in our solution. Agility does not insist that the problem be solved piecemeal. It is not agility that drives a quick demonstrable solution; it is the wrong-headed perception that, for software, engineering is not required. It is an attempt to commoditize software development in the hope that these expensive developers may be readily automated. With that hope, we give up invention and real usefulness. We accept that our applications will bloat and slow, requiring ever faster microprocessors just to service the pointless feature-fluff. We try to normalize the mundane, reduce expectations and assure a continuous flow of new hardware purchases until a profit may be assured regardless the pointless crap we produce.

---

22 This is usually called *versioning* but, of course, no one is paying attention to the backward compatibility of the interface. In an OO design, revisioning of interfaces is rarely needed due to proper application of The Open-Closed Principle.

13: On Reading the Tractatus

What is thinkable is also possible.
Ludwig Wittgenstein

On a dark, icy and foggy night in 2004, my family and I were driving home from an event in southwestern Colorado. We were approaching Monarch Pass when a dense fog set in. There were cars behind us and cars ahead and, as the fog deepened, the headlights behind and the tail lights ahead became indistinguishable from the creamy white that obscured everything beyond the orange frame of our Volvo. Occasionally, our headlights would spot a shiny roadside reflector or the reflective center line of the road but the actual contours of the road were entirely invisible.

To stop would lead to a rear-end collision with the car behind. To speed up would be impossible: I had no idea what was in front of us to begin with. There were vague forms in the white but their distance was unclear. The car was moving forward but only the next few feet of road could be made out at all. Is the road straight for the next ten yards or am I missing a turn and going over the cliff?

The problem immediately at hand was depth perception. There is a similar problem while landing an airplane at night. The pilot forces an awareness of distance by intermittently focusing on the runway numbers and the lights in the distance at the runway's terminus. Knowing this and feeling the adrenaline surge, I desperately clung to that habit. As we moved forward at roughly constant speed, I sought a nearby re-

13: On Reading the Tractatus

flection, isolated it clearly in my line of sight and then sought a more distant reflection. My terrified passengers were moaning and begging me to stop, unaware of the car barreling down on us from behind. I offered reassurances and continued to prosecute my strategy. As I spotted the near target and then the distant target, I really could get a clear enough understanding of the shape of the road ahead to proceed with some confidence.

Near target, far target, near target, far target and the shape of the path formed in my mind. Not fully but clearly and enough. It became necessary to stop worrying about what I didn't know and concentrate on the ragged image of the road that the technique was revealing. While I only had a small percentage of the data I wanted, I had just enough information to proceed. My confidence was firming as we moved forward. Mile after mile we traversed Monarch Pass and began to descend into the town of Monarch where the fog began to lift. The cars ahead and behind were again revealed. They were close but not too close. Everyone on the pass had found their own mechanism for survival and we had avoided a collision together. My sweet spouse spotted a hotel for the night and we welcomed the break.

The next day, I made the connection. The process from the previous night was familiar, not just from night landings, but from something more intimate and precarious. The drive through the fog presented a problem wherein some components were clear and others were completely unavailable. The solution involved paying attention to what could be comprehended and constructing what could be constructed from that. Eventually, the picture became clearer, progressively more nearly complete until we could see our way through to the conclusion.

There was a distinct similarity to problem solving generally. This is often my approach when I address the resolution of a complex problem. It is essential, in such situations, to become comfortable with what you do not yet understand in order to manipulate those portions of the problem you can grasp. To insist upon understanding everything you are thinking is to throw out the whole concept and give up.

Famine In the Bullpen

As a senior staff engineer at Sun, I would always cherish the presentation of the problem. Someone from Marketing or Sales or, in my luckiest moments, a customer would describe the problem that was to be solved. I would receive it as a gift. I would question and take notes, assembling all of the information that could be gleaned from my benefactors into that collection of things that were revealed. I would take these notes back to my office and begin the process. While the actual mental process has never been clear to me, I always imagined myself escorting the problem through hallways, past door after door where occasional ideas would pop their heads out and confront the problem. Sometimes the idea was a bust but sometimes the idea would be able to contribute a new limb or a patch of flesh to the haggard corpus of the problem.

I must confess that, regardless my fantasy regarding my internal process, the most important mechanism is always unconscious. As I lean back in my chair and concentrate on the problem, then turn to my whiteboard and scribble, then return to quiet reflection, then return to the whiteboard, I am only priming an invisible engine that will essentially "take it from there." Knowing this, I nonetheless go home and return to work the next day pretending to cogitate and struggle. I fill my whiteboard with diagrams and I start on a document explaining the solution knowing full well that I don't understand anything.

In a week or two, I know the problem will be solved; but, I am not actually bringing anything of value to the process by pretending to know where I am going. What I do bring to the process is the acceptance of my ignorance. I don't have all of the information I want, but I do have just enough to negotiate the next few miles. Given that, I try to construct what can be constructed on my large whiteboard in my quiet office, building a tattered image of what the problem might actually be.

Alfred North Whitehead in *Science and the Modern World*[Whitehead_1925], reviews advances in modern science and its origins in Greece where rudimentary early concepts were developed. "Alas," he laments, "[the ancient Greeks] genius was not so apt for the state of imaginative muddled suspense which precedes successful inductive generalization." He con-

13: On Reading the Tractatus

firms, for us, that confusion, uncertainty and doubt precede the innovative revelation. For that reason, the engineer must be comfortable with these feelings.

The problem itself is important because until it is understood, the solution will be impossible. In fact, the biggest problem is figuring out the real problem. The customer has no idea what the problem is. They only know that something hurts and they want the hurt to go away. The engineer must first follow the trail of symptoms provided by the customer back to the actual root cause. Without that, the supposed solution is only a band-aid. Any technician can apply a band-aid. The solution to the problem requires engineering.

———— • ————

There is always nervousness when the impossible problem is first presented. One will fake confidence in the discussion with the customer but in the back of the mind is the constant nagging worry that this may actually be impossible. When I'm listening to a customer problem, I have to fight back my tendency to dwell on the impossible problems I failed to resolve. I think back to the high-accuracy pressure transducer I tried to design in Oklahoma City. The failure slaps me on the back of my head during the customer interview reminding me constantly of my inadequacy. I cannot let it in. I have to keep the fear at bay and listen to every nuance of the customer's complaint. I take notes and look at facial expressions and body language. I'm looking for what part of the story has an emotional component and what part is made up to try to summarize aspects of the problem for which I require details. I need to then ask questions that will illuminate the path to the actual problem. The pressure transducer was an early problem. I have more experience now. I have to remember that and know the problem will be resolved.

In the fullness of time, the solution invariably arises, and it arises from the full understanding of the problem itself. Archimedes explained his method for grasping the deep truths of the cosmos as "Motus Orbicularis" (orbital motion). Imagine a hawk who identifies a field mouse in the distance. It circles. It orbits and closes in. It watches and analyzes.

How does the mouse respond to the wind? How does it respond to cloud shadows? Is it calm or nervous? It watches and orbits until it knows the mouse like its own wing. It moves closer as it circles until it is within inches of its prey. It extends its talons and grasps. Here there is a miraculous transformation. The mouse is no longer a mouse. It is supper. This is how the problem becomes the solution.

When Isaac Newton was asked how he developed such ingenious explanations regarding the functioning of the physical world, he responded, "By thinking about it without ceasing." This is what defines engineering as a discipline rather than a procedure. We orbit like Archimedes with relentless focus like Newton until the solution presents itself. Engineering isn't a thing to know, it's a way of thinking. It is a way that is comfortable with incomplete information, piecing together fragments and shadows into a growing picture that will finally resolve into the complete understanding of the problem and then into the elegant solution.

For that reason, I should be shocked that I couldn't read Heidegger's *On Being and Time*. I managed to get about 15% of the way into it but I had to stop. I insisted on dwelling upon every sentence that I couldn't understand until I thought I understood it. It took forever. I struggled, imagining that I could meet the challenge of *Sein und Zeit*, but I failed. Failed utterly.

Many years later, I was listening to *The Partially Examined Life* and I was inspired to read Wittgenstein's *Tractatus Logico-Philosophicus*[Wittgenstein_1922] (*The Tractatus*), a treatise on the subject of language: how we use it and how it may best convey meaning. I was intrigued by Wittgenstein's decision to number his paragraphs. This is reminiscent of a functional specification and implied that each paragraph was important. The podcast discussion wandered all over from ontology to language to metaphysics. It made Wittgenstein sound fascinating.

I bought the C. K. Ogden translation on eBay and resolved to begin my read on an upcoming trip to Washington DC. Settling into my seat on the aircraft, I read the first page, then read it again, then read it again. It was full of simple statements made without qualification. I was

13: On Reading the Tractatus

generally prepared for this because I'd heard the podcast discussion, but it still put me off and made it difficult to move to the next page. A German philosopher was explaining the world in uncompromising terms without supporting data. It was obvious to him. That it was not obvious to me was simply an annoyance.

The story goes that in his oral arguments for *The Tractatus* (*The Tractatus* was accepted as Wittgenstein's doctoral dissertation in 1929), Wittgenstein was confronted by a panel of professors which included the eminent Bertrand Russell. Finally, after hours of interrogation, Wittgenstein rose and said, "Don't worry, I know you'll never understand it," and walked out of the room. He was awarded a doctorate anyway.

So I was in good company as I struggled with the text, but it still took an hour or so to finally give up. I gave up and accepted that I didn't understand anything I was reading. I moved forward from there, reading on and on, jotting down the terms that were confusing me along with best guesses as to their meaning. For the time being, I ignored my confusion. In about ten pages there was a statement that triggered a small revelation. I looked back at page one and realized that I actually understood a fair part of it now. By proceeding without demanding an immediate understanding, I had allowed myself the freedom to get it eventually. The entire book flowed so much more easily after that. In areas I could comprehend, I read carefully and took notes regarding the ideas being presented. When the text became incomprehensible, I read more broadly, looking for familiar terms and taking notes about the general concepts. I reached the end on my way back from Dulles and only then understood that I was finally applying my familiar process for solving problems to reading German philosophy.

This, actually, is not far from the technique used by scholars to read any complicated philosophical text. It is a combination of *close reading* (similar to what I was trying to do when I first opened the Tractatus) and *distant reading* (similar to what I did when I was confused). One approach tries to understand the meaning as truthfully as possible from an analysis of the sentences with respect to the concepts being developed in the nearby text. The other puts the concepts into an understanding of the larger context. Each feeds the other. These techniques, from the discipline called *hermeneutics*, are helpful in reading a specification as well.

While hermeneutics focuses on the treatment of ancient texts, it emphasizes what is useful in any technical reading: controlling bias and grasping the meaning of a document with intellectual innocence. Reading a specification, one does well to take notes, summarizing key points so that as the pieces of the picture are filled in it is easier to see how everything fits together. It is important to recognize one's bias so that it can be managed. If the reader likes Hibernate but the product requires a SQL-laden schema with multiple levels of indirection in order to assure data integrity, one must be able to set aside that bias and choose or write an object-to-relational mapper that will best support such a design.

A well-written specification will require a minimum of suffering but since it is a technical document it will require a certain level of disciplined attention. It is necessary, from time to time, to skim forward without full understanding trying to grasp the overall direction. When the revelation occurs, you will want to return to the earlier text and reread with the renewed comprehension that revelation provided. You will want to avoid matching up issues in the specification with ideas for the implementation since it will bias your understanding of the unread text.

A technical document approached with managed bias and an innocent eagerness to perceive what is there without embellishment will leave the reader with a full understanding of the proposed solution. With that information fully digested, the reader is now ready to critique the approach and consider implementation options.

——— • ———

The Tractatus is worthy reading despite the fact that Wittgenstein himself admitted to some fundamental flaws later in his life. Nonethe-

13: On Reading the Tractatus

less, "What *can* be shown *cannot* be said." [emphasis Wittgenstein] leads undoubtedly to thoughts that had not been thought before, and that is always good. "Causality is not a law, it is the form of a law," provides insight into cause-and-effect and the notion of a form.

Allow me a few paragraphs to encourage the reader to try *The Tractatus* because it exposes the kind of abstract thinking involved in serious problem-solving. Here are a few concepts Wittgenstein explores that should draw you in. The book is comprised of seven sections. Each is organized hierarchically as an initial proposition, followed by propositions intended to support it until the initial proposition is proved. He begins with "The world is everything that is the case." From there, each section takes up a piece of the problem, assembling and associating those pieces until the whole issue may be assessed. Finally, he concludes with a single statement which carries an import that is not clear until one has read his entire thesis: "Whereof one cannot speak, thereof one must be silent." Section 7 is comprised of only that one proposition because it is essentially QED.

He exposes the object as a complete and self-contained thing in the real world. "The object is simple," "The object is fixed, the existent; the configuration is the changing, the variable," "In order to know an object, I must know not its external but all its internal qualities." Of course, he isn't talking about software objects, but his explication reminds us that the object is a natural classification, self-contained and knowable. We design the object to represent a thing in the real world – a thing recognized even by philosophers as tangible and meaningful. The developer knows the object by knowing its inner workings but exposes only its public interface.

The book sets out to question so many things that we often assume to be simple givens. "Ethics and æsthetics are one," "The world is the totality of facts, not of things," "The world and life are one. I am my world." He claims that there is no subject partly because we are too close to what is. What we observe, we are. As an engineer, I feel that I have lived that in a small way. Solving the problem becomes all-consuming. We are the problem. We see the world from the context of the problem until the problem becomes substantial and yields to exploration. Wittgenstein notes that we do not define the world but our language and our failures of perception limit the world. I may be completely misunderstanding Wittgenstein, but this speaks to me and my experience with engineering.

A certain humility is required to actually solve a problem. The possibility of failure is always in the background. If there is no possibility of failure, then the problem can be solved by a programmer: no engineering required.

The idea is to *avoid* breaking down the problem into manageable chunks. By breaking the problem up, we obscure the essential relationships within and the essential wholeness of the problem. That is the ongoing error: the problem is decomposed and then resolved as a set of decomposed pieces. I have never taken a class in engineering but I have interviewed people who have. They explained to me how an engineering problem is solved. It's very simple: decompose, analyze, resolve and recompose: a step-by-step process.

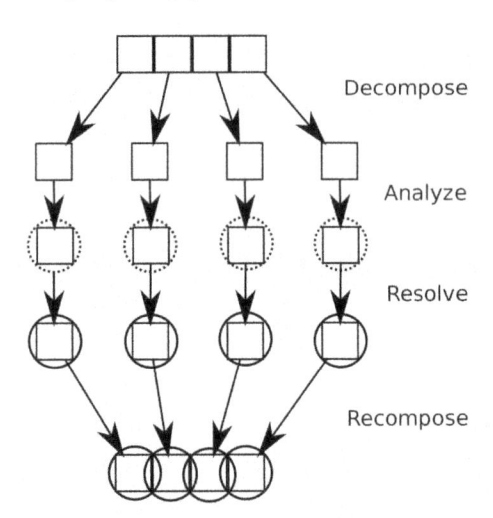

Decompose

Analyze

Resolve

Recompose

This makes it easy. Anyone can do it, and in fact many do. The solution at the end of this procedure is what we might call a *technical solution*. The problem itself has been divided up into manageable chunks, each of which can be easily addressed, then those resolved chunks are

13: On Reading the Tractatus

brought back together into a solution. Once decomposed, though, it is very easy to lose track of what the original problem actually is.

We can see evidence of this process all around us.

———————— • ————————

On January 28, 1986, the Space Shuttle *Challenger* exploded during ascent. Evidence showed that one of the solid rocket boosters' seams opened enough to allow a jet of hot gas to soften and finally sever one of the struts holding the booster in place. As a result it compromised one of the external fuel tanks leading to an explosion that destroyed the vehicle. At the time, I was working in aerospace where this failure struck home in a very visceral fashion. The responsible party appeared to be Morton-Thiokol, but my employer also produced products and services that needed to guard against the loss of human life. We trained the astronauts and we monitored their progress, so it was personal.

The problem was described as a failure of the primary and secondary O-ring seals. As a former user of O-rings as high pressure seals, this struck me as fundamentally telling. The design appears to have followed the process identified by my interviewees. The tell-tale indicators include that the solution addressed individual specific components of the problem without addressing the entire problem.

The analysis showed that the Viton™ seals failed due to the extreme cold prior to launch. That explanation required a little suspension of disbelief on the part of valve manufacturers but it satisfied the public. Viton seals don't suddenly shatter when the temperature moves below their specified limit. Instead, they gradually become less effective but not immediately useless. They are used in the petrochemical industry in valves that are mounted on top of U.S. pipelines. Occasionally they experience lower temperatures than expected and on those days, the valves do not all suddenly fail. Looking at the specific design, though, there are a number of problems.

It appears (since I wasn't there) that the problem decomposed into the following pieces:

1. The solid fuel will apply high pressures and temperatures at the inter-segment joint especially once the flame-front reaches it. That joint must be sealed.
2. If the gas gets past that seal, there needs to be another one (redundancy is required).
3. Dual redundancy is required for designs involving human safety.

The first problem is resolved with a topologically complex mating surface sealed with flame-resistant goop. To deal with the possibility that the goop might melt and flow out, someone added an O-ring seal. The problem is that the O-ring presumes (indeed requires) that the fluid it is sealing in be free of particulates. The O-ring is an *energized seal* meaning that it seals a joint by preceding the pressurized fluid into the gap. To this end, the O-ring initially joins the flow of the fluid allowing a small amount of fluid to move past it as it enters the gap. If there is any particulate matter in the impinging fluid, the particulates may move past the O-ring lodging against its sealing surface and defeating the seal. The seal following the O-ring seal (the seal intended to work if the O-ring didn't) was another O-ring which was going to encounter an even dirtier fluid consisting of combustion byproducts, melted and burning goop and melted and burning Viton. It was bound to fail as well. In fact, the Morton-Thiokol engineers admitted that this was a problem but that there was sufficient molten rubber moving through the interface that it was bound to eventually seal sufficiently.

Considering each seal as an independent issue, the design makes sense. Considering the entire problem, a completely different design would result. In all likelihood, a serious design would require gaskets and only gaskets – a type of seal that is not energized but instead seals without encouragement.

Ironically, the *solution* to the Challenger disaster was to add a third O-ring.

13: On Reading the Tractatus

The automaker Tesla has made the electric car not only popular but technically feasible. Their research into battery technology and sturdy yet light-weight auto construction with extremely low wind resistance at highway velocities has revolutionized the industry. The one remaining problem resides in recharging such a vehicle over a long trip. Here, we decompose the problem:

1. For a long trip, people need to refill their battery regularly.
2. Batteries take a long time to charge.
3. Some electric cars have a range of less than 100 miles.

These look like a fair decomposition of the problem. We can solve the first problem by installing lots of charging stations. The second problem is addressed by improving battery technology. The third by packing more batteries into each car.

Until we consider the whole problem, we don't come to realize that the original problem was the wrong problem. The problem to be solved isn't how to refill my battery. The problem to be solved is how to get the next 200 miles down the road. You don't want to refill your battery at all, you want a new battery.

Tesla engineers aren't slouches. They've figured this out. The battery in the Tesla can be swapped by a robot in only ninety seconds. They tested this concept on the road between San Francisco and Los Angeles with no success. They discovered that, for that stretch, the drivers welcomed a thirty minute break while their Tesla recharged.

As is often the case, this doesn't mean the solution is wrong; but until passenger cars and heavy trucks are mostly electric, the solution won't be popular enough to make sense in the market. In time, this will be the approach we use for all vehicles. In the meanwhile we've applied a technical solution, addressing components of the wrong problem without actually addressing the real problem.

Famine In the Bullpen

The issue of the Java language is, like my previous examples, more complex than can be fully addressed in this chapter, but the gist of the problem can be summarized effectively, I think. Decomposing the problem James Gosling was addressing, we come to the following (very) partial list:

1. When multiple parents are inherited, you don't know which is providing the method you are calling.
2. When the base class is modified in an incompatible way, all of its children are broken.
3. Once compiled, the program can only be run on a particular architecture.
4. Browsers run on all sorts of different underlying operating systems the idiosyncrasies of which introduce complications into the software stack.

That, of course, is a very short sample of the complete list, but let's work with it as best we can. We will see that each problem has been addressed more or less individually. To deal with the problem of multiple inheritance, it was simply disallowed. The fragile base class problem remains in Java and even Gosling once lamented his failure to orient the language to a JavaScript-style *prototype* architecture. To deal with the apparent problem of compilation, it was built upon a virtual machine (VM) which would isolate the Java code from the underlying operating system. The issue of the browsers pushed that even further, leading proper Java design to utterly ignore potentially useful features of the underlying OS, meaning that, unlike other VM-based languages, the underlying OS was, for a time, inaccessible.

These approaches, if we include the desired prototype typing method, are all fine solutions to the individual components of the problem but until the overall collection of components are reviewed as a complete thing, the real solution is not clear. I have mentioned the language Eiffel before and it has some problems that have not yet been entirely addressed, but the problems Java was intending to address are addressed in Eiffel without isolation. Multiple inheritance in Eiffel sup-

13: On Reading the Tractatus

ports aliasing of parent methods meaning that you always know which parent method is being invoked. Following Bertrand Meyer's principles, the fragile base class isn't fragile at all, it is improperly designed in the first place. The Eiffel IDE runs on a VM that could be distributed exactly the way that the Java VM is. As to isolating the program from the underlying OS, that's fine as long as you really don't care that the underlying OS was selected for a reason. Sometimes the OS is really useful and provides services you may want.

The larger problem is that in order to develop an OO solution to a problem, you have to fully understand how to develop software using OOM. An assessment of the problem as a whole would reveal that. People who want to use procedural methodology should use it, but a piecemeal examination of the problem only produces a language that claims to be OO for people who don't really like OO.

———•———

That's not all. For example, installing software was a major problem until the development of OS images that could be installed to a slice of a computer in minutes. Despite this appearing to be the ultimate solution, it doesn't compare to the failed ZIP project at Sun wherein the bare metal computer would boot and immediately (within seconds) begin running its OS. The Sun engineer realized that installing the software wasn't really the problem. The problem was booting the computer and using it. That conclusion was not obvious from a simple analysis of the parts of the problem.

Random drug-testing of bus drivers fails in the same way. The problem to be addressed is bus drivers operating their vehicles in a manner which is not consistent with the requirements of public safety. Testing for drugs addresses a minuscule part of the larger problem which is, basically, behavioral. Yes, your bus driver isn't drunk but did her husband sue for divorce this morning? Is our bus driver worried about his finances? Did she spend a sleepless night dealing with a croupy child? All of those are key factors in distracting a bus driver; but by looking at individual issues, one was picked out and "resolved" making the whole problem look solved.

If bus companies or airlines actually wanted to solve the real problem, as understood, they would institute a test of reaction time, reasoning and tactics that could be administered before each trip. They would address the root cause. While they wouldn't know about the blood chemistry of their drivers, they would be assured of the safety of their passengers. They also wouldn't be infringing upon the assurances made by the fourth and fifth amendments to the U.S. Constitution. They would be solving the whole actual problem and not just a few symptoms.

From *The Tractatus*, we observe an analysis of the broad problem of what we know and how we communicate that amongst ourselves. Wittgenstein begins by decomposing the problem. He addresses each of the components and then, prior to offering a solution, brings them together as a whole for a final overall understanding. It hints at the method used to resolve any complicated problem.

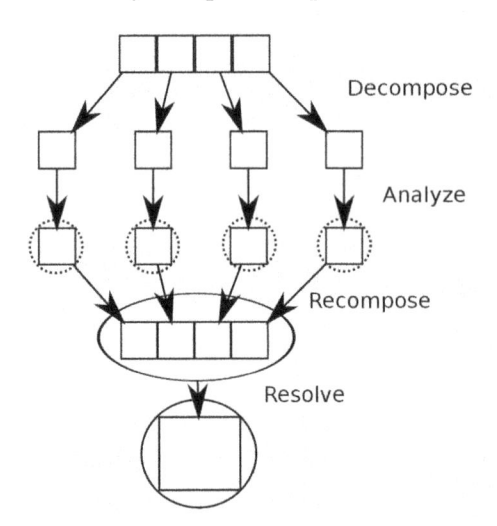

Certainly it is necessary to analyze the problem fully and that does involve decomposition; but the final resolution must take into account the entire problem. At the point where we are assessing the problem as a whole, the delusion of the step-by-step procedure becomes difficult to

13: On Reading the Tractatus

maintain because that's when you step into the realm of free-thinking whimsy. To accomplish this we use a rather different approach: Decompose, Analyze, Recompose, Resolve.

You understand the whole problem. You've analyzed all of the pieces and you have a keen understanding of how all of the parts fit together. You are not yet ready to solve the problem. You are now ready to *understand* the problem well enough to *begin* the process of developing the solution. The *Resolve* part of the process is iterative – moving from problem to options for a solution to the problem and back to options again until the solution works and fits.

In the end the result is an engineering solution. It will be simple. It will resolve the entire problem and it will apply well to other similar problems. It will also adapt to the problem as it changes with its environment. The engineering solution is as intimate with the problem as the desert hawk is with its meal. It has arisen from the problem organically as a result of the engineer's disciplined analysis. Like Wittgenstein, we analyze incisively from parts to the whole; but we ultimately resolve only the whole.

14: Software As a Surface

Language is the amber in which a million subtle and precious thoughts are safely embodied and preserved.
                              Frederic W. Goudy

A Chicago consulting firm, one of many that exploit the Salesforce.com infrastructure, made a serious error in 2010 and offered me a job. Their interview consisted of setting me a complex task and instructing me to develop a solution. I was to present it to a team in Chicago. I worked diligently to understand the Salesforce.com data architecture and divine how it could be applied to the problem at hand. I devised the solution and a slide deck which I would present to them from my T42 ThinkPad in their Chicago office.

They flew me out for the day and I hurled my mighty spiel. The questions were incisive. The faces were grim. When I was finished, they sent me away and deliberated. I was invited back into the room after a few minutes and informed that I had the job. I was elated. It was easily half the thrill I felt when I got the job at Sun. Everyone with the company seemed brilliant and disciplined. I was thinking that I was back at Sun (or close enough). Everything they did used the Salesforce.com back-end but they seemed interested in solving serious problems for real customers. This would be good.

I went to Chicago for a week of training. I was informed that it all started with a document from Sales identifying the nature of the problem and the customer needs. The instructor was using unfamiliar

14: Software As a Surface

terms but she seemed to be describing a *requirements document*. As I listened, I was thrilling at the idea of once again working for a company that would take a requirements document seriously.

Clearly this was a company interested in the engineering discipline. I imagined, as this document was being described, that the next topic must be the *functional spec* (the engineer's response to the requirements document). I listened intently as the instructor moved on to a document which, based upon her explanation, was exactly what I was expecting. They didn't use the familiar words, they had their own words for these documents, but the description was definitely that of a functional specification. I was joyous. After all of this time at a fast follower, I was working for a technology leader: a company which, like Sun, used true engineering methodology to develop solutions for customers.

I was assigned a mentor, a twenty-something senior architect, who started leading me through the process of interpreting requirements and writing a functional spec. Of course I'd been doing that for twenty four years; but, I took my position as his junior seriously and listened and learned. I'm afraid, though, that I didn't understand a word he was saying. The requirements document he showed me didn't provide any useful information about the actual problem, nor did it provide enough information about how the customer perceived the problem. It provided a salesperson's solution without any serious information about the problem that drove the solution. The actual information I needed was not there.

I asked my mentor if I could talk to the salesperson but he had already moved on to a different project and was not able to spare the billable hours. My mentor was shocked that I couldn't work with what I had. I began writing a functional specification to the best of my ability. My mentor was again shocked at this terse, technical document. "This is for the customer, he'll never understand this." He pointed me at some of *his* "functional specs" with lots of pictures and color graphs. It included plenty of reassuring words about how cool this solution would be. I suddenly realized that my enterprise was likely to be a disaster.

Famine In the Bullpen

I copied his flashy full-color style and produced a worthless yet comforting document that conveyed to the customer the sound delusion that everything was in hand. I was assigned a developer a day after I finished that marketing document. Steve, the developer, called me and basically said, "I'll take it from here."

I asked him what he was going to do since my document was obviously useless. He said that he'd worked with less. I asked, "Wouldn't you rather have a functional spec?" (I used the correct term).

There was a brief pause followed by. "Could you do that?" The tone in his voice was startled with a hint of hopefulness.

"Well yes," I said, "I'm an engineer. That's kind of what I do?"

"I have to start coding now. How can you get me a spec in time?"

I told him that I'd start writing the spec now, and at the end of the weekend I'd have the definitions and the first few sections. I was thanked profusely by a skilled developer who had given up on ever having enough information to do a good job: a man who had become accustomed to doing the job the architect should have done by pulling together all of the threads and hoping upon hope that he had guessed correctly about what was needed.

I started the work that evening, pulling together what I could from the initial requirements-like document, putting myself in the position of the customer and trying to imagine what they must have been seeing that would lead to the bill of particulars provided by the salesperson. That Monday, I had something from which Steve could at least start. For the next few days, I put time in on the spec until my supervisor informed me that I was being assigned to a new project. I responded that I hadn't finished the technical documentation for the previous project. He told me that my customer document was excellent and so I was done.

I then realized that the ridiculous fluff-piece I had put together for the customer was actually all that I was expected to do. It was the developer's job to figure out the actual functional specifics and code something up. I was assigned to a new project with a soft drink company and

14: Software As a Surface

a team in Poland. The lead engineer in the U.S. was also named Steve. Since I was already writing a functional spec for the first Steve, I decided to run this project using Scrum as purely as I could manage. I scheduled daily meetings and wrote stories with explicit acceptance criteria so detailed it may as well have been a piecewise functional specification.

Scrum works fairly well on projects for which requirements are well-defined and for which the solution can be specified as a set of short simple tasks. Since I was working from a poor requirements document, I had to guess at the nature of the problem but I thought I had a good enough grasp to serve. The problem was that I was also dealing with language issues and technical gaps. For instance, we needed to know the actual practical speed of 3G versus 4G versus wifi. I wrote a spike (a Scrum investigation) to assess this. A developer was to take a 3G and a 4G phone into the field and download a very specific set of payloads to each phone from each of a set of specific locations. Without a clear understanding of experimental design, though, the developer provided a mixed bag of downloads from various locations. I had to spend a few days teasing the variables apart.

By now I was working sixteen hour days, writing the functional specification for Steve; researching the actual problem and likely solution for Steve; generating highly detailed stories as the understanding allowed and addressing the responses and questions associated with those stories. Lacking sleep, fighting off panic and unable to reserve time for anything except work; the nightmare was threatening to pollute my entire waking life. I put up with that for five months: sixteen hour days without a break, monitoring one smart team with a smart Steve lead and one smart lone Steve. I generated documentation and resolved discrepancies, meeting regularly with the customer and adjusting requirements as my understanding of the needs changed.

In the end Steve's customer was praising the results in ways that were deeply moving and the team with Steve leading had also seen warm accolades. When my supervisor told me I was moving to a third project, I quit. Every hour of every day was already consumed. There was nothing left and I was not willing to reclaim those hours by conforming to the expected behavior, painting pretty pictures for customers and taking advantage of developers.

Upon leaving I realized that this company was like a child who, upon watching his mother writing a mystery novel, would sit at the computer and type at length believing the motion and the concept identical. It was clear that the company was taken in by the basic notion of engineering method; but, they had no idea what it actually was. It was all show and bluster and could not possibly have succeeded without a brilliant stock of developers who were able to figure out the actual engineering and thanklessly and flawlessly deliver.

The technical architect at that company was simply expected to write a marketing document, throw it over the wall to the developer and move on to the next project. This wasn't an insult to engineering; it was a sad childish pretense. So how were the customers taken in by this failure to grasp the concept? In the same way, perhaps, that the child's friend, also knowing nothing of the process of writing a novel, delights at the young boy's apparent skill. The customers were bankers and marketing people. Without actual experience in the discipline, any process, executed with confidence, would appear to be competent engineering.

This isn't the tattered cliché of the blind leading the blind, though, because the consultant, in the back of his mind, really understands that this is a show in much the same way that the novelist's son will eventually realize that his output is not identical to his mother's. Pretending at engineering discipline is not engineering discipline, it is marketing – or at least indistinguishable from it.

———•———

Documentation is intimidating, enigmatic and important. The problem, unless it is trivial, and the solution, unless it is obvious, must be described. Any problem complex enough to be actually solved has earned the right to stain some paper. The problem and the solution must be described separately, because a solution developed prior to a full understanding of the problem will be flawed by ignorance and yet,

14: Software As a Surface

since it is in the same document, will restrict the process necessary to develop the real solution.

A project begins with a statement of the problem. Unfortunately, this is often encapsulated in a requirements document. The problem with a requirements document is that it tends to combine problem and solution in ways that are often inappropriate. I remember, when working in aerospace, the requirements received from NASA and the military. We would build a massive functional specification which contained numbered paragraphs which corresponded to each of the numbered requirements. In other words, NASA said, "you shall do this," in their document and we said, "We will do that," in ours. Neither document provided much illumination but instead served more as a contractual binding. The engineering was described in book after book of technical documentation, none of which would ever be read.

This is the understanding of documentation held by most software people and it explains our aversion to it. The problem is that *no documentation* is just as bad as *poor documentation*. Any documentation that is not read is equivalent to no documentation. Nonetheless, the process of explaining a problem precisely reveals details that a face-to-face discussion cannot. The process of describing the solution precisely is also illuminating. It is in the process of writing paragraph five that you realize your description in paragraph three was missing something. It is in the process of adding that something that you realize there's something really basically wrong with your concept. Without the process of writing the document, that connection would not arise until it was too late.

Bertrand Russell once said, "Everything is vague to a degree you do not realize until you have tried to make it precise." The engineer constructs that precision when he writes the functional specification. I don't write functional specifications any more because it frightens the kids. I still write documents, simple prose descriptive documents, to explain the design, but it's hard to get modern developers to read even those.

The functional specification should be the engineer's response to the detailed description of the problem. When the description presumes to propose a solution at the same time (as in the NASA requirements), the resulting engineering is more an accounting procedure than anything else. The requirements are typically provided by someone in the sales or marketing department. They are often the result of an extended discussion with the customer. Sometimes the requirements document is a formal thing with a scope and definitions and paragraph numbers. Other times it's scribbles on the back of a napkin. In the latter case, it is essential to collar the person who made the scribbles and talk it through in depth.

The engineer has to fully understand the problem and the problem is sometimes described, usually just hinted at, in the requirements document. The problem of figuring out what the problem is has already been discussed, but to begin that process, details about the environment where the difficulty first arose and the tribulations of the people confronting it need to be reviewed with care. It is then necessary to pull together the description of the solution.

I have always felt that the requirements document itself is a misplaced concept. What is needed is a document exclusively dedicated to the problem-space. Certain well written requirements documents may do that; but generally, they span problem and solution in ways that are not helpful. I'm used to figuring out the nature of the problem myself, but a formal problem-space document composed by a customer liaison skilled in ferreting out the problem details would be extremely useful.

So, an engineer or salesperson (sometimes with the help of an engineer) assembles a document of some kind identifying the problem-space. The engineer responds to that with a functional specification. The functional specification describes the surface features of the solution. It does not – indeed it must not – describe the implementation details. It does not explain why this solution is so cool. It does not include boiler plate contractual statements. It just describes the surface features of the solution.

By surface features, I mean interfaces. Every public interface including the user interface must be described in the functional specification as well as any publicly exposed network protocols or library

14: Software As a Surface

procedures. Everything under the surface, such as procedures or processes that are used to implement the described signatures and behaviors, are left to the developers. Good developers working on a complex implementation may well put together a design document for review in which the implementation is described.

Such a design document is often useful, but not always required. It is the surface features that are critical because they comprise the contract with the customer. A long tedious functional specification will not be read and is therefore useless. A functional specification must be accessible and doing that requires some practice.

Sun Microsystems delivered software patches for its systems which conformed to a functional specification reviewed and approved by the ARC. The patches were unique, in the UNIX arena, because they could be applied one by one and then "backed out" one by one. The specification guaranteed that, after applying ten patches and then backing out each one, the Sun system would be returned to its pre-patched state in pristine fashion.

A customer, for example, could write their own C compiler and place that special compiler where the Sun C compiler used to be. Running for several months using that compiler, the customer might accidentally apply Sun's C compiler patch which would replace their custom C compiler with Sun's. Upon realizing that they had done this, the customer could back out that C compiler patch and they would discover their custom C compiler restored to its original place exactly as it had been prior to applying the patch.

The functional specification described this behavior in sufficient detail to allow any number of implementations in any number of programming languages all of which would function in exactly the same way. That functional specification complete with a few appendices of examples was twelve pages long.

———•———

As a member of the ARC at Sun, I was assigned to sponsor a project that I will denote by the code name *Tigris*. When I pulled up their functional spec, I decided I'd go over it on the bus and red line it as needed. I printed it out and dealt with other business.

That evening, I went to the printer and was shocked to find that the spec was nearly three hundred pages long. Reluctantly, I lugged the stack of paper into my briefcase and headed to my bus. On the bus I began to thumb through the tome. It was chock-full of pictures and marketing explaining how excellent the project was. Normally, I concentrate pretty well on the bus but the more I thumbed through it, the more confused I became. I was ARC sponsor and so I had to be able to explain it, yet it was all a muddle.

When I arrived home, I pulled out a notebook and started over. This time I was taking notes to try to tease the meaning out of the document. After ten pages, I had no notes. There was literally nothing there. This spec, written by an engineering director, was three hundred pages of dead air. In the end it was approved by the ARC, not because it seemed important and well conceived but because it seemed harmless.

A few months later, I was attending a Sun conference. I was sitting with Alka, a friend and fellow engineer, listening to the lead engineer for Tigris as he explained the architecture. The concept remained elusive but Alka and I listened closely trying to assemble some overall view of what he was talking about. When the presentation was finished, we filed out quietly. Sitting in a coffee shop, still puzzling, one of us (I forget which) had a revelation.

"I know the problem. It's so amazingly versatile that it's almost useless. It's *a grand architecture for doing stuff with things*."

We laughed over that for some while and I return to that description on a regular basis every time I encounter a framework so versatile it provides no real value. This is what happens when no time is invested in figuring out what the real problem is. The specification for Tigris was clearly structured as a series of filled-in templates describing each piece of the conceived design. Had the responsible engineer undertaken to actually write an original work, the incongruous portions of the idea

14: Software As a Surface

would have become obvious and the specification would have been useful and much shorter.

———•———

As with any document, there is always a certain difficulty in getting started. It helps to understand the general structure because the first few sections of any functional spec follow a kind of formula and having a well-tested starting point is always helpful. Different organizations will use different terms but the general approach will remain fairly similar. We always start with something like scope, related documents and definitions.

Scope: This is where you avoid creeping elegance. This is a few paragraphs explaining the problem being solved and emphasizing that you are solving that problem and not every other problem associated with it. If possible identify similar but unrelated problems that are *not* being solved in order to mark your perimeter. This is where you would make it clear that this is a Content Distribution System and not a Content Management System which is defined elsewhere.

Related Documents: Here list any documents to which this one refers. If you don't refer to any other documents, that's OK. The importance of the other document, though, is not to be discounted. It saves a lot of space if you can simply type "the message shall conform to RFC2616." Seriously, "HTTP protocol" is somewhat open to interpretation but the actual defining document is unambiguous, or at least far less ambiguous.

Definitions: This is a crucial part of any specification. It is used to assure that words in the text may be simply stated. In poor specifications, obscure words are either used and not explained or they are clumsily explained in the text. Often, the actual meaning of a word will change as the document proceeds. This leads to tremendous difficulty understanding the document.

The rest of the document is a little more specialized to the problem. I typically entitle the next section *Provisions* and use that space to identify the behaviors supporting each interface. In order to assure the distinction between this and a requirements document, I strive to avoid the term *requirement* in favor of the term *provision* or *provides*. Be sure to number each paragraph so that any paragraph may unambiguously refer to any other paragraph. Hierarchical numbering (e.g., 1.0, 1.1, 1.2, 2.0) is useful but not required.

This section will fully and unambiguously describe all the behaviors underlying the interfaces. It defines the semantics behind the syntax. This is where you indicate that the two provided integers are to be multiplied returning a product. It does not describe the implementation or the coding style. If there is a key internal feature that is essential to the functioning of the architecture, then it should be at least recommended as a possible implementation option. If this underlying thing is truly innovative and essential, it should be fully described in a separate specification, one for which that ingenious construction is described in terms of its interfaces, so that *this* ingenious solution may refer to it while describing its interfaces.

In a section called something like Exposed Interfaces or Exposed Components, describe the publishable signatures such as endpoints and objects that may be passed to or delivered by a client. This is the signature – the syntax part of the interface. The ontology does not belong in this document since it will undoubtedly include private objects that are not exposed to the client. The ontology is essential but is developed after the functional specification for the purpose of *providing* the exposed interfaces described therein. Such an ontology (often a set of UML diagrams) is part of the engineering design and will be implemented in the software.

Finally, in a section we might call Use Case Scenarios assemble all meaningful examples of how this product will interact with the outside world. If you like the UML graphical approach to the use case, feel free to use that. I've always preferred to simply describe each scenario in text form. Identify what the user (whether human or machine) will do and then exactly what the product will do in response. This puts the interfaces into context providing not only a justification for the design but

14: Software As a Surface

also clear examples of what must be tested and in what way in order to fully verify the product. This may also form the basis of a software warranty, if that seems reasonable. You would warrant all defined scenarios and no others.

———•———

A usable document gets to the point. It is well-structured and readable. A functional specification describes the surface features of the solution and only that additional information necessary to convey key underpinnings of the design. Everything that a user may see, access or invoke will be defined. The functional specification describes the product interfaces only.

The language is terse but rich. Since important words are defined unambiguously in the Definitions section, fewer words are required to get the point across. The paragraphs are numbered because it must be possible to unambiguously reference a paragraph providing information related to the current paragraph. The paragraphs are numbered for the same reason they are in *The Tractatus*: each paragraph is important. We bear that in mind as we write each paragraph, if it isn't imparting critical information, it's wasting the reader's time.

In my experience there are two common documentation strategies, the list and the vague rambling prose. We could describe a system for storing, editing and deleting newspaper content as a list in the wiki:

Objects:
- *Story*
- *Title*
- *Content (part of a story)*
- *Author*

Actions
- *create (version = 1)*
- *read*
- *update (version + 1)*
- *delete (all version?)*
    Question: What about intermediate versions?

Famine In the Bullpen

TBD: How to read a whole history?

Here the basic concepts are listed as words along with an implied promise that all questions would be eventually answered. Alternatively, we often see the description expressed in vague essay form like this:

> *We produce stories for publication and we modify those stories. Each story may go through multiple changes on the way to publication. Once published, we may still make changes. Whenever we make a significant change, we want to keep track of it so we will always keep a version associated with each story.*
>
> *Whenever we change the story, we'll write out the changes and a version number so we don't lose track of the change. We will be able to pull up a story by version and see that version. We should be able to merge versions too.*
>
> *When we pull up a story we'll be able to see the story and all the versions prior to it. The UI should display the final in black and the versions in other colors. To undo a change, we just go back to the previous version.*
>
> *When we create the story we'll start at 0 then with each change we take the version up one. If we delete a story, we'll delete all the versions too. We won't be able to recover a deleted story so we shouldn't do that much.*

This form is a rambling explanation of the developer's undisciplined concept. It includes a little implementation and a little commentary all intermixed. That kind of specification requires a lot of guesswork and in the long run, the implementation will need to be inspected by the author and approved because the design is really only in the author's head.

Both approaches reveal that the author really honestly isn't sure what is wanted. The general idea is presented as a muddle of images – a blotchy collection of disconnected concepts that describe the end product as if in a dream. Neither approach provides enough information to produce an implementation; especially for a complex design wherein a number of developers will provide solutions in parallel that must communicate with each other.

An actual functional specification would explain this as follows:

14: Software As a Surface

4.5. *Content Revision*
A limited history of editable content is kept so that erroneous content may be quickly retracted in favor of the last accurate revision. All history is retained during the editing process so as to facilitate detailed review. A mechanism for publishing and unpublishing allows for quick replacement of erroneous content.

4.5.1. Each editable shall be associated with a revision. Said revision at initial creation of the editable to be 0 and incremented by one each time the modified editable is stored.

4.5.2. A single configurable integer shall be retained specifying the maximum number of revisions to be retained for any editable.

4.5.3. *Publishing*
An editable is published (made presentable) by setting a boolean for that editable indicating that it is published to true. Setting that boolean to false indicates that that editable is not published.

4.5.3.1. The current published editable shall be defined as the editable having the highest magnitude revision with the published boolean set to true.

4.5.3.2. If no revision of an editable has published set to true, then that editable shall not be available to any presentation.

4.5.4. An editable may be retrieved with reference to a revision or without.

4.5.4.1. If without a revision, the editable having the latest (greatest magnitude) revision and published set to true shall be returned unless no such editable is stored in which case an error shall be returned.

4.5.4.2. If with a revision, the editable corresponding to the specified revision shall be returned unless no such editable is stored in which case an error shall be returned.

4.5.5. *Saving an editable*

4.5.5.1. The act of saving an editable shall be transactional as regards all operations identified in this section.

4.5.5.2. Saving an editable shall comprise storing the content and its

> *revision as a new entity, leaving the prior entity and associated revision unchanged.*

4.5.5.3. *If the published boolean of an existing entity is set to true, then all editable records between that and the previous published editable shall be deleted.*

4.5.5.4. *If a new published entity results in the total number of published revisions exceeding the maximum defined in 4.5.3, then the oldest prior revisions shall be deleted until the total number of revisions equals the specified maximum.*

4.5.6. *The act of deleting an editable shall be transactional and shall comprise the deletion of all revisions of that editable.*

4.5.7. *No support shall be provided for deleting intermediate revisions. A valid editable shall comprise the current and all prior stored revisions.*

The terms *editable, content, transactional, publish, revision* and *entity* are already defined (in the Definitions section). The key is to write it once, write it well (unambiguously), and never write it again. What is important is the fact that the functional specification may apply to a newspaper story but, with reference to the form of the problem, it could apply to any other aspect of the presentation that is subject to routine modification. It takes a little practice to get to the point that everything that needs to be explained is explained without rambling, but the process of distilling the operation to its essentials clarifies the mind and helps to assure a fully functional design.

The details of the implementation are left to the skilled developer. Knowing precisely what is expected, now is the time for face-to-face discussion and whiteboard work. A plan for the coding of the product is developed through individual creativity and extended collaboration. Often the concepts involved may be recorded in a fairly informal document that we may call a design spec. This collaboration is constructive only because the course has been unambiguously charted by the functional spec.

Documentation is important, not only to convey the design to those executing it but also to help the person writing the document to fully

14: Software As a Surface

form the idea. The human mind tends to fill in blanks with fluff that may easily be mistaken for understanding. By composing a document representing the complete idea, the mind is forced to disgorge all of its content and, when the fluff spills out, it is easily recognized as failing the test of reason. It forces the writer to think through that missing part.

The fact that a person will write any given document doesn't define the process as arbitrary or dictatorial. One person needs to take responsibility for proposing a consistent solution. Committees can throw together ideas but only an individual can turn those ideas into a consistent narrative that others can read and understand. Fundamental to the process (regardless the type of document) is a formal review by interested peers. That review will uncover problems and inconsistencies that the original author undoubtedly missed. The original author will go through iteration after iteration until the document conveys a meaningful solution acceptable to the attentive team.

An agile team will insist upon a documented plan, because, quite simply, if you don't know your current course, you cannot execute course corrections. A truly agile team *does* respond to changes in the needs of the customer. It does not respond to customer whims. It establishes clearly what solution will be provided to resolve the customer's problem. It will deliver that solution in a reasonable amount of time and it will build in allowances for likely changes. The document doesn't freeze the solution, it provides the instrument whereby the solution will adapt in an orderly fashion: without version 1.0, you cannot comprehend version 3.2.

15: The Science of Desolation

The modern practice of assuring that software engineers provide simple, predictable, incremental results is a desolate science. It has given up on human potential. There is a famine in the bullpen which has lasted so long that the boney ribcage is regarded as nothing more than a fashion statement. While a large swath of the population may be content to apply their end-effectors to repetitive mechanical production and then celebrate in the evening with beer and football, that doesn't mean that the system itself must confine even those to the role of meaningless subordinate. In the same way that Sun Tsu wrote of the enemy that "A surrounded army must be given a way out," so must each human be allowed a way out of the mundane expectations of the machine. Their humanity must be able to at least see the exit signs that identify creative outlets.

Agilists often refer to *The Toyota Way* (Appendix A) as the inspiration for modern software Agile practices. While there are some similarities, Toyota's truly noble principles do not define a feature factory. They define a manufacturing line where each individual human is valued and is responsible for assuring continuous improvement through direct active participation in what would otherwise be a soul-numbing repetitive grind. While Scrum reduces all participants to the same level, presuming that all are equivalent and contribute the same mundane qualities, Toyota differentiates between the contributors, acknowledging the value that each role (manufacturing engineer, harness technician, assembly worker) uniquely provides to the process.

The assembly worker cannot override the engineer's design, but she can force the engineer to reconsider a questionable fender securement.

15: The Science of Desolation

The process allows anyone to stop the line and challenge the choices of the higher ups. Most importantly, The Toyota Way emphasizes long-term thinking. Principle #1 is:

> *Base your management decisions on a long-term philosophy, even at the expense of short-term financial goals.*

In a Scrum shop, the emphasis is on solving the immediate problem with a minimum of analysis with the goal of finishing the task within the iteration. Consideration may be given to the next iteration or, in a pinch, the next few iterations, but that's as long-term as Scrum gets. Even within the SAFe framework, only the next quarter is considered. There is little reason to think too far ahead when your output is simple features answering customer requests. In such a system, the long-term thinking is left largely to the customer

———•———

I was sitting in on a discussion between two senior architects with a local publishing company. They were arguing over microservices. One was saying that they needed to use microservices because they isolate concerns. The other said that microservices was a good idea but they needed to distribute the data in the isolated databases using a message passing bus rather than services. They went on for some length and I finally decided to scratch an itch I'd been nursing. I asked them what a microservice was.

Their definitions were roughly similar but their conceptions of the term "microservice" were not detailed enough to be able to fully explain why either of them thought it made sense for the use case they were describing. I asked the question that had not yet come up. "What problem, at your company, does a microservices architecture solve?" Solving problems is not part of the modern curriculum, so there was an uneasy pause. Presently, they both returned to explaining why a microservices architecture is good and I had to draw the discussion to a stop. "Look," I said, "unless you understand what problem you're trying to solve, you can't possibly make a case for a solution."

"Lots of companies are turning to microservices," one responded. "They isolate concerns and promote a modular componentry."

"No, no, no," I retorted firmly, "If you're going to decide that microservices makes sense, you need to assess the problem. What is the business requirement? Are the processes CPU-bound or I/O-bound? Is the system primarily passing messages or analyzing complex data? Are the data schemas tightly coupled or do they represent isolated data pools? Until you understand the answers to those questions, you can't even begin to speculate regarding the best possible software infrastructure for the company."

I was expecting that to start an interesting conversation but instead it resulted in a few seconds of blank stare followed by a change of subject. I was disappointed but not really surprised. Solving problems has been entirely supplanted by slick general solutions that plug into any problem: frameworks sold like Nineteenth Century patent medicines. Dr. Stephen Jewett's Health Restoring Bitters: *Gives great tone and vigor to the digestive organs*. Heroin: *The sedative for coughs*. Microservices: *Isolating concerns and promoting modularity*.

If we are not solving a problem but we are arranging the components of a solution, we are dilettantes at play. This delusion, that we are being scientific and technically rigorous when we are discussing the next toy we want to pull out of the box is probably not an isolated phenomenon. I have to guess that psychics, faith healers and Scientologists also spend a good portion of their time reciting hollow jargon and weighing the merits of obscure and unproved technologies as though they serve some vague mythic purpose.

The desire to speak with authority on some topic, whether one has the discipline to understand it or not, is the product of a lazy, self-centered eagerness to be valued. In the engineering realm, the accolades go to the person who solves the problem. The problem is that no one is being trained to understand problems. For that reason, the nature of the problem has to remain a nebulous threat lest the final solution be proved inadequate upon analysis. This leads to the proliferation of reli-

15: The Science of Desolation

gious rituals which, when practiced, encase the value proposition in an incense-like fog of respectability.

———•———

This preoccupation with the minutia of the mundane seems to be an ideal distraction from the possibility of creative exuberance. We see established norms within the culture that appear to be contrived for this purpose: the feature factory, the innovation sprint, the step-by-step procedure. Why would a company settle for being a fast follower; and why does religion replace reason in our technical processes?

A review of papers by well-heeled economists shows a general agreement that U.S. innovation is in crisis. They disagree, however, on its cause and how to fix it. *Competitiveness At a Crossroads*[Porter_2013], a Harvard Business School 2012 survey, claims that the lack of competitiveness may be laid at the feet of government regulation. Not surprisingly, the survey included only C-level executives who clearly expressed their certainty that they themselves were not at fault. You should read that study just for giggles.

The more interesting studies, the ones that don't begin with the preconception that management is a victim, reveal more plausible theories. Nobel Laureate, Edmund S. Phelps, noted, in his New York Times opinion piece[Phelps_2013], that this started in the early 1970s, with U.S. innovation dropping by nearly 50%. He indicates that the period of peak innovation ran from the 1820s to the 1960s, a period that saw extensive changes in taxation and government regulation ranging from nearly none to as much as ever. He finds an inverse correlation between innovation and the increased popularity of corporate austerity programs beginning in the 1970s as companies laid off workers and reduced long-term investment.

Mihir Desai, Mizuho Financial Group Professor of Finance at Harvard Business School, wrote about *The Incentive Bubble*[Desai_2012] and the mechanism whereby corporate innovation is tamped down by skewed executive compensation packages. These packages emphasize short-term over long-term goals, but he also identifies the deterioration of competitiveness as corporate executives collude to assure a pot large enough for all concerned. He quotes a former Morgan Stanley executive who said, "[A] given party is often at the same time a competitor, a counterparty, a partner, and a customer." In other words, the top executives were focused entirely on with whom they could negotiate their next big bonus. Competitors and partners were equally likely sources of wealth, meaning that actually competing was no longer a worthwhile distinction.

This reflects a mystifying attitude common to many wealthy people which was driven home to me on July 15, 2012 when Chris Hayes interviewed a former Mitt Romney business partner, Edward Conard on *Up with Chris Hayes*. He was explaining that Romney had "created a lot of franchise value, and we were going to pay him for that." Romney was leaving the firm, but he wasn't going to do what you or I would do, he didn't just quit, he did what rich people do and negotiated his exit fee. He had already delivered value and had been paid for that, but now he was owed more for leaving. Conard summarized Romney's negotiating position as "'I created an incredibly valuable firm that's making all you guys rich. You owe me.' That's the negotiation." This led other wealthy functionaries in the firm to insist upon renegotiating *their* remuneration too. With all of them satisfied, all was well. Of course, if their very best welder from their most profitable factory had approached Conard to negotiate *his* exit bonus, the guy would have been summarily fired. Rich colleagues deserve a hearing. It is unlikely that ordinary people would receive the same courtesy.

My point is that as people accumulate wealth, they start to think differently. They get stupid in ways that are inconvenient for the rest of us. They become comfortable and lose their drive because, even if everything goes wrong, they can simply retire in luxury. With that as your worst case scenario, you will become complacent. As a complacent CEO, you will locate and install timid middle managers – ones that will not threaten your hard-earned security.

Allan Murray joins us in thinking through the timidity of management in his August 21, 2010 Wall Street Journal article[Murray_2010]. He

15: The Science of Desolation

quotes research by strategy consultant Gary Hamel who advocates rethinking management generally and has established an online laboratory for that purpose. Murray summarizes:

> In corporations, decisions about allocating resources are made by people with a vested interest in the status quo. "The single biggest reason companies fail," says Mr. Hamel, "is that they overinvest in what is, as opposed to what might be."

Clayton Christensen, in a lecture at the Gartner Symposium IT-Expo, explains some of this as a side-effect of ill-educated business schools which emphasize techniques for maximizing short-term profits to the exclusion of long-term goals. He notes that the math itself is tilted to construct ill-conceived formulae (ratios) that favor best results for short-term gains while reducing long-term assets like actual capital and research.

He notes that at the religious behest of well known business schools "We measure profitability by these ratios [because] it 'neutralizes' the measures so that you can apply them across sectors to every firm." This drives divesting assets of long-term value in favor of short-term gains. He concludes, "They still think they are in charge, but they aren't. They have outsourced their brains without realizing it. Which is a sad thing."

He tells the story of Dell, which, in order to increase profits, transferred property and intellectual capital to a company in Taiwan called ASUSTek, letting them take over costly key areas of expertise a chunk at a time until they were eventually able to rise up as a competitor selling their Asus computers to Best Buy and undercutting their former benefactor.

There are other specifics as well. In Peter Cohan's 2013 blog on forbes.com[23], he takes Apple to task for how little actual innovation they have provided. He identifies Apple as clever at integrating and marketing, but that actual serious innovation has become a series of simple features added to their existing products. Cohan reviewed, with minimal enthusiasm, Apple's future plans.

---

23 http://www.forbes.com/sites/petercohan/2013/02/22/apples-innovation-problem/

Famine In the Bullpen

The commentators proposed various solutions to the problem. One suggested that lower taxes would do the trick; but, most were thinking along the lines of reducing executive incentives and encouraging an "old-fashioned" ethos among executives to get their blood boiling to compete. Some economists proposed that modern companies should establish a position for a Director of Innovation or that they should *train* their employees to innovate.

It's nice that everyone is thinking through the problem but, for the most part, these solutions expose a failure to understand what innovation is. It's hard to encourage an employee to innovate for the good of the company when the median tenure at a software company is about 4.4[24] years, meaning that once the employee has put in the six months needed to figure out how the company works and then come up with an innovative solution and then promoted it within the system, she'll only have a year or so to enjoy the benefits of her cleverness before she moves on. When workers are asked to innovate, the time is typically used to expand understanding of a popular framework. With the new framework on the resumé, that next job is bound to be better than this one.

Companies sometimes offer profit-sharing plans, but your contribution to the success of the company won't count for much if the rest of the employees are slackers. You need everyone to innovate unless you can negotiate a personal bonus based on your personal contribution. I'm sure this is done, but I've never figured out how to do it.

Most studies seem to agree that the early 1970s marks the turning point. What caused it? If current behavior is rational, what manner of irrational behavior drove the previous century of innovation? How would one assess this data in order to understand what the problem actually is?

---

24 United States Department of Labor, Bureau of Labor Statistics, Employee Tenure Summary, Table 6, 2016/09/22.

16: Root Cause Analysis

We address a problem by first identifying its root cause. Believe it or not, there are formal methods for performing a Root Cause Analysis (RCA). *A3* and *RCASE* are among the more popular at the time of this writing. They provide useful tools for addressing manufacturing faults and they are a valuable part of the *Six Sigma Process* promoted by Motorola. I must confess that I've never used a formal method for RCA and this will become clear shortly. I have, however, worked at a Six Sigma company, Martin Marietta. RCA and Worst Case Analysis were fundamental tools in reviewing problems in manufacturing and spacecraft design at that company. When applied after the spacecraft crashed, they were informative, but of no use to the crumpled hopes of the project. When applied to likely potential problems, they were of great value.

Even at Martin Marietta, my analyses were done with interviews, reading technical documents and lots of scribbles on lots of scattered papers leading to some statistics followed by a report explaining the nature of the root cause. There was mathematics and certainly there were guidelines regarding where to start; but, even for the rigorous procedural methods required by NASA, human imagination played an important role. We will attempt such an analysis now regarding the issue at hand.

The problem to be analyzed is the one we have been reviewing up until now. Why are companies paying people like me a six figure salary to plug together the software-equivalent of Lego® blocks? Why does U.S. industry seem so barren that it would be difficult for a modern teenager to fathom an industrial film of the 1950s? Why do my former teammates still reminisce about how cool it used to be solving impossible problems? Why is the U.S. economy so sluggish despite low corporate taxes[Rubin_2015] and record corporate profits[Ghanbari_2016]? While the first question is more personal to me, the assessment of the previous chapter implies the possibility that the questions may all be related.

I begin this chapter with no good idea what the problem is. I thought the last chapter would lead pretty naturally to that, but no such luck. The more research I did, the more muddled became my conclusions. Oddly, that is typical of my attempts to understand any difficult problem. After my disappointment with the last chapter, I left the problem to simmer. While waiting for a test to run or for a workspace to compile, I'd return to the problem. Falling asleep at night, I'd review the possibilities. As ideas came up, I'd check duckduckgo.com and then go to the library to pull old magazine articles.

What was different? We recognize 130 years of innovation growing out of the tail end of the First Industrial Revolution and kicking off the Second Industrial Revolution, leading to advances in textiles, transportation, factory processes and automation. We saw the development, during that time, of the train, the automobile, the airplane and the rocket. Canning and refrigeration preserved foods for transportation to remote consumers. The vacuum tube revolutionized the use of electricity and established the basis for the Twentieth Century field of *electronics* (a term coined originally by the publisher of the magazine, *Electronics*, in 1930).

One-hundred-thirty years of fundamental discoveries leading to the modern motorized transistorized world of the 1960s, then we stalled in the seventies. Having lived through that transition, I'm reflecting on memories and testing any idea that seems to apply. It seems that the cause must relate to the way companies do business. It seems that this would be driven by economic incentives because it seems to relate to the motivations behind theoretically profitable corporate practices. As I escort the data along the hallways in my head, various concepts will open their door and pop out. If there's a match of some sort, that idea will join the group. Eventually, as the ideas congeal and break apart and congeal again, a form will arise that is familiar. If I can latch onto that,

16: Root Cause Analysis

I'll have something I can mash against something else which might give me something more tangible to drag through the hall.

That's how I think of the process of addressing a difficult problem. Others will think of it differently, but the common factors remain gathering data, musing, synthesizing and testing. That process has not changed since Newton. As I mused, I considered the Clayton Act, designed to encourage competition and forbid competition-killing mergers. I reviewed how the inflation of the early 1970's might have influenced industry or Nixon's sudden abandonment of the gold standard. Nothing seemed to have a clear connection to the failure of U.S. innovation.

Root Cause Analysis, I have found, also involves babbling. While talking this through with my long-suffering spouse, I was reviewing the economic and business data I was considering. I started complaining about how no change around the 1970s seemed to match up with the observed reduction in innovation. I threw out some loosely connected terms as they popped into my head: neoliberalism, the gold standard, the Clayton Act, Johnson. As I was jabbering on, my spouse started reading from Wikipedia. She had found the connection. Something did happen in the late 1960s that drove fundamental changes in business and the government's treatment of business, not only in the U.S., but everywhere. An important part of this change was that it was *not* a strictly economic or political change, it was a global change in attitude.

———•———

In the 1960s, Milton Friedman was active in the Chicago School as it began its philosophical transition from modern monetarism, wherein the government regulates the amount of available money based upon production and demand, to modern Neoliberalism, wherein the natural regulation of a laissez-faire market functions with minimal interference. Friedman and the Chicago School became active in influencing government officials, insinuating the notion of free market libertarian ideals into administrations as early as that of Richard Nixon.

Famine In the Bullpen

Neoliberalism began in the 1930s and was heavily influenced by the childish ramblings of Ayn Rand. The philosophy basically claims that acting solely for one's own best interests, through some ill-explained mechanism, yields good for all of society. Her short article, *Objectivist Epistemology*, reads like a junior high school paper, flitting from example to example with enough speed to assure that no actual argument would form. For people who like the idea of doing whatever they want to, though, this looks like high philosophy.

In the aftermath of Richard Nixon's near impeachment, many young republicans of the time, such as Dick Cheney, John Bolton and Paul Wolfowitz, experienced the humiliation of Nixon's losses very personally. They cringed at the perceived failure in Vietnam as well as the threatened impeachment for what seemed to them to be fairly mundane campaign shenanigans. They resolved to restore the Republican Party, the power of the Presidency and the respect of the rest of the world, even if attained through military force. They and their cohort combined Neoliberal economics with a hawkish foreign policy to form what became known as *Neoconservatism*.

Influenced by Neoliberalism, they took the boorish tenets of Ayn Rand and the surface features of random writings and utterances from Friedrich von Hayek and Milton Friedman, cobbled together a consistent story and began to preach the gospel of small government, low taxes and unrestricted capitalism. The Neoconservative movement in the U.S. advanced on several fronts and influenced many leaders.

In 1971, Lewis Powell Jr., later to be named to the Supreme Court, wrote a memorandum to the U.S. Chamber of Commerce. It begins with "No thoughtful person can question that the American economic system is under broad attack..." and proceeds from there to advocate a department of propaganda be established for U.S. businesses. He makes it clear that environmentalists, labor unions and civil libertarians are the enemies of business and that their voices must be openly opposed "without embarrassment."

Powell's characterization of business leaders, as employers and "good citizens" who "improve the standard of living" and "serve on

16: Root Cause Analysis

charitable and educational boards," was incorporated into the canon and concepts like "greed is good" and references to the rich as "job creators" became common tropes. Taxes were further reduced making it practical to become a multi-millionaire in a single year. Prior to this, tax law assured that several years of dedication would be required to do this.

The Clayton Act was largely on holiday and it became fairly straightforward for a company to avoid competition by simply purchasing its competitors. Every company for which I have worked since 1985 has used this strategy. Even Sun Microsystems bought up small companies that threatened specific niches it was eyeing. It incorporated their threatening technologies and stopped further innovation along those lines.

Generally, it appears that the problem is one of attitude. It permeates the entire system, from the CEO who hires timid top management, to the corporate president who is terrified of risk and invention, to the lowly programmer who just wants to code up the next feature. There is a lethargy here that seems to be borne of a passive acceptance that this is "just what we do."

The Neoconservative movement has had an impact that is visible even among those purported to be "liberals." It was Bill Clinton who said, "The era of big government is over" and it was Barack Obama who opposed *card check*, inhibiting labor union expansion, and the election of Keith Ellison to the DNC chair to suppress the progressive wing of the Democratic Party. All of this despite the fact that an avowed Socialist almost became the Democratic nominee, clearly exposing the underlying progressive leanings of the average American. Despite this, the common knowledge remains that the status quo (meaning right-leaning moderation) is essentially OK and we would be unwise to move too far from it.

We see it everywhere: passive, accepting, comfortable with what is. Let's not push this too far. What might happen if we do that? Well, what will happen is a world where problems are directly confronted and actually solved. A world where people cannot be complacent because the environment makes that kind of comfort uncomfortable.

By relaxing rules that support competition, no company needs to take risks. They just wait for a competitor to threaten and they buy them. Modern companies start up with the explicit intention of being purchased, meaning that they don't have to sweat a long-term plan. By allowing riches to flow to the highest paid CEOs without penalty, the CEOs have no reason to press their company to continually contribute, only to stay in play.

We the people, through our government, may assert the rational claim that wealth must be earned. In order to become rich, one must prosecute their project and guide it wisely for decades, reaping the rewards over time while assuring the best possible product to satisfy the real needs of the consumer. When the competitor threatens, the company must survive by innovating and surpassing the competitor's offering.

This is not a fiscal, economic or policy problem. It is a cultural problem, which is why it has achieved such acceptance at all levels. It arises from the values introduced with and by Neoconservatism, namely that all good is assessed by its cash value. Companies are not worried about their competitors; managers are not worried about solving complex problems and developers are not concerned with the dull grind of the feature factory because the good is easily attained and soundly verified by the size of the paycheck.

I claim that this culture is corrosive; that its damaging effects must be resolved and that those goals and capabilities that we have lost must be rebuilt. A company that exists to do good is stronger and healthier than a company that exists only to make money. The fast follower is a stumbling doddering geriatric, muttering to itself about its imagined import, pushing its belongings in a stolen cart along the avenue. It begs on the street corners from gullible consumers and contributes nothing of value.

17: Not Google Timber

In 2007 I managed to get a phone interview with a Google guru (that was apparently his actual job title[25]). He asked me a question about building a hash table. Despite never having written hash table code, I provided an answer that I thought was at least correct.

There was a pause followed by a pronouncement from the guru, "Well, you're obviously not an engineer. You should probably look into purchasing or sales." He then cheerily ended with the standard invocation, "Do you have any questions for me?"

At this point, I could ask a question that had been on my mind for a while: "Yes, I've read that Google engineers spend 95 percent of their time coding. When do you design?"

Here the pause went on for some while. I wasn't watching a clock but I remember it as a slow count of ten. He then abruptly responded, "Good engineers design."

From this response, I learned two things. One: I am not Google timber; and, two: every developer has an innate understanding that engineering goes beyond hacking out code. In fact, most developers know that a well-conceived design calls for far less coding than a common ad hoc solution.

Later that day as I was talking with Mark, a fellow engineer, I told him about my conversation with the guru, to which he responded, "Why would any company hire a guru? The guru goes to the top of a mountain once and waits for supplicants to come up to him. What a

---

25 I shouldn't make fun of that. My last official title at Sun was "Architect Wrangler." Really. I'll show you my business card.

company wants is a sherpa: someone who can negotiate any mountain whenever he needs to."

The term *guru* is a clear conceit intended to convey the notion that the company is exceptional in some way; but hubris is not confined to Google. When I interviewed at Sun Microsystems in Colorado Springs, I was occupied for five hours shuttling from office to office answering highly technical questions on whiteboards until I was exhausted. Dragging back to my car for the long drive to my home in Aurora, a suburb of Denver, I was despondent. I knew that I had failed. It was not possible that I could have answered enough of those questions correctly to have won that rare prize: a job at the innovation powerhouse that was Sun Microsystems in 1993. I reviewed and reinvented each grueling question, spotting errors in every one of them and living the fantasy of the imagined historical correction.

Slouching into my home that evening, I gave my spouse the bad news: I was stuck at Martin Marietta for a few more years. When the phone rang, I answered glumly only to learn that I had been allocated an office along those revered halls. I went to bed that evening knowing that I was a mid-level programmer at Sun Microsystems.

Much of the thrill lay in the rigorous ordeal. It was the difficulty of entry that established an early bond with the other members of that team. In a word, I had been *proved*. The interview with the Google guru left me quite unmoved. The single question followed by the almost comic dismissal of my previous twenty five years of experience simply satisfied me that this was not a person with whom I could work. The Google mystique had slunk away like an exposed street magician.

The hubris of the single question and the hubris of the day of relentless interrogation are two very different species. The first enters with the knowledge that you are not worthy while the other challenges the worthy response and is open to the possibility that you may measure up. I became part of that interview regimen. We asked lots of questions and passed the supplicant from office to office just as each of us had been passed. We recognized the nervousness and saw our role as understanding the strengths and weaknesses of each uneasy candidate. Fi-

17: Not Google Timber

nally, our decision was not based on who was good or bad but whether there was a fit. Those who did fit entered our company with the same possibly delusional pride that each of us had once experienced before easing into the simple satisfaction of working competently with competent companions.

The Sun environment was, in the most interesting ways, innovative. It exposed a corporate-wide mastery of human behavior. The CEO was a brash but lovable rogue who appeared to believe in all of us. His *Parade of Bozos* speech remained in everyone's memory. His motto: "To ask permission is to request denial,"[26] drove daily risk-taking and constructive rebellion. On every April first, there was an April fools joke so beautiful and elaborate that it captured the imagination of every employee. It also had an innovative communication strategy.

—————•—————

According to a 2015 study, humans and alcohol have been together for thirteen thousand years, possibly longer than humans and leavened bread. Alcohol, therefore, is a natural and appropriate component of successful human interaction. It grew up with us and is a long-treasured companion. The monthly Sun beer bust was where you figured out who was actually working on what. You found out that Tim Goff was already developing the software update architecture you were going to use to impress your boss. Sun's communication infrastructure was better than most but without the beer bust, you would never get the IT guy to admit that he had developed a technique to clone a Solaris system in ten minutes.

You would never have heard about the project to deliver a fresh Solaris installation to bare metal in twenty seconds. Project ZIP would have been a killed mystery and cache-only client would have been released before your project could have effectively exploited it. Sun was a unified, well-oiled machine and essential communication was facilitated, at least in part, by the beer bust. Indeed, there was a rule and a

---

26 Strikingly similar to the Jesuit credo, "It is more blessed to ask forgiveness than permission."

beer fund. If, in a meeting, you made a sarcastic comment, you were expected to put a quarter on the table. That quarter went into the beer fund.

You can develop all of the process and mechanism you want in order to assure smooth communication and properly directed flow of information, but it can't deal with the unpredictables. No matter how scientifically precise your system, people introduce variables that cannot be accommodated without introducing randomizing agents that defeat the overarching process. Any rigid well-designed system for extracting maximum value from people is bound to fail; and that is, inevitably, the downfall of such systems. Unfortunately, the inherent unpredictability makes management very nervous. Unenlightened management sees employees as unpredictable components of a machine: a clockwork machine that would eschew the fallible human were it not for the fact that there are tasks that only humans can do.

―――― • ――――

The latest trend, in my experience, is to give an applicant for a development position a programming test. In 2014, I was looking for a position, so I did what I always do: I updated my LinkedIn profile and waited for potential employers to contact me. The first company spoke with me over the phone and then indicated that they would be sending me a project to complete. I received the project and unzipped it on my Linux machine. It was a Java project, which meant that I had to spend about an hour downloading and installing Maven, Spring, Tomcat and various other frameworks of the Java Complex that I don't need for any of my Python projects.

With that done, I started looking over the software. It was an intentionally poorly designed project that required significant refactoring. I started reorganizing the objects more appropriately. I cleaned up any captive throws and consolidated unnecessarily redundant code. I began modifying the tests, removing mocks that masked bad behavior and adding assertions to indicate what was being tested. Then I realized that the test included a set of integration tests that had not been completed.

17: Not Google Timber

In order to complete them, I would have to incorporate something like Jersey in order to set up a local web server. I checked the time and realized I had been working on the project for six hours.

Exasperated at the loss of my Saturday for a potential job that was clearly intended for a basic coder, I stopped. I sent the hiring manager an email informing him that after six hours, I had lost interest in his company. He called me on Monday and apologized asking if I would come in for an interview anyway. I politely refused.

Of the other four suitors, two asked me to take a test. This time I asked how long the test was expected to take. One said "no more than twelve hours," and the other demanded three. At this point I asked each of them how desperate they thought I was to get a job at their company? They seemed surprised at my reluctance.

In almost every case, the phone interview started with a question of the form: "Tell me how much you love technology." To all of these questions I answered that I'm not interested in technology. I'm interested in solving problems.

In one case I asked, "What problems do you need to solve?" to which the interviewer responded with, "Lots; and we use the following technologies to solve them..."

Two of the interviews ended with me telling the interviewer that what he really wanted was a kid fresh out of college who loves Java and all the frameworks. While that should have seemed like excellent money-saving news, both interviewers insisted that they needed a highly experienced programmer to wield their mighty technologies. I remained unconvinced.

Eventually, I interviewed with Rosetta Stone. After a serious hour of lively discussion regarding how I solve problems, I was relieved to find that not all companies are simple tech dabblers.

Just in case my career path has puzzled my reader, I tend to enter any company as a mid-level programmer, no matter my prior position, for reasons I do not entirely understand. Certainly I don't know where to look for a senior position, and I have tried. I am told that I need to

Famine In the Bullpen

tap the shoulder of a high-ranking friend, but I don't want to work in any of the companies where I *have* high-ranking friends. Obviously, I won't take a written test, I won't take a drug test[27] and at my former employers I tend to anger about as many managers as I delight. For that reason, I tend to enter as a mid-level programmer, get promoted to senior staff in a year or two, get bored and start somewhere else as a mid-level programmer. God knows what sort of test I'd have to take for a Director position.

───•───

When I was promoted to Senior Staff at Sun Microsystems, I was assigned to a mentor named Sam Pierson. He resembled, in both voice and demeanor, the character played by Jude Law in the otherwise unremarkable film, *Sky Captain and the World of Tomorrow*. Competent and clear in his communication, he undertook to introduce me to the Senior Staff mindset.

We were in the San Francisco area when his team and mine met for a joint dinner at Fuki Sushi. Before the meal, we chose to spend some time at the bar. We gathered around a large raised table and Pierson stood next to me. He leaned over and, in his sonorous accented voice, quietly informed me, "You will buy the first round."

Confused, I revealed myself to be the idiot that I hope I no longer am. I asked, "How do I expense this?"

Pierson stared at me for several seconds. A shallow smile crept across his face as would be expected when an intelligent man concentrates on the witless movement of a specimen. In the fullness of time, he responded.

"You do not expense this," he explained. "This is personal. You personally must clarify your commitment to your team; and, you must do this from time to time as the opportunity arises. This is your *manage-*

---

27 The right to privacy, embodied in the fourth and fifth amendments to the U.S. Constitution, are actual rights and should not be violated by anyone, even your company. I don't take drugs; but I do believe that privacy is fundamental to personal liberty and a strong community. See https://thegreatcollaboration.org.

17: Not Google Timber

ment tax. It is a price you pay for the privilege of directing these brilliant minds."

The statement was unexpected. His firmness drove it deep into my brain. There was a moment of revelation. I had always appreciated the engineers on my team; but, this message carried a deeper implication. In the haze of my satori, I saw myself as the simple navigator and my team as the real engine of invention. I reviewed Pierson's team and realized that some were developers I had, in the past, dismissed as inadequate. If Pierson could work with them; if Pierson could bring them to the level of performance he would demand; then there were no losers; there were no failures.

As I directed our waiter to take the drink orders, I was filled with an exquisite calm.

———•———

Human beings are not to be taken lightly. They produce magnificent works of art, spellbinding stories, transcendent music and other products of the active self-aware mind. Even industry must confess its utter dependence on human value. Since the job of the corporation is to make money, it must choose only the resources that yield greater value than their cost. It is for this reason that companies are so enamored of automation. Human beings are expensive, and so to replace one with a machine is to elevate the expected profit.

So, why isn't everything automated already? The answer is, of course, that even an intellectually challenged human being makes a modern robot look like a garlic press. Perhaps the chubby guy in the tee-shirt on aisle five of the Walmart is not capable of developing a solution for global warming, but he can drive a truck, and the last set of confusing directions he got were resolved when he realized that *Wad Road* had to actually be *Ward Road* because there was no other road near the turn with a similar name. Self-aware or not, college educated or not, his brain has accumulated programs for resolving a plethora of common problems that would flummox the most complex computer.

Famine In the Bullpen

These skills did not need to be taught to him in a formal fashion. Based on his initial wiring, he found certain things interesting and naturally sought to better understand them. He may have learned to drive a truck because his mother drove a truck. He may have learned nuclear physics because a good teacher introduced the subject provocatively. She may have picked up bee keeping because a friend challenged her. People exploit their potentials in odd ways and unpredictable timeframes.

Robert M. Pirsig in his 1974 novel *Zen and the Art of Motorcycle Maintenance* advances a view that may be tested fairly easily with ordinary people. It is the view that human beings have an inborn understanding of quality. With a little experience a human can tell, when listening to an engine or reviewing a manuscript or tasting an old brandy, that something isn't quite right. By the smallest variation in the sound of the tappets or the tiniest hint of unfamiliar acidity even below the threshold of conscious awareness, a human will understand that something is wrong.

Scientific studies give us some clues to this mechanism. What about the strange but common case that every engineer has experienced: that glorious moment when the impossible problem is described – you know it can be solved, you just don't know how. You feel it in your bones. The problem looks utterly impossible, but you know there's a solution.

In the early 1960s, Sarnoff Mednick designed a fascinating experiment that he called the *Remote Associates Test* (RAT)[Mednick_1962]. Subjects were wired up to sensors that would detect any slight inflection in the muscles that control smiling and frowning. The subjects were told that they would be shown three words. If there was a common term that would apply to all three words, they were to tell the experimenter what that word was. For example if the subject were to see:

        cottage   Swiss   cake

they would be expected to say, "cheese." To the triplet:

17: Not Google Timber

salt   deep   foam

they may respond "sea" or "ocean." These triplets, which share an association with a common word, are called *coherent*. Not all of the triplets presented, though, shared a common connection.

If presented with an incoherent triplet like:

sleep   mail   switching

no word will come to mind. Some times the shared term arose in only a few seconds. In others, like:

dive   light   rocket

It took up to fifteen seconds for the subject to realize that the common term was "sky."

Here's the interesting part. In each case there was an instantaneous response. In the case of the coherent triplets, each subject smiled almost instantly. The smile was miniscule and not noticeable except for the sensitive instrumentation reading the subject's facial muscles. In the case of incoherent, triplets, there was a nearly instantaneous frown.

In other words, the solution to the presented problem was known to the subject's unconscious mind almost immediately, even when it took several seconds for the fully formed solution to show itself. Could this be similar to the engineer who knows there's a solution even when the actionable design is weeks away?

Could it be that the unconscious is where we figure out everything that is really important; and that, if we receive that conclusion innocently, we might rigorously determine if it is grounded in fact? The special awareness of the skilled motorcycle mechanic results from years of practice – a practice that trained the massive neural network in the mechanic's brain. While the conscious mind can juggle no more than seven variables simultaneously, a neural network excels at extreme multivariate analysis. The mechanic's brain closes its network around the problem and immediately recognizes a match. In due time the resolved solution will surface, ready for conscious refinement. Only very complex purpose-built machines share such a capability with the ordinary human.

Isaac Newton was recounted to have been a fairly average student. At the age of 22, during the plague, he became isolated on a rural farm where over the space of a few years he developed a deep understanding of light and gravity. Kepler, founder of orbital mechanics, stumbled along for decades claiming, at one point, that the orbits of the planets described a sequence of Platonic solids – they do not. Poincaré worked for two hours every morning and then for two hours in the early evening. The rest of the time he spent walking about and conversing in bars and cafés. From unlikely origins, fertile minds may yield great produce.

Any good manager knows this. Every human may prosper if provided the needed encouragement and resources. When I was at Sun, we were provided a new member for the team. I was told that I should not expect much from Terence but they didn't really have any other place for him. After a few conversations with Terence, I found him to be hopeful but shy. On his other teams, he had sat back and waited to be assigned a task.

With only a little encouragement and the welcoming nature of the existing team, he was soon suggesting new ideas and constructively critiquing others' work. Within a year, he was taking on responsibility for full subsystem designs and stretching into areas he did not yet fully understand. He was taking risks and committing to resolve complex problems.

The team was agile but not Scrum. We spoke every day and adjusted our documented understanding of the plan over the early Internet. At one point we recognized that we had a very serious problem to solve. Terence claimed it.

I was in Denver and Terence was in Menlo Park. He took on the task and went dark. I waited a few days and, having heard nothing, became a little concerned. I called Terence who said that everything was fine. He thought he had an idea how this could be resolved. Reassured, I

17: Not Google Timber

went on with my responsibilities. Distracted as I was, I didn't talk with Terence for another week. At that point, I called him again. This time he sounded a little distracted. He made it clear, though, that he was entirely into the problem and was making progress.

A week later I called him again. This time he sounded disconnected. His answers were short and he wasn't responding constructively to my questions. At this point, I was no longer reassured. I called his officemate and asked her what was going on. She told me that, in her opinion, he was just entirely focused on his project. Thinking this through, I realized that this was how I acted when I was in the middle of a vexing problem. The problem occupies every waking minute until the solution reveals itself. With the solution in hand, there is a panicked rush to record it and implement it before it becomes muddied by doubt. The full definition recorded and verified, the tweaking and reviewing begins, taking sometimes days until it is ready to present for peer review.

Three days later, Terence called me to triumphantly present his solution. It was beautiful. It was so clean and well-conceived that two other departments incorporated his program into their projects.

Terence wasn't dull. He was misapplied. A person's potential cannot be revealed by a single question. It cannot even be revealed by a grueling day of interviews. It's hard to fully assess a human until you've worked with them for a while. I have been generally more impressed by my coworkers than I would have expected. I have found that most people, when challenged, eagerly meet the challenge and prove themselves its superior.

18: Runner's High

A true revelation, it seems to me, will only emerge from stubborn concentration on a solitary problem.[...] Suddenly, miraculously, it will reveal itself as something we have never seen before.

                                                             Cesare Pavese

When I was fourteen, I was handed a pamphlet from some mysterious society. I don't remember the name but the message stuck with me for the rest of my life. It was simply that thinking is hard and unnatural. Most people are capable of doing everything this world requires without once having to actually assess abstract concepts and derive some sort of conclusion. I was having a lot of trouble relating to people and this concept proved comforting, although not practically useful, for some time.

It is easy to take an idea like that and turn it into cynical evidence of one's natural superiority since, of course, I *like* to think. Then as one gets older and looks back on that dismal road of heartbreak and embarrassment, one begins to question its validity since it starts to hurt about then. In my moments of clarity, I return to that message and try to process it lovingly, since the way people think really does border on unfathomable.

At Sun Microsystems, I worked with an engineer who was highly skilled in designing secure networks. We'll call him Cyril. His mastery of cryptography, breech methodologies and network protocols was inspiring. It was always an education to review technical issues with him.

18: Runner's High

One afternoon, I was in my office talking with my friend and colleague, Sarah, about natural selection. We were apparently talking loudly enough that we were overheard and Cyril poked his head in, eager to join the discussion. He went to our whiteboard and started drawing a graph. As he was drawing, he was explaining how the Earth was no more than 4000 years old because there was no evidence to support any other conclusion. Sarah asked about carbon-dated fossils to which Cyril responded confidently that God had placed those bones to test our faith. Other engineers started popping in now and questioning Cyril's claims only to be confidently rebuffed with mind-numbing claptrap. Eventually the interchange became obviously pointless and everyone moved on.

Several minutes later, I walked into the break room where one of Cyril's friends was explaining exactly the same thing to someone else. Clearly they had both attended the same revival meeting the night before.

How could this man appear to be so intelligent and yet not have any concept of science or logic? Good engineering always begins with science. Finding the root cause of a problem is nearly impossible without a disciplined application of scientific method and yet our secure networks pal was clearly incapable of distinguishing between reason and the ridiculous. I was left so puzzled that I returned to memories of that pamphlet from my childhood. Is it possible that the human brain is capable of solving complex problems in software architecture without once actually thinking? Is it possible that the kind of problem-solving people do every day is purely algorithmic? Is my thinking (my self-awareness) just an overly complicated program from which I derive the illusion of consciousness?

———•———

I had a revelation about this as a result of Sarah persuading me to become a runner. She ran every morning and daily effused about how wonderful she felt afterwards. For her, it seemed the most natural activity in the world. Soon after taking on the runner's discipline, she was sprinting through the long winding streets of her Colorado Springs neighborhood every morning, breathing in the crisp mountain air and reveling in the vigorous movement.

After delaying as long as I could, I was finally persuaded. Every weekday morning, beginning at my front door in Nederland, Colorado at 8650 feet altitude, I ran for thirty minutes. It hurt a lot. The first five runs, I ended coughing up blood due to the dry air I was gasping in and out. Over time, my lungs adapted but it didn't stop hurting. I was not deterred. Sarah had assured me that in time it would be great. I would become addicted just like she was. I continued religiously week after week through the Summer. I gained no muscle and lost no weight. I could not increase my distance and barely increased my speed. For four months, I continued and it just hurt. Finally, I gave up. I am clearly not built for running.

A few years later, I was recounting this experience to an engineer friend and our conversation eventually wound around to that pamphlet explaining how hard one needs to work to bring about this unnatural skill we call thinking. He noted that he had always loved to analyze things and study them. He was a dedicated reader and enjoyed exploring the latest theories in physics. Abstract thinking had never been hard for him. I'm not sure which of us brought this up first, but we both began to consider whether thinking might not be genetically predisposed. Some people, like Sarah, were natural runners while clumsy clods like me would need to practice for years until it became tolerable. Some people like Sarah and my friend were natural thinkers while others would need to struggle for a fair portion of a lifetime to master the skill. Most would never see the value of it and would simply give up, just like I did with running.

When running, the body is dissipating about 1000 watts (W). It is uncomfortable to dissipate that kind of power. You are clearly aware of the work required to make the muscles move beyond their convention. People become accustomed to working past that discomfort because they perceive a reward at the end that is worthy of the effort. That reward eventually translates into a direct enjoyment of the strenuous ac-

18: Runner's High

tivity. The human body at rest dissipates around 100W. The human brain dissipates over 25W, even more when concentrating. Dissipating power takes effort. When you expend effort, you expect a reward. When the brain is focused on a serious problem there is, without question, discomfort. Thinking hurts, so why would anyone do it?

William James wrote: "Many people think they are thinking when they are merely rearranging their prejudices." Aldous Huxley wrote: "Most of one's life is one prolonged effort to prevent oneself thinking." Bertrand Russell wrote: "It has been said that man is a rational animal. All my life I have been searching for evidence which could support this." Indeed, a perusal of any web page of quotations from Bertrand Russell will reveal a sizable count of comments regarding the mental insufficiencies of Man.

In other words, questioning peoples' intelligence is no new thing. What may be new is the idea that common actions viewed by most as brilliant skills are actually easily performed using only a small portion of the brain without actually engaging any of its higher faculties. How else can we explain college professors who treat the adolescent whinings of Ayn Rand as philosophy? How else can we explain the surprising success of Donald Trump in the 2016 presidential election?

When Hegel, early in the nineteenth century, was writing about logic, he made a distinction between the kind of thinking that gets us through the day and the kind of thinking done by a philosopher. The job of the philosopher was clearly to further Man's deeper understanding of the world and this required a special kind of thinking. Hegel called it *speculative reason*.

It was speculative reason the philosopher would use to understand the meaning of life or the nature of God or the actual meaning behind commonly misunderstood words like *truth* and *freedom*. Ordinary people could do ordinary things with no notion whatever of this kind of thinking. The cooper was oblivious to solving these kinds of problems as he skillfully shaped and treated the wooden planks, formed them with steel bands and rivets and sealed them to assure a sound vessel. The seamstress mended clothing and the sailor stitched up sailcloth while wasting no time at all worrying about the nature of democratic processes in the modern monarchy. The blacksmith formed red hot iron into shoes and fitted them with precision to the horses of farmers and kings with no concern at all regarding the reification of abstract concepts like *roundness*.

As we look back on those activities from our smart phones and electric cars, it isn't difficult to see how Hegel could see the world as he did; but it isn't that simple now, is it? Smithing and barrel making have transmuted into cashiering and auto repair in the modern day, but many modern occupations have moved way beyond those. You *have* to be able to really think to develop a web site or a marketing campaign or design a ten story building. Don't you? Hegel had no exposure at all to the kinds of minds required to function in the modern age. Cyril's mastery of encryption and network strategies was far beyond any skills required in Hegel's era and yet it is obvious he was not thinking. How is this possible? What algorithm could look so much like intelligence without actually being intelligence?

───── • ─────

Allow me to propose a hypothesis: the human brain is basically a goal-seeking engine and we solve most technical problems in much the same way that a competent spreadsheet assembles the provided data and fills in the hoped-for blanks. In fact, the human brain craves a straightforward goal and enough information to close around the problem. I haven't been able to piece together a better way to explain how fundamentally stupid people can be imbued with highly complex programs which they run with absolute fidelity while utterly incapable of engaging their higher faculties. It is possible that such people are not actually *self-aware*, not actually capable of observing their own program in order to assess themselves dispassionately within their environment. They (what we might call their *self*) may actually be defined only by their algorithms.

Uncle Bob didn't have to explain to Billy that when he grew up he would need to kill an abortion provider. He just expressed a vague goal

18: Runner's High

by muttering constantly that those people kill babies and someone needs to stop that from happening. Without thinking anything that Hegel would recognize as cognition, Billy's brain closed a loop around that goal, adjusting it mechanically as positive and negative feedback was processed. It filled in the missing aspects of the goal until it was actionable. If positive feedback loops predominated, the drive to action would successively amplify and finally the goal would resolve to a complex strategy combined with an irresistible drive which, when prosecuted, would achieve it.

No one would suspect a magpie of being intelligent. A magpie cannot read or devise a mechanized vehicle. It can, however, recognize a situation where a particular tool would be useful. It can obtain that tool and use it to extract a morsel of food from a deep crevice. An ape can use a stick to pull termites from a termite mound; a beaver can build a sound water-proof structure; but none of these creatures could explain why Communism doesn't scale or why bacon tastes good.

This goal-seeking is biochemical and takes place without serious intervention. Once started, it moves on its own yielding art of great beauty, impractical inventions and skillfully executed courses in differential equations. All of these outcomes appear to require thought and, in a trivial sense, they do. Everyone's brain does this. There are people who live their lives cradle to grave without ever moving beyond it: never thinking an original thought and never questioning their motivations. There are well-designed studies that seek to explain the mechanism behind this behavior.

In 2003, David Dunning, Kerri Johnson and associates presented a study which contrasted people who were recognized by their peers as competent against those who were recognized as incompetent[Dunning_2003]. The key difference between the self-assessments provided by competent people and those provided by incompetent people appeared to be that incompetent people were the ones who did not describe themselves as incompetent at any of the defined tasks. These openly incompetent people are part of the cadre who cannot assess themselves – who cannot step outside of their algorithms. These comprise part of the population we wish to consider but they are not the ones that present the real puzzlement. Any decent interviewer will identify the incompetent applicant. The interesting cases are ones like Cyril, who appear competent at every level until they are driven to express an opinion outside their realm of expertise. At that point, Cyril had to engage his ill-practiced mechanism for reasoning. That's where his algorithmic brain failed him.

Honestly, Cyril was a valuable employee and he earned his pay daily. He recognized what complex and inscrutable tool he needed and applied it effectively. I'm not questioning if Cyril should be employed, I'm wondering what it would take to make him put on his running togs. Is there a way to cause him to voluntarily step out of his normal operating zone so that he spends some time pushing beyond the comfortable feedback loops he has worn so smooth and begins to self-assess in a manner consistent with real creative action? He has demonstrated skill: clean, analytical, well-oiled skill; but could he demonstrate genius?

This attitude may appear arrogant and exclusive, but in fact it is deeply humbling. None of us may be certain that we have moved beyond the algorithm. This book may derive from wisdom, experience and true self-reflection or it could easily be my brain closing a simple loop around my dissatisfaction with my job which resolved to this tasteless fruit. Even if we are certain that we are self-aware, we will look back to a time when that was not the case – when we were following prescribed paths; proud to be part of a defined group; living to satisfy recognized superiors. We may look back to an extended childhood spent in the service of others' expectations. Every one of us was a child and many of us may be able to place the moment that childhood became adulthood. This transition will most likely be associated with a trigger: something changed in our environment and the childish understanding of the world became untenable.

This is humbling because none of us may be certain that we have made this transition. It is also invigorating, since it means that we may yet experience that transition and that we, whether transitioned or not,

18: Runner's High

may provide such a trigger to others, unleashing their repressed brilliance.

I learned, after a sweaty aching Summer, that running yields no reward worth the effort. I cannot imagine any event that would change my mind on that. I know people who have learned the same attitude toward thinking. I have worked with them in close quarters. I have tried, sometimes successfully, to get the most out of them and even seen them struggle against their limits in order to gain the praise of their peers. What did I do when I was most successful in that regard? I'm not a manager, I'm an engineer, so I don't know how people work. I only know that shortly after my angry-young-man persona wore threadbare, I started working better with people. I found that by accepting people and treating them as if they could be ingenious, I began seeing genius peer out from time to time. I stopped giving orders and started asking for suggestions. I do not know how to turn that into useful advice.

I do know that not everyone can innovate. Not everyone can apply engineering discipline to the resolution of a complex problem. Whatever the company, there is a place for those who demonstrate skilled use of tools and for those who see the world differently and press their sweating bodies against it until it is oriented so that everyone can see it with the same clear vision.

―――― • ――――

Gregory Berns, in his book *Iconoclast*[Berns_2010], proposes that in order to think differently (he would likely say *envision* differently) a shock is useful. It often helps his iconoclasts to go to places they've never been or to view art that is unusual. Some of the inventors he catalogs were shocked by circumstance, like the glass artist Chihuly who had an auto accident while in Great Britain and lost sight in one eye. Berns proposes that this unexpected change was at least partly responsible for his seeing differently and thereby being able to perceive and conceive differently. He notes that the developer of Magnetic Resonance Imaging had the necessary revelation in a Big Boy restaurant. He describes space explorers, baseball greats and medical innovators, and tends to draw each story back to some eye-opening event.

I find much of his argument persuasive partly because he provides excellent references to experimental evidence, but also because it is consistent with my experience. Berns seems to define the event as cause for the revelation, but I think that the unusual stimulating events are part of a larger unconscious process. When I'm mentally blocked, I go to a bar or a coffee shop. The change of scene almost always shakes me out of my stupor. In more difficult cases, I will go to a museum or go for a drive into unfamiliar parts of the mountains around my house. In every case, that change restarts my process, but it has rarely resulted in the revelation itself.

Berns' story of Kary Mullis, inventor of the process called *polymerase chain reaction*, includes Mullis' own account of his revelation. It happened while he was driving up the northern California coast. Now the scenery on such a highway is undoubtedly beautiful, but not significantly different from other roadside scenery all over California. I suggest that the highway was one of many diversions that fueled an ongoing process which could have yielded its bounty at any point, but in this case, did so on that drive.

I have had at least three serious shocks in my life. I know that while wrecking a small plane in a field near Sayre, Oklahoma, my view of the world changed. I experienced a similar adjustment having an Oklahoma policeman train a shotgun on me while screaming "Get outta the car! Get outta the fuckin' car!" When the rear tire of my motorcycle seized up in an oil slick in the rain on a highway at speed with cars on either side, that was pretty enlightening, too. While I do not satisfy Berns' definition of an iconoclast, I have to say that believing you are going to be dead in thirty seconds rewires a lot of brain circuitry. Unfortunately, I can directly associate no revelations with any of those shocks, but the shocks may have prepared the way for future revelations.

My revelations tend to occur randomly days or weeks after I begin my ruminations. While writing *The Flying Crossbeam*, a novel that explores the development of a unique belief system and the people who

18: Runner's High

adopt and advance it, I conceived of a koan (a cryptic phrase) that might be posed to a practitioner of that belief system for use in meditation. The koan came to me while I was crafting a sentence. There was no good place in the book for a story about a koan, so I left it out. Working years later on another book, my main character found himself in a spot where it seemed my koan would play a role. The problem was this: in order for it to contribute to the plot, I had to know what it meant.

The Zen Buddhists have developed many koans which have no meaning. Indeed, they *must* not have a meaning. Their purpose is to instill uncertainty. There is no answer to the koan, *"Why is a mouse when it spins?" "Stop that bell in the distance,"* is not an instruction to invent a mechanism to do that; and while Bart Simpson proposed a simple answer to *"What is the sound of one hand clapping?"* the Zen master would not be amused.

My character's dilemma required a rare case of a meditator discovering, through a revelation, a useful meaning for a koan that had been told to him years earlier. I decided that I would meditate, then, upon my koan which is simply this: *"If one more person enters the house, it will be entirely unoccupied."* I treated it like I would any intractable problem, I thought about it without ceasing. Driving to and from work, going to sleep and waking up, at restaurants and grocery stores, during scheduled periods of quiet meditation, I would think the koan and puzzle over it.

After weeks of this, I was on my morning drive to work over ground I had driven hundreds of times, seeing nothing of note when an understanding struck me. I was thinking the koan and suddenly I understood it. I had been prepared for the answer to have nothing to do with my plot, but fortunately it did. When the understanding hit me, I began immediately to weep. Wiping the tears from my eyes in order to maintain control on the winding road into Boulder, I repeated and reviewed with satisfaction that this was the answer and this was how my character would retrieve the contraband that he was commissioned to recover.

The koan clearly had an emotional attachment for me since, otherwise, I would have forgotten it. Six years later, though, my unconscious mind paired it up with my character's plight in this particular story. It wasn't like I had been shopping it around for everything I was writing. It came to mind while thinking through this and only this plot. The answer arose while driving a familiar road and it arose as a result of relentless concentration very much like any solution I've managed to develop.

In the same way, I conceived of the title *The Flying Crossbeam* at least three years prior to deciding what the book was about. When I began writing it, I was having trouble seeing how the title fit the plot. I knew the story was about religion and I assumed it was referring to some variation on the flying buttress, a common construction method used in medieval cathedrals. It wasn't until I wrote chapter four that I realized what it meant. I literally had to stop typing and read back the protagonist's statement as if he were explaining it to me. I stared in awe at the obvious explanation that had been hidden for all of that time.

As a neuroscientist, Berns brings fascinating evidence about how the brain actually responds to challenge. I do not doubt his data in any way, and I only question a small part of his proposed cause-and-effect relationship. Clearly the brain is wired, as Berns proposes, to take the path that requires the least power for the same reason that I prefer to bike rather than run: expending an excess of energy is uncomfortable.

With a shock (even a mild one), people may discover hidden resources. The brain may remap its connections and different ways of thinking may become possible. It may be possible for one to step away from one's algorithms and begin rewriting them – to acquire one's *self*. How do we impose therapeutic shocks for the purpose of stimulating the creative side? Drudgery is a part of every job but there has to be a way out. It must be possible to give Cyril regular opportunities to tackle a challenging problem, to question his comfort and stare down his fear. Like the *runner's high* Sarah described, there is an elation at the end of solving an intractable problem. With repeated experience of that reward mechanism, thinking creatively may become a natural state.

18: Runner's High

Instead, I know brilliant engineers who, after demonstrating their exceptional abilities, were politely thanked and never challenged again. Over beers, they lament their loss and ask me where they could find another interesting project, to which I can only sympathize and confess that I too live that craving every day. We must explore how the healthy society may feed this yearning maw. Innovation is a drug and the more people we can burden with this addiction the better off the world will be.

———— • ————

When smart managers talk about "vision," they're really meaning a goal that everyone can understand and appreciate. The hope is that the internal goal-seeking machinery of each employee will be engaged. As with any community of people, there will be reliable laborers, administrators skilled at wise planning, and some high-energy brilliant inventors. All of these have a place in any organization, the trick is to place them in the roles wherein they may best serve, not only for the good of the organization but also for their own satisfaction and well-being. Every person performs better and enjoys their work more when they have a meaningful goal.

While nearly every company can show you their vision statement, it should be obvious that no one takes them very seriously. They are bland and lifeless simulations of a failed aspirational grasp. The problem lies in the fact that most companies are in place for a reason that no one wants to identify openly. If we were to simply use the actual fact as the vision statement, it may actually be easier to prosecute. The real vision statement of most companies would look like this:

> *We act with great caution to advance only when required in order to assure continued high income for our top stockholders by maintaining our current value proposition through regular updates and acquisition of viable competitors so that we may avoid the need to innovate while providing a product adequate to our most likely consumers.*

Famine In the Bullpen

This may not prove inspiring to the more creative members of the crew, but it could be sufficient to a fair number of employees. This being a very common unstated vision statement, it seems reasonable that more companies should adopt it. The creative people will leave, which saves money, and the folks that are comfortable with repetitive dull work or strategic acquisitions will remain.

If the company really does have a challenging vision, then it should be able to hold on to its innovative component by stating it. That vision will set the goal and, if presented clearly, can inspire everyone. As even I will run if my life depends on it, people will prove their genius if the goal is clear and applies personally to them. The organization, though, must actually have a vision. It must actually express a meaningful goal.

19: Onramp

Humans are underrated.

Elon Musk

Creativity comes in all sizes and shapes. We often think of the inventor as the ultimate exemplar of creativity, but that limits our understanding significantly. I worked with a brilliant fellow named Jeff, who was not much interested in developing things from scratch. His primary skill was in taking other people's inventions and making them work the way they were intended to. He was generally called in to get this application server to talk to that caching repository or to get this Enterprise Service Bus (ESB) to talk to that identity server. He pored over the manuals identifying and working around obscure discrepancies and showed all of the developers and IT folks how it was actually done.

His clear and concise definition of the procedure for getting these tools to do what they were supposed to required an ability to assess and analyze, but also the creativity to fathom what was in the inventor's mind when he put this tool together and subsequently failed to explain it to the poor fellow who ended up documenting his ingenious device after the fact. Jeff's tutorials regarding the latest coolest frameworks we had decided to take on, were filled with insight that the sparse documentation failed to reveal; and once he had set it up, it just worked. It was for this reason that I always tried to invite him to discussions regarding technical strategy. I was never disappointed.

Famine In the Bullpen

How do you interview for a fellow like this? How do you assess whether the new guy can perform this kind of service? Did you even know that this was a skill you really needed? The technical realm isn't the only place where finding the right person is a challenge. In the first part of the Twenty-First Century, public school teachers have taken the whip for the failures of parents and governments. Public schools have had their funding cut and teachers are blamed for the failure of students to excel. Rigorous testing of these students is put forward as the means to determine the effectiveness of the teacher.

My fifth grade teacher at Russell Dougherty Elementary School in Edmond, Oklahoma, was Mrs. White. She would often call upon a student to stand and answer a question. If any student interrupted their answer with "uh" or "ya know" she would respond quickly with, "Thank you. Does any one else know the answer?"

As a result, each young person in this class learned, over nine months of intense conditioning, to speak with authority, to use no fake sounds for filling the silence. Instead, we learned to relish and nourish the silence. Thirty children learned to pause thoughtfully as we were constructing our next sentence. To pause, and look wise as we reviewed all options for our next statement and finally, slowly, authoritatively, to state the certain truth as if handed down by God Himself.

Mrs. White released class after class of children fully educated with the fifth grade curriculum but also trained to speak in a manner that would persuade the listener that there was no alternative explanation – that the statement made was the clear and obvious fact. "These are not the droids you are looking for," was a pale and pitiful imitation of the Jedi skills taught by Mrs. White; and yet, no formalized test would ever have identified this priceless education.

As I progressed to sixth grade, I retained those skills. Teacher after teacher responded to my well-practiced narrative. I did well in classes wherein I was initially stymied simply because I could sound like I understood what was happening. Those special skills were used to buy me time, the time I needed to catch up to my more clever peers and actually master the topic. How many of Mrs. White's students are now serving

19: Onramp

in high-ranking offices because all they needed to advance past their competitors was that breathing room? In the same way, without a college degree, I picked up a job as an electronics engineer and later as a software engineer, a field where I am still employed as I write this book.

While working for a newspaper publisher in Denver, we hired an excellent programmer named Joe Henry who could quote Shakespeare flawlessly when the need arose. We discovered that he had been an English major and mocked him shamelessly for this.

When the problem became how to read an English language newspaper article and figure out if it identified a location, and whether that location was important to the rest of the story, it became clear that his education was the ideal fit for the problem. I asked Joe if he could resolve this and he took it on eagerly. After a fairly typical day of coding on his other project, he arrived the next day quite subdued. He wasn't quite moping, but he was reserved and quiet. We were all busy finishing our previous job and so I took little notice of his new mood. After three days straight of this, I asked after him and he said that everything was fine. He was just quiet.

The next day, he arrived at work ebullient. He looked over my cubicle wall and said, "I know how to do it." I remember him that day as excited and gregarious. Always focused and sardonic, that day he was best described as effervescent. He had spent the past days deeply submerged in his unconscious, reviewing the problem over and over. Following the route proposed by Isaac Newton, he was thinking of nothing else so deeply as the problem at hand. Allowing the problem to periodically slip away and then to innocently return for further review. His revelation, he told me, presented in the shower.

He explained his solution and it was brilliant. It was based upon a fundamental rule of grammar that revealed with good facility likely locations, and provided a means for testing their relevance. He built our lexer and I built our parser, eventually identifying the important places in the newspaper article for pinning on a web-page map of events. He had experienced the elation of solving a problem that very few others had solved. In fact, at the time, only one other company claimed anything close to this capability and, in comparison, their algorithm proved to be easily confused by the communication style of the newspaper reporter.

Once his solution was implemented and running successfully, he became interested in solving other problems. He became frustrated with the reluctance of the company to take an interest in solving problems and was dismissed after annoying some higher ups with enlightened criticism. Now a mid-level programmer at a major bank, he has not been asked to solve a problem since.

What test would have revealed Mrs. White's exemplary skills? How would the school board even craft the job description for her? How would we interview for someone who could pull locations out of an English-language document before we even knew we needed it? If people are commodities to be plugged into the machine, are Jeff, Joe and Mrs. White single-use specialized parts?

In my experience, those sorts of people find rare brief stints at companies with a particular need but then are relegated to the common pool where their actual talents are wasted for extended runs of desperate boredom. Modern companies have no problems that would require that kind of creative energy on a full-time basis. Problems are to be avoided, not solved.

There isn't a way to assure that a particular person is the one you want to hire: not the twelve hour test, not the day long interview, not the single question followed by the pointless insult. Instead, the environment must be constructed to select and drive expression of the qualities that are needed when they are needed. As long as you select a generally competent person, they will be amenable to resolving any kind of problem when it arises as long as the corporate culture is designed to drive that.

———— • ————

Certainly, it must be possible to distinguish between an ingenious innovator and a borderline madman. The two will undoubtedly share many common characteristics. While I am advocating the encourage-

19: Onramp

ment of innovation, I would be remiss to leave my reader with no tools whatever to figure out when you are being duped. Both the innovator and the madman will explain the world in unique and sometimes enlightening ways. Both may speak with great confidence presenting their ideas as if experience informed their conclusions. Both may demonstrate the ability to master complex concepts, but there should still be techniques for distinguishing the charlatan from the real thing.

Innovation, like evolution, is comprised of three components: a creative component, a conservative component and a selective component. To envision this clearly, we may enumerate these components with respect to evolution. The creative component is mutation. Environmental factors will raise a force to knock an allele out of a cell's DNA. The DNA remembers this mutation and seeks to replicate it. The DNA is the conservative component, retaining the essential data of the mutation and allowing it to be replicated. After the DNA has been modified, the selective component begins to come into effect. In all likelihood, the mutated cell will not be able to replicate because the DNA no longer encodes a viable being. That particular mutation has been selected out. If the cell can replicate, does it fit its environment well enough to survive? If not, it is selected out a little later; but it is still selected out. Sometimes the cell may survive and thrive until the environment becomes inhospitable. A mutated cell whose progeny prospers for centuries may well live long enough to be enshrined in the fossil record. This mutation, we may call "successful."

This is the anatomy of innovation. A person who excels at this art will have developed skills that push her thought process off kilter, encouraging mutations in linear thought. She has learned to retain those mutations for future comparison and she will invoke a selection process for weighing their relative merits. She has learned to maintain detachment from her mutations. Regardless their apparent beauty, she will "kill her darlings" before they corrupt the final enlightened conclusion.

People who have never before been asked to innovate and are yet clever, will cobble together their version of this process fairly quickly. I have described this sudden and unexpected mastery of the process in

Joe and Terence (chapter 17). I've left out many other examples simply because they did not fit the flow of the narrative. In my experience, supposedly average people, when challenged to excel, do so effectively and with great enthusiasm.

There have been rare cases, in my experience, of team-members for whom this has not occurred. These anomalies seemed more driven by my deficiencies than lack of ability on their part.

In one case, the fellow had focused his energies on explaining the flaws in our plan without being able to suggest an improvement. Finally, he took a weekend to hack out his solution which he could not explain and which, in the long run, needed to be rewritten. He resigned after failing to persuade management that my services were no longer required. The other case was one wherein I failed to position the engineer where she could thrive. I misread her skills and put her in a position wherein she could not have succeeded. She resigned to return to aerospace. Her background in that rigidly-controlled environment should have led me to move her in the direction of implementation rather than design. She had no background in design and I had pushed her into it so quickly that she could not adapt.

In both cases, I failed. I should have engaged the young man and sought to draw out his criticism. By calmly reviewing his concerns, a position where he could succeed was possible. Unfortunately (and very childishly) I simply didn't like him. This was not only unprofessional, it was wrong. It forced him to make unpleasant decisions he should not have had to make and it deprived the team of a potentially effective member. Regarding the young woman, I should have recognized her unease and either assisted in her design duties or moved that task to another team member.

Competent people who are managed competently are happy to be directed as required. They will take on the impossible with gusto and proudly wrestle its corpus to ground, proving the unassailable utility of the prehensile mind. To oversee the commitment of human beings to anything less is the inexcusable corruption of their value and meaning.

19: Onramp

An assembly of humans dedicated to some purpose can do only so much to select the right people for the job. The selection process must look for the qualities that distinguish the competent peer from the bombastic egotist.

Remember that everyone with whom I have worked has been filtered through a vetting process. I cannot claim that I know how to get high quality software out of a skilled accountant. I have never had to inspire a plumber to take on the role of project lead. There is not a role for every kind of skill in your company and I accept that. What I mean to impress upon the reader is that there is a wide array of options for pulling competent people who understand the field into a space where they can succeed.

So sure, get a feel for the applicant's knowledge of the general field; but once you know he has some experience, forget what he did. Figure out what he can do. You are looking for a few closely related characteristics: the ability to understand things differently than they are presented (this often shows itself as a sense of humor), the ability to explain complex concepts and enough self-confidence to spontaneously explain these concepts as they are understood. Ask questions that show you the thought process. I'm not talking about the volumes of gotcha questions that comprise the dull legacy of the large tech companies. I'm certainly not talking about requiring a twelve hour project. Come up with challenging but non-threatening questions that will show you what this applicant can do. The applicant shouldn't be terrified, but should certainly understand that she is engaged in something serious.

Discuss with others what sorts of questions will reveal the necessary qualities and try to standardize the questions for each applicant so that they may be easily compared. You are looking for responses that illuminate the following:

Competence: Someone who is competent is capable of recognizing their deficiencies and correcting them. It means that they take and offer criticism well. They are humble enough to ask advice and confident enough to offer it. In a review of any concept, competence is essential.

Emotional Intelligence: When reviewing ones own ideas or another's, it is important to be able to respond constructively to emotional states. An innovator needs to be able to recognize if their attachment to an idea is rational or poignant. When the developer whose design is being reviewed begins responding guardedly, one with emotional intelligence will have the tools at hand to reduce the tension.

Skill: It saves time hiring folks who already understand how to do what is needed, so please do that; but, remember that you are going to eventually need a skill you don't think you need now. A competent person with emotional intelligence can pick up whatever skill is required in a minimal amount of time. Skills may be acquired, competence and emotional intelligence need to come with the package.

While competent people with emotional intelligence should comprise a large part of your organization, there will be cases where an otherwise deficient hire may be necessary or appropriate. You may have an immediate need for a particular rare skill or you may encounter a particularly needy applicant whom you are hoping can be redeemed. Not-entirely-competent people need to eat too and we, as humans, will sometimes reach out the hand of favor in exceptional cases.

If surrounded by fellow employees who satisfy our criteria, these not-yet-competent people may be brought around. I have worked in many varied environments and I have seen this happen more often than not. An inspiring team works as a unit and while a faulty bearing in a rotating mechanism will only get worse, human beings on a competent team tend to build up new capabilities from repeated exposure to the good behavior surrounding them.

Once competent people are assembled, they must be implemented. They must be given a purpose and a goal. They must be able to understand how their actions will influence something important and they must be driven to accomplish things that they do not think are possible. A skilled technical lead can do this for a team. A skilled manager can do this for a department. A skilled director can do this for a division.

19: Onramp

Under the most exciting conditions, a CEO can do this for an entire company. The workplace must be an *onramp* to a network of meaningful destinations. It must establish an environment that draws the best out of each employee, that shows by example what constitutes a rewarding and stimulating creative life, that wields with supreme benignity the power of the individual.

20: A Culture of Innovation

Information will never replace illumination.
                                            Susan Sontag

I would like to conduct an exploration of a theoretical institution which promotes and nourishes innovation by recounting and refining my experience of an actual institution that did this to a fair degree. I experienced its strengths and weaknesses first hand. I ask my reader to consider, as I illustrate this example, what lessons may be learned. Between the two of us we may be able to conceive of a reproducible framework for invention.

I base my exploration on this: Never in my life have I worked so hard for so long in an environment that burgeoned with innovation as when I worked for Sun Microsystems. The environment was fundamental to everything that happened there. People were put in a position to advance as they felt appropriate. Some, preferring coding to design, mastered that art as no other and when the design was presented, like the workers in the Toyota plant, they brought their special expertise to the critique and improvement of that design. Others, like me, were driven to take on fresh problems. There were plenty of opportunities and there were clearly defined ways to present your problem and your solution so as to get them noticed and evaluated.

I would often inform a new employee that Sun was basically political. I would mean that in the best possible sense. Like the Greeks, who invented politics and tested it under a wide variety of circumstances,

20: A Culture of Innovation

the politics at Sun was in the wide variety of forums wherein ideas could be proposed, argued and demonstrated. It was easy to get the ear of a higher up and if your proposal was sound, that political relationship would propel you and your idea into an opportunity to advance your cause.

No organization should adopt the Sun model without review. There were problems that should be addressed, but there were also exemplary practices that worked well. I will try to present here an amalgam of good practices and lessons learned in hopes of suggesting a set of practices likely to promote a culture of innovation.

There are rare companies for which high profits and exorbitant executive salaries do *not* constitute their primary vision statement. Such companies are active and well known in the second decade of the Twenty-First Century. SpaceX and Dyson are two companies that thrive on innovation because their top officers have chosen to take on the risk of innovation. That choice is not necessarily the one that will lead to further riches. Indeed, the projects may fail and leave their founders merely rich as opposed to magnificently wealthy. Each of these companies does this because their top officer is driven to do what others claim is impossible, and he is prepared to challenge his people to do the impossible simply to disprove the accepted view that it cannot be done.

Other organizations like the developers of the Lighttp web server[28], Dallas Semiconductor (now part of Maxim Integrated Products) and certain departments within Google engage in innovative endeavors for the same reason. While innovation stands a better chance of more rapid advancement than "following fast," there is risk of failure and in the current business climate, most CEOs have been persuaded that they are better off to avoid such risk.

Nonetheless, if not the company, a division may organize for innovation. If not a division, a department may budget for creative risk taking. If not a department, a team may choose to think outside the re-

---

28 Pronounced "lighty." See the project at http://redmine.lighttpd.net/

strictions of Scrum and tackle full well-planned agility. What I will propose here should be applicable, in one way or another, to any group who seeks to make full use of their human potential and possibly to actually solve problems that higher management may be content to simply accommodate. As with all great labors, there is risk, but the reward is that elation that arises when the impossible is accomplished and the naysayers are vanquished and humiliated. The real underlying goal is at least as old as Galileo, who confessed that ultimately he hoped 'to win some fame.'

This is your opportunity to change the culture of your company. While studies indicate a high likelihood that your company's owner or CEO is a sociopath, incapable of understanding your needs as a creative being, there are practical reasons to emphasize innovation. Throughout this book I present evidence that the innovative company is more interesting and, in many cases, more profitable than the fast follower. An argument can be made that by promoting innovation, the jobs of the top executives are actually easier in that inspired underlings tend to take on more of the responsibility. Also, an innovative culture will tend to have reduced employee turnover which will result in higher profits overall.

Suffice it to say that a rational argument can be made to promote innovation even to an emotionally stunted scrooge. Fortunately, not all CEOs are sociopaths. The CEO of your company may be very open to innovative options. Examples include New Belgium Brewery and Harpoon Brewery whose owners were reluctant to sell their creations to Big Beer when they retired and chose instead to convert their companies into worker-owned coops promoting legitimate worker ownership and improving participation. Stack Overflow and Teamwork.com provide private offices for developers opening the door to concentrated "flow" and to productive creativity.

If the CEO is non-responsive, you can make your argument to a director or to your own boss. You can suggest changes on your own team and then when your productivity impresses others, the innovative culture may spread.

20: A Culture of Innovation

So, there are practical possibilities for the bored team-member. Start a conversation within your company, propose approaches that test the envelope such as OOM or careful design prior to implementation. If that fails, look elsewhere with an eye toward companies that better support innovation. With enough skilled workers focused on developing or finding innovative options, it is possible that the industry may begin to shift. Culture is driven by attitude and if our attitudes and behaviors may be adjusted, the culture may as well.

———•———

There are three key components that support innovation within an organization. To understand them we return to our previous review of evolution. There must be a creative component, a conservative component and a selective component. They must all be present and fully functional or the whole thing falls apart. Too much creativity without selection and you are shipping the most beautiful of crap. Too much conservation and the recording of facts slows everything to a crawl. The balance is important and while I hope to provide some suggestions, experimentation within your culture will nonetheless be required.

I would like to prosecute this exposition in reverse order, beginning with selection. Whatever happens there must be a scheme for discriminating between crazy ideas that will command a market and brilliant ideas that no one will ever understand. At Sun Microsystems, the technical side of the selection component was addressed by the Architecture Review Committee (ARC), which reviewed all projects for technical merit. The essential business review was much less transparent. In my experience, your manager would take you to some director somewhere who would, in most cases, hear you out and bring it into the budget process. This made it clear to many of us that a standing committee responsible for reviewing the merit of the concept in the market would have been very useful. For this reason I suggest that any organization intending to promote innovation establish these two committees to meet at designated times to review ideas on those two dimensions – technical and business.

Famine In the Bullpen

Therefore, the other piece of the selection component is the Business Review Committee (BRC). The BRC will consider if the proposed idea has a place in the market. If it has no potential value in the market, it doesn't matter how technically excellent it is. The reviewers must be both practical and creative. They need to be able to fashion appropriate budgetary constraints and also be able to assess the potential of the product in a fickle and often unpredictable market. They may review it as a product or they may review it as a component to be used in future products. It is possible that some members of the BRC will be competent to review the functional spec for a full understanding of the technical principles of the product; but the document describing the market potential of the idea is a separate and important instrument. Since the development team responsible for the product also needs to understand its importance in the market, there are many good reasons to produce a brief document covering that subject. The complexity of the functional specification should not be necessary here. Instead, a clear explanation of the problem to be solved and the solution that solves it. In fact, this document is probably already written – it is the *onepager* used to initiate a project, as will be discussed later for the conservative component.

One could imagine the BRC requesting a larger market analysis for projects whose merit is not clear. This would be generated with the cooperation of the person who wrote the onepager, but would probably come from skilled personnel in marketing or analytics. In that process, the merit of the onepager may come into question resulting in rejection. One may argue that this sort of rigor would not be necessary with Scrum; but, of course, in a Scrum shop market analysis is still required. A Scrum shop that doesn't engage in market analysis is wasting more money than it is saving. This analysis will be performed and a document published in an easily accessible spot.

The BRC will not be interested in a detailed description of interfaces. It will focus on projects and major updates to projects. The approval of the BRC will designate budget and a rough schedule for each project, and will call for regular status meetings so as to adjust expectations with experience.

20: A Culture of Innovation

Regarding the technical dimension, Sun maintained, on average, three ARCs for the entire company. They met once per week for a few hours. The ARC's job was to review projects but also to review any change to any exposed interface including user interfaces, localized messaging and APIs. Their basic purpose was to assure the technical integrity of every project, both in its inception and in its evolution. The ARC did not care if the change was marketable but they were ruthless in their assessment of how each change affected the user and the product's interaction with other Sun or industry standard products.

As we gained experience with the process, two routes through the ARC were provided, one very lightweight and one more rigorous. The lightweight mechanism was called a *fasttrack*. The developer implementing a change to an interface that was obvious and non-controversial would deliver a short document describing the change to the ARC. The ARC members would review it and if none of them *derailed* it, it was approved. The other mechanism brought the engineer into one of the ARC meetings. A functional specification would be submitted for review and it would be discussed within the ARC and approved, approved with modifications or (rarely) rejected.

In order to avoid surprises, engineers were encouraged to meet with the ARC for a *pre-review* before writing the full functional spec. Often, the applicant would simply talk through the idea in that meeting. The ARC members would make suggestions and the engineer would head back with a good idea of the technical expectations for the project. At that point development could proceed with reasonable certainty that the project was on the right track. Once the functional spec was done, another meeting would be scheduled and, with ARC approval, the team would make whatever adjustments the ARC may have required and move to delivery.

If the reader is suspecting that this is a very heavyweight process, I would ask how he would implement a project of any size without a functional spec. If the answer is "a stack of stories," I would suggest a review of the preceding pages of this book. I have been party to a number of Scrum teams that took on large projects and I would counter that it is instead a stack of stories followed by another stack of stories to finally figure out how to patch together the shards that the previous stories spewed out followed by yet another stack of stories to finally correct the brittle bird's nest yielded from the prior hack-fest. Something was delivered but it was not good, and it was not maintainable.

Someone needs to design the whole solution. The idea that the market is moving so quickly that that is impractical is balderdash. It takes two weeks to a month to write a functional spec. It takes a week or so to have it reviewed, first by peers and then by the ARC. In the meanwhile, your team is prototyping and researching the solution. You are moving as quickly as you would have using Scrum, but your solution is actually objectively likely to solve the problem and be maintainable. If the problem is sufficiently complex, the real time-sink is figuring out what the problem actually is, which can take months. The Scrum notion of a two-week spike followed by full-scale coding simply ignores that fact.

While developers complained about the ARC, it imposed a discipline that most engineers appreciated. It provided the engineer with time to think the problem through and propose a complete solution since that was required by the process. Knowing that any change to any exposed interface had to be reviewed by an ARC, caused every developer to think carefully about every change. If it was possible to fix the problem within the existing interface, that was always preferred. That kind of discipline would have saved a couple of my prior employers serious money. The developer avoids writing the fasttrack, if at all possible, by actually thinking through the least disruptive solution. If an interface change was truly needed, the fasttrack required a very simple explanation of the change and writing it out sometimes provided me with an inspiration that resolved my original problem more cleanly and made the fasttrack unnecessary.

Does this mean that all projects are a massive undertaking complete with burdensome documentation and oversight? Not in any way. A simple project will involve a short onepager and a short spec which would be fasttracked through the review bodies. The fact that the

20: A Culture of Innovation

project is simple doesn't mean that it should be tackled blind. For heaven's sake, just write it down! Let smart people review it and then implement it.

The ARC and the BRC each respond to their projects with an *opinion*: a short document explaining that the project has been reviewed and the final dispensation. The opinion is necessary in case some future engineer has a similar idea or seeks to change an existing project. It is essential that the reason for the approval, rejection or modification of each project be understood in context. None of these documents need to be long, but they should be recorded and readily available to anyone inside the organization.

The BRC and the ARC require a significant investment in time from their members. At Sun, ARC members were expected to fulfill serious obligations to other projects while serving. This led to burn-out wherein members were unable to engage in the disciplined review required to provide the necessary support to the submitting project teams. After four years, I know that I burned out. I didn't realize it until I made an utter fool of myself in an ARC meeting. I had not done my homework and I made a statement exposing that fact clearly to all concerned. There was an uneasy silence at which point I apologized and resigned.

The members of the BRC and ARC need to be taken very seriously. Once assigned to one of the review committees, the member must be relieved of serious non-committee responsibilities for the duration of their tenure. Since actual experience is necessary in order to serve effectively, this implies short, concentrated stints for all members. Perhaps six months followed by a real project, followed by a cycle back through the committee. Some experimentation should reveal the best balance for your organization. I am fairly confident that four years is too long and four months is too short, since it takes about that long to figure out the process.

The conservative component is provided by the documentation regimen. Each document needs to be numbered so that it can be unambiguously distinguished from the documents of similar projects. The specifications at Sun were not numbered until they were published externally and even then they were rarely referenced by number. We refer to *The Java Language Specification* and not JSR-000901[29] rev 7. Each project was numbered when submitted to ARC (e.g., PSARC-1544) but the specific internal documents associated with each project were available in the wild with only their sometimes-conflicting titles. Confusion could have been easily avoided by having a central authority (person or program) assign a unique number to each technical document and make it available in an index.[30]

Ideas aren't like banknotes. They aren't issued by official sources. Anyone in the company may have an idea that could improve the world and turn a profit. How would anyone put such an idea into motion? The tool at Sun used to initiate a project was a onepager. People who wanted to identify a problem but hadn't yet figured out a solution would write a halfpager which clearly explained the problem. When a halfpager was augmented with a solution, it became a onepager.

This turned out to be a very convenient system which would be even more convenient using modern searchable storage methods. An engineer looking for a next project would peruse the halfpagers. Finding one that looks challenging, he may add a solution and submit the corresponding onepager. The BRC would assess the onepagers and decide which are appropriate for pursuit. If they find the solution to have potential, they will assign budget and the technical process will begin in earnest.

I worked at an aerospace company which had a very useful tradition. It too required a document similar to the halfpager and onepager and once per year it would call upon their submitters to post them in a large auditorium. The ceremony was called *cover the walls*, and it allowed everyone in the company to review the proposals and vote on

---

29 The number optimistically anticipating another 999,098 documents.

30 Fifty years ago, this numbering would be provided by the *chief draftsman*. There was a reason for that canonizing identifier and that reason has not gone away. It allowed a document to be unambiguously referenced and it allowed for an unambiguous association between the document and its revision in order to assure that everyone was referencing the correct technical information.

20: A Culture of Innovation

them. This would be an excellent tradition for any innovative company. Give each employee five sticky stars and have them put one or more on each proposal depending on how profitable they think it might be. That doesn't need to determine the direction of the company but it should be a meaningful influence to the BRC which will consider or reconsider these onepagers based upon their final ranking.

The halfpager, the onepager, the functional specification and any other technical documentation will be organized into a common repository. It will be searchable. The halfpagers and unassigned onepagers will be indexed and when a project is initiated, its onepager will be associated with it. This index will not be a wiki in that it will be maintained by a dedicated person responsible for assuring that it is up-to-date and correct.

The documentation defining the project life cycle, both active and inactive, will remain in the index over the foreseeable future. It will be referenced regularly by engineers looking for a project, by marketing people looking for a solution to a particular customer's problem, and by developers looking for their next cool project. The conservative component is critical to an organization. It avoids duplicate projects, it connects customers with their solution and it connects developers with their next job. Documentation isn't a problem as long as it's valuable. The innovative company provides as much documentation as is necessary and no more. This is the conservative component of innovation.

The creative component is ensconced in the creative energy of all of the employees. Every employee must have the option of submitting a halfpager or a onepager. Some pagers will be brilliant but inappropriate to the organization. An innovative organization may well collaborate with other innovative organizations to exchange such proposals looking for a match. An engineer who finds a halfpager she can turn into a onepager, may complete it and submit it. The BRC will pick up the onepagers as they are submitted and, for those that merit consideration by the organization, may notify the submitter that they should proceed. This would result in a functional specification which would go to ARC and the assembly of a team which would begin the technical work.

Famine In the Bullpen

———•———

The innovative organization draws from the special skills of all employees. The interview process strives to exclude the incompetent and the emotionally immature. Surprisingly, though, such individuals may serve well in specific niches of the organization. Anyone who finds a productive niche is worthy of retention. How would an innovative company retain worthy employees and continually screen out those who are inappropriate? Is there a way, without draconian culling, to assure a reliable collection of good fits? Is there a way, without requiring uncertain managers to select and reject specific employees, to close a loop around excellence? I think there may be.

21: PROSE

In response to the general concern regarding the stodgy mundanity of modern business, many creative entrepreneurs have been experimenting with an environment that will be conducive to an innovative culture. These numerous experiments strive to establish a diverse, open, and free-thinking assembly of team-members. The goal is tricky since, by striving to advance free thinking, unified agreement becomes a highly dubious goal. An authoritarian company can easily organize people into rank and file and direct them to their well-ordered goals. Free thinkers need to be drawn carefully into consensus and inspired to a goal.

Creative people are hard to lead but when they are skillfully persuaded to a particular target, they pounce upon it in aggregate with an enthusiasm that makes leadership irrelevant. In order to support this sort of skilled persuasion, people need to find themselves in a place that is safe and yet challenging; that is respectful of individual privacy but open about incidental information; that promotes communication while strictly avoiding insult and invective. This would not be the creative company of the 1950s where the IBM engineers wore the white-shirt-black-tie uniform and sang the IBM theme song at communal breakfasts. We've moved beyond that. Modern creative people are not as easily fooled into camaraderie. There must be a clear commitment to honest exchange. If there is a uniform, it will arise spontaneously. If there is a theme song, it will be composed on-the-spot and bellowed in the nearby bars with each satisfying competitive victory.

While such a company is a complex mix of initiatives, there seem to be two key areas of concentration: assessment and compensation.

These seem to be a small part of the business infrastructure but, in fact, they are part of (and indeed not possible without) an entirely new approach to business protocols. There may still be a hierarchy, but it must be a shallow, highly communicative hierarchy. There may still be a chief officer, but her compensation must be justifiable as something she truly earned rather than an undeserved gift from her wealthy cohort. Strategies will still be secret but the process whereby they are developed will be clearly understood.

There are some studies that demonstrate this, but there are even more actual examples. In the traditional company, the manager is easily influenced by his boss who passed this particular employee to him. He is easily influenced by the employee who brings him coffee every morning. It is fairly easy (and relatively cheap) to buddy up to one person, but it's hard to buddy up to everyone in your department. The employee assessment and the employee compensation package needs to be determined as scientifically as possible while isolating personal biases and misconstructions.

———— • ————

If we were to begin with modern approaches to employee assessment, we will find a confirmation of an observation most of us have already made: the boss doesn't know the employee nearly as well as the employee's peers. The experiments performed by Dunning, Kruger and associates[Dunning_2003] demonstrate that employees are very effective at differentiating between competent and incompetent peers. Modern companies are harnessing that fact to their advantage.

A quick web search will show numerous companies offering services in support of peer review. That is to say that, rather than the employee reporting on his work and the employee's boss reviewing and adjusting that resulting in an agreed upon summary of the year's accomplishments, the employee's peers will submit the report. According to Inc. Magazine, in their July 1, 2000 issue, this began as early as 1990 with companies like Risk International introducing universal peer review. The process they used was refined from a general review to a packet of more specific reviews for only the employee's closest associates. By 2000, the process had been refined to the point that the entire culture was tied to collective, open-minded pursuit of superior value. Reports tend to confirm that this process promoted better interdepartmental cooperation and improved employee morale.

By putting employees into the assessment process, each felt an improved ownership of the problem of maintaining a skilled workforce. The manager doesn't have to break the news to the disgruntled employee about his unsatisfactory performance; instead, the job of the manager is to work with each employee using the incontrovertible evidence submitted by his peers with a goal of constant improvement.

This is not easy and is not possible unless the commitment to a transformation of corporate culture is understood and genuine. Amazon attempted this in a halfhearted and perhaps cynical way, by encouraging anonymous criticism by peers. The result, after a few years, was a tedious litany of complaints about coworkers with no constructive improvement possible due to the angry and derisive nature of the complaints. That peer review program was discontinued.

In response to this trend The Committee on Publication Ethics has published their guidelines for peer reviews which encourage constructive comments only, and an improved corporate communication regimen. Some companies have taken this even further. George School in Newton, Pennsylvania enacted a peer review program that was *not anonymous*. They required that all criticism be constructive and, in support of this, the critiques were curated to assure this rule. The HR director, Karen Hallowell, reported that after a few years of soothing hurt feelings and negotiating between employees in conflict, the system calmed down and now reports a unified and cooperative community of skilled and effective workers. She believes that their peer review process has played an important role in forming that team.

Each organization has its own approach. In some cases, the peer review is one of several inputs into an assessment delivered ultimately by the supervisor. In others, peer review is the largest component of the final assessment. Clearly, though, this approach forces the organization to faithfully expose its actual goals. It would be impossible to accurately measure any employee's contribution to "whatever it is that has to get done." Such assessment demands a clear goal for the business against which the behaviors of the employees may be meaningfully judged. Thus, taking employee assessment in a radical direction leaves an indelible mark on the larger corporation.

Even when it is not basic to the company's process, the value of peer review still peeks through. Sun did not have a formal peer review process and so, after several years at the company, I was surprised to discover that a number of employees deeply resented me. These were people who had responded negatively to one of my white papers or one of my dissenting ARC opinions or whose project had been affected negatively by one of my projects. This became clear to me only after the manager of a team I was hoping to join informed me that I was "universally loathed" by all concerned. While this criticism does not appear to be very constructive, it made it clear to me that there was a problem. In response, I undertook to review how I communicated and how I built relationships with others. I was able to examine and correct the more abrasive aspects of my personality. At later companies, I was accepted much more warmly. Peer review is good because only your peers know what you are doing. It contributes to a better corporate culture and to meaningful improvement.

In the same way, the traditional means of compensation falls short for a number of enlightened companies. The deleterious effects of exorbitant executive salaries on the productivity of modern companies is moving conscientious executives to orient their companies to improve employee commitment by distributing both ownership and compensation more fairly.

Even at Sun, there was a reason why Scott McNeally's official annual salary was $100K. Everyone knew his primary income was from stock, but the fiction that he was just another specialized worker provided immeasurable value in morale and team spirit. The fact that the

21: PROSE

Costco CEO, James Sinegal, took a salary of $350K[31] and offered his employees a living wage as well as benefits allowed Costco to show excellent profits even when compared to its parsimonious nearest competitors. Employees who are treated fairly contribute more value than employees who see themselves as compensated parts of some rich guy's machine.

The private Chinese network and telecommunications company, Huawei, distributes ownership across all of its employees to the point that the founder, Ren Zhengfei, owns less than two percent of the company's stock value. On annual revenue of over $60 billion with a profit of over $5 billion, its 170,000 employees receive salary distributions designated at over twice the net profit of the company.

In the U.K., the John Lewis department stores, Waitrose supermarkets and several other retail-related enterprises are driven by the John Lewis Partnership, an employee-owned coop with 2015 revenue of £10.94 billion and profits of £299.7 million. As with Huawei, the employees' income is largely comprised of their share of corporate profits.

Many companies, like the software companies Fog Creek and Stack Exchange, have established transparent salary structures which they describe with rightful pride in executive blog posts. Up to sixteen salary tiers are defined with the CEO in the top tier and the novice programmer in tier eight. The requirements to move from one tier to another are clearly defined and the review process, while conducted privately, is consistent and well-understood. One of the CEOs made it clear that while individual salaries are a private matter, if all of their salaries were exposed on WikiLeaks, no one would be surprised.

According to blog posts from 2014, Zappos, a shoe manufacturer, Github, a software repository, and iwantmyname, a web domain name registrar, all implement some variation on a single salary wherein the number of salary tiers is greatly reduced, sometimes to only one for the workers in a particular office. These processes have been in place not as

---

31 As with McNeally, his full take-home compensation was closer to $2 million; but, the perception that he was not compensated grandly, was essential to the culture and morale of the workforce.

an experiment for a quarter, but for multiple years with good acceptance by the participants. This, too, isn't that unusual: many government departments and school districts payment schedules assign a single predictable salary to each employee, adjusted only by simple modifiers such as tenure and job definition.

These long-running experiments have not been widely accepted, even though their positive effects on profitability have been widely demonstrated. They imply that there is an approach that might provide the ideal environment for the culture of innovation. It involves these well-tried components but it combines them and seeks to better define the environment that many of these companies have already developed through practice. The process is very likely to work well for small companies; but large companies may use it on a by-division or by-department basis.

———— • ————

If we were to learn from these experiments and construct a complete solution, how would we harness the knowledge of each employee's peers in a constructive way to assure a competent workforce? Along with that, how would we welcome and encourage free thinking while constraining actions borne of that thinking to those that are most likely to benefit the company? Employees should be taking risks, but there should be constraints that would cause all teams to weigh those risks in a balance imposed by the environment illuminating both rewards and penalties.

It should be an environment wherein a manager does not feel the urge to dress down an employee who has erred. The environment itself should contain the rewards and penalties within its processes. This drives a collaborative team with minimal interference from judging and resentment. In a well-designed system, the disgruntled worker won't think, "that manager needs to be fired." Instead he will think, "the system won't tolerate him for long," confident in the reliability of the environment which will make the poor manager's position naturally uncomfortable until he either improves or leaves. The manager will not

21: PROSE

"write up" the employee in preparation for dismissal, but will instead trust the system to make her uncomfortable enough to go of her own accord.

I propose my system, as did Jeremy Bentham. I admit that I have not constructed this organization. I have tested bits of the concept as well as I could, but the aforementioned progressive companies have already tested the basic principles. I propose to assemble those tested parts, in which we have confidence, into a recognizable whole. I call this concept PROSE.

The PROSE company implements five principles: Peer review, Respect, One salary, Shared contribution and Equal treatment.

Peer Review: It is rare that management has enough insight into their underlings to be able to assess them fairly. Their peers, on the other hand, generally have a keen understanding of each the other's contribution. Peer review should play a key role in assessing individual contribution.

Respect: We encourage a culture that accepts the contribution of all participants. They each have different skills, different strengths and different levels of competence. We criticize quickly, incisively and constructively. We praise quickly, incisively and honestly (no false praise to build people up). We encourage so as to remind people of their legitimate potential. When talking about people, we focus on the positive. When talking to people, we speak lovingly and bluntly.

One salary: Every employee will receive the same base salary. It must be sufficient to support a family of two, providing the necessities of life as long as they watch their expenses. This salary will be adjusted with inflation. That means exactly what it appears to mean. In a period of deflation, the base salaries will decrease. For this reason, it must be adjusted using a market basket that reflects the likely purchases of the affected population.

Shared contribution: The organization will set aside an apportionment of money which should be tied to real goals. Those should include such worthy intentions as profit, customer satisfaction and charitable giving targets. For a non-profit, the profit component may be replaced by contribution reserves or some other indicator of good financial governance. Peer review will determine each employee's rating (this includes the janitor and the top executives). That rating will be converted to a percentage using a simple linear formula. Each employee will receive that percentage of the reserved pool of money. The janitor at this organization will probably have a higher overall salary than the average janitor. The CEO will probably have a lower overall salary than the average CEO; but each of them has actually earned their pay as determined by the people who are best qualified to assess them.

Equal treatment: Anyone may propose a project. Anyone may comment on a project. The president and the chief engineer are employees with specialized skill sets just like the marketing director's administrative assistant. This also means that everyone bears the same responsibility. If the janitor submits a onepager, he will be expected to go before the BRC and advocate for his proposal. Everyone gets the same benefits and vacation. The budget and most accounting, excluding that which would reveal personal information, is available to all employees. The Board of Directors includes a fair cross-section of the workforce.

In such an organization, the top officers have no special benefits. They compete with Tiffany, the graphic designer, for their portion of the allocated cash reserve. If they do their jobs well, everyone will assess their essential contribution to financial success fairly and their allocation of the resources will be commensurate with their contribution. It is entirely reasonable to expect the wise guardians of the corporate vision to be well paid; but, if Tiffany has proposed a brilliant logo for a well-paying customer, she may well receive an unexpected bonus as a result of her favorable peer review.

This peer review will be best accomplished using a well designed computer program. When the quarterly review comes due, each employee will be presented with a graphic representation showing all employees within their ranking group, except, of course, themselves, having the same proportional ranking. If there are eleven employees being ranked, this employee will see only the other ten and each will be ranked at 10%. The employee will rank each employee up or down based upon that employee's recognition of the others' accomplishments toward the goals. As each employee is adjusted upwards, the others will ratchet slowly downwards so as to assure a constant 100% between them.

This *could* all be anonymous but remember our Amazon example from before. Anonymity in such a situation can quickly become toxic. For that reason, each assessment should probably be accompanied by comments and suggestions from the person making the assessment. These should be encouraged, without anonymity, from all employees doing the ranking – a short message of encouragement or a brief suggestion. The comments should be moderated to assure that both positive and negative comments are constructive. Of course, if any comments are a surprise to anyone, management is not encouraging the right kind of communication within the workplace. A culture of innovation is a culture of constant review and open discussion. Excellence and areas requiring improvement must be topics that arise naturally and easily as each team-member seeks to improve and to help others improve. Remember that with respect comes a welcoming openness to criticism.

There is a practical upper limit to the number of people who can be meaningfully ranked in this way. There are a couple of ways to address this. One would be to include everyone in the ranking and invite each employee to adjust up or down only those people they know. Face it, that might be twenty to thirty people. The other is to divide the rankings up, allowing ranking by department with top management included in each ranking. Some math would be required to normalize the rankings, but it would not be challenging math. In the end everyone is ranked indicating the percentage of the allocated funds to be distributed.

Famine In the Bullpen

If an employee is contributing consistently to the good goals of the company, her salary will be high. If an employee is slacking or faking their contribution, their salary will be low: it may be nearly the subsistence base wage. Any employee relegated to the subsistence base wage will eventually leave since regular (non-innovating) companies will easily exceed that compensation.

This is not intended as a rigid specification. It would be entirely consistent with this proposal if a company were to apply peer review as seventy percent of an employee's assessment combined with, say, customer review for the other thirty percent. The point is that the people who actually work with the employee should judge the performance. If a company were to allow review of top brass and then only the immediate coworkers of each employee, that would be consistent with this proposal as long as all assessments were combined fairly into a final company-wide assessment.

If the one salary were higher than suggested with somewhat lower shared contribution or lower than suggested with somewhat higher shared contribution, there should be no conflict with these basic principles. New employees should get around six months on a typical fixed salary while establishing themselves. More time or less is, of course, up to the organization. The point is that all tenured employees are paid from the same pot based upon an objective assessment of their contribution to the company's well-defined goals.

The proposed system closes a meaningful feedback loop around fitness to the position. Good fits are well compensated, poor fits are poorly compensated and naturally encouraged to move to other companies which they might serve more effectively.

———— • ————

Once you have established your PROSE organization, you will encounter a problem. You should find that you are accumulating effective employees eager to adhere to the challenges that arise from the system itself. It is possible that you will encounter employees who abandon the process of hopping from job to job in order to pump up their salary.

21: PROSE

You may end up with long-term employees. Knowing that their recommendations are taken seriously and that their compensation is tied to their direct contribution, the only limit will be their creativity. While the Shared Contribution portion of PROSE may seem draconian to some, my experience with peer review has generally been very positive (both when reviewed well and when reviewed poorly). I would leap at an opportunity to be paid based upon peer review. I suspect many others would as well.

As long as I am healthy enough to contribute, I would be happy to apply myself energetically to such an organization. It is correct, morally correct, to exploit this kind of enthusiasm to the organization's best advantage. The team-members themselves would encourage such exploitation since they share in the reward. At this point, therefore, it becomes necessary to address the problem of employees who cannot contribute due to sickness or age. For such a company, provisions must be made to guarantee reasonable support during long-term illness as well as benign inducements to depart when the natural enthusiasm begins to sag under the weight of time.

If that sounds like a pension, yes, I am suggesting a pension plan. At least some modern companies, tired of dealing with rapid employee turnover, are exploring a renewed interest in the pension plan. According to an Aug 22, 2016 posting on bloomberg.com, Woodford Investment Management, co-founded by Neil Woodford and Craig Newman, is reintroducing the pension. They found, partly from their own experience and partly through research, that the traditional bonus was not reflecting deserved compensation in a way that was encouraging retention.

The pension isn't as expensive as people often suspect; but, it is an investment that requires serious study. It provides additional incentive to apply oneself to the long-term goals of the company, but most importantly, it provides an inducement to leave after a productive run and make way for new team-members with new ideas. Regardless your choice of a pension, a 401K or some other approach, your goal should be that: retention for a reasonable amount of time followed by a benign separation. The feature factory doesn't care much about retention because there are plenty of other workers with those same mundane skills ready to plug right into that open socket. An innovative company wants to retain the special skills they have nurtured and keep their technical edge sharp and well-honed.

We hear horror stories about the old guy who hangs on until retirement producing no value. He is *Retired In Place* (RIP). At a PROSE company, though, this would be difficult since without contributing, his salary will naturally fall to an uncomfortable level. Is this a cruel scheme for clearing out employees who can't contribute? It could be, if insufficient care is applied to the company's overall plan. Take care, your goal is to extract maximum value by providing a unique and rewarding experience from employment to retirement. To burn out your team-members is to waste their most valuable years (for them and for the organization).

PROSE drives a dynamic and challenging environment. In a 2013 study[Sheinert_2012] (most recent of several), very old rats, when placed into an interesting environment, actually developed significantly more neural interconnections within their brains than rats in simple cages. I propose that with age, the excitement of the ongoing creative endeavor will make RIP very rare. As employees age, places where they may contribute will be found. The nature of their contribution may change with age; but, its value does not need to diminish.

Innovation is not limited to technology companies. A company that sells oatmeal may still use PROSE. The creative focus may be in sales and marketing. It may be in more efficient ways to store or transport the product. It may be in ways to encourage sales agents. It may be in the advertising campaign that distinguishes your company from the other commodity vendors. Invention is applicable to any company. Close a feedback loop around it and amplify it.

22: Informal Methods

There is nothing so permanent as the temporary solution.
Russian saying

I moved from an aerospace company that applied the Waterfall method with uncompromising rigor to Sun Microsystems which seemed to have no method at all. I began as a mid-level programmer fixing errors in the software that was responsible for delivering their software. There was a bug reporting system, and my manager saw to it that I always had a satisfactory backlog of bug reports to address.

Checking in my tested correction, I turned to the next bug report and began working on it. I reported to my manager every week to review progress and plans. While that sounds a little like a Scrum-offshoot called Kanban, it was much simpler than that. Without daily meetings or story points, I cranked out fix after fix, reliably checking off eliminated errors and added features just like all the other mid-level programmers were doing.

There were minimal meetings and while an occasional high-profile problem may command special attention, management was generally not concerned about gathering statistics regarding my bug-fixing skills. My manager knew what I was doing and reported that to her manager who trusted her to keep her department functioning smoothly. It was a method but it was an informal method.

We have reviewed some ideas for constructing an organization that may thrive on invention and we have reviewed a process which may be able to make such an organization self-sustaining. Within that organization is the inevitable (but likely small) feature factory as well as manufacturing and engineering and those processes that allow any team-member to propose and even direct a unique creative project. From the macro to the micro we now consider how such a project may be organized.

To the reader with a history of problem-solving, I offer notice. This chapter will not contain any surprises. I will discuss techniques for understanding the problem and solving it with a skilled team. The chapter is intended for people on the periphery of the engineering process or, perhaps, for developers who have been dragged through a pointless long-march by an unskilled engineering lead. If you are an experienced problem-solver who opts to proceed through this chapter anyway, I will feel immensely gratified if you find a single new technique or think of your process in a slightly different way as a result of my ramblings. To you I offer my thanks. To other experienced problem-solvers, I sincerely offer that you may skip this chapter without guilt.

My first ARC-approved project at Sun was a one-man-show. I refactored the Sun patch architecture originally in my spare time and, after a month or two, as a sanctioned project. I took on the problem of automating patch delivery and accumulated a small team of three skilled engineers with whom I prosecuted that project. We read *eXtreme Programming eXplained* early in the project and adopted several of the recommendations. The project required that certain parts of the problem be resolved immediately followed by lower priority parts which we could address more thoroughly, eventually subsuming the emergency parts of the problem into the larger better-conceived solution. We took a *Napoleonic Strategy*: advance, consolidate and repeat.

Each advance demanded a fasttrack or a functional specification. Initially, I wrote the spec and my team reviewed and corrected it. Eventually different team members contributed parts of the spec, making it a communal document. We organized our work around sections of the

22: Informal Methods

spec. I would write the portions of the code that were more complicated (probably best read as "least well explained in my part of the spec") while the other team members wrote the parts that communicated with that. Over time, I found that precaution to be unnecessary. I soon learned how clever and trustworthy my team was. Willy Hui, Terence Leong and Mahima Mallikarjuna joined in on all aspects of the work as we joined teams all over the world developing the earliest of the Java application servers.

We submitted tests with each new class. We communicated informally almost every day, even though my team was in Menlo Park and I was in Broomfield, Colorado. We pair-programmed when needed and we quickly modified our specification whenever we encountered an error or misunderstanding. We were agile but we were not Scrum. I openly admit that we were *cafeteria-agilists*. We didn't agree with all recommendations in the eXtreme Programming challenge. We tested them, assessed them and went with what worked for us.

On the plus side, we rewrote very little because we knew our course from the spec. On the minus side, to be fair, even though we were together for some years, we never figured out a good scheme for predicting how long a particular task would take. I now know that a variant on story points may have worked well for us.

Aside from lacking a pointing process, my Sun team was not wanting for a method. We were still able to predict pretty well when we would deliver and the resulting products were reliable and popular with customers having a large and diverse stable of Sun systems. For the most part we did what seemed reasonable. The team was competent and emotionally mature. We established a respectful rapport, we communicated regularly and we operated from a written spec. This method was effective and decidedly informal.

Of course, any of the formal methods discussed in chapter 6 may be considered and applied as appropriate. Competent people should be allowed to organize teams and projects as best suits them. Agility should always be fundamental and should come naturally to such a workforce. The gathering of data to assess the effectiveness of processes within the organization makes good sense as long as such gathering doesn't disrupt those processes too much. The Scrum-style daily assessment of status is essential when you don't have a well-understood plan. With a plan, less frequent meetings suffice. In other words, your project may choose to use an interrupt rather than a polling strategy. Most formal methods use daily meetings (polling). In my experience, the interrupt strategy has always been more efficient and effective.

Beginning with a problem, an engineer will assess it and determine what solutions may be applied. This often starts in an engineer's spare time until a reasonable proposal may be assembled. Some enlightened organizations encourage their engineers to take time to muse on-the-clock but usually, there are eight hours of serious work to do and the initial proposal has to be assembled elsewhere.

The problem of understanding the problem is fairly personal but it is not an undefinable art. There are widely accepted tools that assist in that process. This leads me to a brief exposition about Gerald Weinberg. Mr. Weinberg is the consultant's consultant. He has dedicated his life to solving problems for clients. He has developed, and fully documented, very clever methods for figuring out the nature of the underlying problem.

Weinberg's understanding that the problem must be fully understood is essential and his techniques apply well to preparing the way for resolving the problem in an engineering fashion. In Gerald Weinberg's seminal work, *The Secrets of Consulting*[Weinberg_1985] he explains some of his most effective methods for understanding a problem. Anyone solving intractable problems would do well to find a sturdy copy and read it dog-eared.

To help his reader remember the methods, he provides mnemonics in the form of memorable rules. *The Credit Rule*: You'll never accomplish anything if you care who gets the credit; *The Bolden Rule*: If you can't fix it, feature it; and my favorite, *The Harder Law*: Once you eliminate your number one problem, you promote number two. That means

22: Informal Methods

there will always be problems. What an excellent prospect for the engineer!

---•---

Understanding the problem begins with the potential customer. If you don't know who the user will be, you may actually have nothing useful. For that reason, the customer really does need to be figured out first. Veblen's Principle carries real value: *There is no change, no matter how awful, that will not benefit some people and no change, no matter how good, that will not hurt some.* That means that for any product you produce, there will be adherents and detractors. It is essential to consider both.

Weinberg reminds the reader of questions so deep that they are often ignored. Who, for example, is the customer? What would be the result of providing the perfect solution? What would satisfied users say about such a solution? What would unsatisfied users say? There is always a loser; who is it?

If answering those questions proves difficult, then the problem may require further analysis. Pull together some incisive folks or, in a pinch, do this alone in your office. Write out sentences stating the problem in different ways. Recite the sentences out loud while emphasizing different words. In each case, explain out loud what the sentence means with that emphasis. See if that triggers a better understanding. If not, try replacing each significant word with a synonym and repeat the exercise.

Once the problem is well enough defined, consider what causes the problem. How isolated is it? Are there other problems that seem to appear simultaneously or under similar circumstances? Could they have a common cause? Could one of those other phenomena be the cause of the others? If a prior cause is determined, then repeat the problem analysis from above. Continue until the most fundamental cause has been determined. At that point, you've determined the *root cause*. That is the actual problem to be solved.

Famine In the Bullpen

Once the problem is defined, a solution must be developed. That process will be carried out in a manner unique to the engineer. Some may begin with a discussion among interested peers to think through possibilities. Some may prefer to put together an initial written proposal prior to review. Sometimes the idea is so revolutionary that it may be hard to explain without a nearly complete specification to pull all of the threads together. It is hard to predict how long it will take to come up with a solution to a difficult problem, but you will be expected to do that anyway. Here Scrum-style story points will probably not contribute much. The engineer or contributing engineers will need to rely on past experience to guess at when the solution will be available. My only advice is to be pessimistic no matter how sad your manager's face may look, it will be worse if you miss your deadline.

With the deadline set, your only option is the time-honored one: think about it without ceasing. Take notes, use automatic writing, work at bars and coffee shops, shake up your environment to keep your mind active. Meditate quietly. Babble loudly to yourself. Fall asleep thinking about the problem and wake up muttering about it.

Don't focus on the problem, focus on the form (the very nature) of the problem. You can't say anything about everything and you can't say much about something, but mastering the form of a thing allows you to describe effectively anything that honors that form. In understanding the problem, it will become clear that it is part of a family of root causes that are similar enough that they can be identified. Back when I was paid to engineer solutions, I would tell my team to "solve the class not the problem." We would concentrate on that family of problems adding in relatives as our understanding progressed. We did not design our solution for something. We designed it for anything, leading to a solution which would be already prepared for the next complaint.

22: Informal Methods

After the ecstatic elation of the discovered solution, will come the need to document it. As you write the functional specification, you will find the holes in your design. You will realize that your URI doesn't include enough data for a serviceable request. As you add in the data you will realize that you don't actually need that data. As you craft each numbered paragraph, the other paragraphs will become clearer. It will pull itself together into a whole that can be clearly explained. Then it's time for review.

Don't accept recommendations from reviewers who can't explain why their correction is necessary, but joyously accept well-founded recommendations. Face it: despite your ingenious solution, your initial spec is crap. You were too close to it. With help from smart people, it will become proper and actionable. While you are working on the specification, members of your team may be experimenting with some of the concepts, building out prototypes, researching existing tools that may be compatible with the solution and contributing sections to the specification.

When the reviews are complete, the specification is divided up and different team members will implement designated sections.

•

During implementation, keep communication simple so that any concern may be aired as soon as possible. Constantly refer back to the documented specification and reserve a public space where the team may write up issues, concerns and problems encountered and describe how they were addressed in order to assure that everyone is comfortable with the coding style and derived patterns. Write tests to verify all new software and all changes and incorporate those tests into the workspace where they will execute with each build. Do not sequester your unit tests from your integration tests as if that distinction were fundamental. Divide your test suites based upon meaningful categories. Test (preferably automate a test) for every product use-case assured by the specification. Test corner cases as well, but feel free to sequester the corner cases into a separate suite which you may run less frequently. Be agile and use a formal method if you feel comfortable doing that.

Outside factors will begin imposing constraints. A third-party interface may not become available in time, a piece of hardware will be discontinued, a subject matter expert will move to a different company. You can't know what will happen but you should prepare for the unexpected with a *Red Flag Review*. In the Red Flag Review the team lists everything that may go wrong. It actually isn't as hard as you might think. Given a little pondering, the team members will come up with a long list of potential problems. For each of those the team will establish two things: a red flag and a plan B. The red flag is the distinct, agreed-upon event indicating that the current plan has failed. Plan B is, as would be expected, the alternative plan. For example:

Risk	Red Flag	Plan B
Security team may not deliver the SSO solution on time.	No delivery by May 23.	Integrate Identiview SSO solution.
The message queue is unproved and may not be able to accommodate large messages.	Large message test planned for April 10. Test fails.	Implement Barry's plan to fragment and sequence messages.

In this case, on April 10, the engineer responsible will verify the test passes. If it fails, that engineer will throw the red flag. At that point, the team will switch to plan B. The process is terribly satisfying. At Sun, I had the privilege twice to receive report of a red flag and confidently call out, "Go to plan B." The projects delivered on time with only minor deviation from the original goals.

In some cases, part of the plan was so unstable that we developed a plan C as well. In that case, we added the new line to the table with a red flag along the lines of "plan B is unsuccessful as of April 15" and an associated plan B (C). Scrum is one method that allows a simple project to

22: Informal Methods

stay on schedule. For a challenging project, Scrum may fall short; but, Red Flag Review is an excellent method for helping a team to look ahead and plan for eventualities. It emphasizes the fixed/variable triangle. You can slip schedule, features or quality. Where schedule is fixed and quality is rightly sacrosanct, this allows a clean and reasonable way to gently adjust features just enough to deliver what is needed.

———•———

There has been a recent fascination with Continuous Delivery (CD), wherein each fragmentary change is immediately deployed into the wild. It further promotes the feature factory by driving developers to build only simple components. If an entire software product can be deployed in pieces then why aren't vacuum cleaners deployed in pieces? Why aren't aircraft deployed in pieces? The idea that each little part of a larger solution must be delivered in usable form immediately, obscures the legitimate beauty of the complete product. The idea that an individual tune from Pink Floyd's *The Wall* is meaningful without the entire work, trivializes the masterful execution of the album. It requires, in fact, some sort of scaffolding wherein someone would need to explain what leads up to the tune as well as what follows. In the same way, continually delivered pieces require additional throw-away scaffolding that could be avoided if we just had the patience to develop the entire product and deliver it as a whole. It carries the underlying myth that everything is so changeable that no real solution is possible and any delivered solution is really just a necessary pretense to ward off the abiding suspicion that nothing can be done.

With each minimal release we advance our commonly accepted belief that we cannot produce a masterful whole. An accomplishment as grand as a well-executed rock album is beyond our capabilities because we only see the solution in fragments.

A well-designed product requires fewer hours coding up software than a product that is hacked out without a design. More time spent designing the product results in a fairly quick and efficient coding cycle. Nonetheless, coding is required for any software product, so an important part of any method is assuring that your code is sound. There are no surprises here. Tests should be written to verify proper functioning and all software should be reviewed by at least one other pair of eyes (a code review).

There are some studies that support the effectiveness of *pair-programming* in which two developers share a single computer. One is the driver (the one writing the code) and the other is the navigator (watching each keystroke and commenting if the driver goes off course). In a sense, it is a continuous immediate code review (we may say eXtreme Code Review). The research is not definitive. Many of the studies are from academic environments and are conducted by professed pair-programming advocates. It is suggested, by some studies, that even though two people are doing the work of one, the savings in coding errors and debugging are significant, improving code delivery speed by 15% and reducing errors by 15%.

Many companies brag that all of their software is pair-programmed. I always wonder if those companies also advocate pair-management. If two heads are better than one, then that should apply to any human activity requiring thinking and decision-making. Why aren't managers sharing a desk, pair-writing each employee review, pair-commanding each responsive tactic, pair-presenting each divisional progress report? Could it be that managers don't pair-manage simply because they don't have to? Could it be that they advocate pair-programming because they don't trust developers to work alone? I don't know and I offer no critique one way or another, although I do look forward to an authoritative pair-management study.

I worked with a skilled engineer at Sun who advocated *code-free software development*. His claim, "where there is no code there is no error" is, on the face of it, a true statement. The problem was that his concept still involved code, it was just someone else's code. What he meant was that if there is an existing product, such as a web server or a message queue, that could simply be configured to do what you need, you should use it. There is no question that if you do not need to write new software, if you do not need to produce a new product, do not.

22: Informal Methods

That is a key reason for designing the software first. Once you have a thorough design, it is much easier to determine if there is an existing solution. Do not produce a product if one already exists, but be sure of that by first designing your solution.

———•———

Several years ago, during my days as a contractor, I was in a meeting with senior engineers who were discussing how to implement the new concept of microservices for their company. I provided my usual response, reminding them that the discussion was irrelevant until they understood the problem they were solving. I made the mistake of using the term "business rules" which led an engineering manager in attendance to quip, "You know, our business is mostly made up on the fly, so we don't have any business rules."

While the quip may have been in jest, it nevertheless stopped any discussion of analyzing the problem itself and the discussion continued along the original lines. Of course, that manager didn't really understand what I meant by those words but, more importantly, I was already bored with the discussion and had no interest in pursuing it. Companies all over were switching to microservices and no one yet had died; so I just didn't care.

The manager was sitting in on an architectural discussion and even though it would be in his best interests to save some money by promoting a well-designed architecture for his company, he preferred to put that off until he knew exactly what his business model was. This is the kind of thinking that led to the notion that the world is moving so fast that all designs must be constantly adapting to the constantly changing environment. He was suggesting that until we knew exactly what this twenty year old company was going to do next we couldn't develop its infrastructure. He believed that solutions were designed for *something*.

This, of course, is bunkum. The data in that company was stored somewhere already. It was routinely accessed already. It was processed and provided to clients already. The processes for doing all of those things were put in place ad hoc on an as-needed basis. In each case, someone solved something but missed the big picture. The resulting system (and this was the unconscious awareness of the architects) was very rigid and intolerant of change. This was not because *that is the nature of solutions*, it was because the assembled solutions were *poor*.

The details of the business dictate the constraints, not the parameters, of the well-conceived architecture, which brings us back to *form*. Can the engineer assess the form of the business? Based upon what has happened in the past, can a set of likely future scenarios be reasonably predicted? If not, the business is probably doomed. If so, the well-conceived architecture is possible.

The skilled engineer, like a skilled tailor, would design it to fit the body while accommodating the effects of age. It would be stitched loosely at joints likely to require a wide range of movement. Additional material would be sewn in where growth was likely and thicker material where appendage moved against appendage. The engineer would establish configurable options for areas of uncertainty. She would optimize those operations for the current use-cases but would allow for reconfiguration as those components grow or shrink.

The counter-argument to this is YAGNI which would dictate solving the immediate problem today and tomorrow's problem tomorrow. That assures constant frenetic activity with no underlying engineering design. Developers who work in such an environment tend to be frustrated and bored. What they do today will be thrown out tomorrow. They know that they are producing nothing lasting, that all of their solutions are temporary and that they themselves are only valued as patch artists.

Inasmuch as everything is temporary, this may be the natural way of things; but a well designed product that performs flawlessly is simply cheaper and better accepted than a slap-dash solution. The customer complaints are demoralizing and will not be addressed. The slap-dash solution will not be refactored. It never is.

23: Health and Wholeness

Enough is plenty to the wise.

Euripides

David Bohm, in *Wholeness and the Implicate Order*[Bohm_1980] page 3, comments on our word for *health* as follows:

> *It is instructive to consider that the word 'health' in English is based on the Anglo-Saxon word 'hale' meaning 'whole': that is, to be healthy is to be whole.*

To be whole is to be not only complete and intact, but also to be fully functional. Surely many fresh corpses are intact having all of their original parts in their original places. The fact that those parts are non-functional defines the entity as *not healthy*. We see a person as healthy when all of the parts are functioning at optimum efficiency and effectiveness. *Effectiveness*, in that the part is doing what it is supposed to do as opposed to some extraneous activity. *Efficiency*, in that the energy consumed is being used maximally for the intended purpose of the part.

We accept without argument that to be healthy is better than to be unhealthy. We accept this for humans and we often anthropomorphize inanimate objects as well and tell friends that our car is sick, or identify unhealthy corporate practices or question a developer's *coding hygiene*.

This book has been almost entirely focused on problems associated with a culture wherein innovation is damped and controlled due to the fear among the higher authorities of the explosive glory that may need to be sopped up once innovation yields its intended goal. This drives the institutional body to suppress the functioning of key parts: preferring anemia and withering degeneration in place of the unpredictable vibrancy of glowing good health.

The problem with this approach is that human beings thrive on innovation, and once exposed to the opportunity to do the impossible, are loathe to return to the desolation of the mundane. To watch the lights go on in a programmer who is invited to innovate, and then see the glorious result as the innovation yields value, and then to watch the lights extinguished when it is made clear that this will never happen again, remains the deepest sorrow of my career. What remains clear from all of these sorrowful experiences is that there is nothing so valuable as human labor. Human beings are called upon to do work for one and only one reason: the profit returned from human labor continues to exceed that of automation. An institution is healthy when all of its parts are used to their fullest potential. A company that treats its humans as if they were machines, restricting them to repetitive mundane work, is not practicing efficiency, it is practicing desolation. It is unwhole in that it is preventing its parts being functional. Such a company, such an institution, such a nation, is ill.

———•———

I have outlined a likely root cause for this pervasive attitude and I advocate changes to government policy in order to encourage a return to a creative culture; but, this attitude is not driven inexorably by public policy. Periods of high innovation occurred before corporations or the rich were taxed at all. They occurred before any laws were passed to limit monopoly control. They occurred, dare I say it, before the U.S. Constitution was written.

I do believe that public policy will play a useful role in restoring our effectiveness in solving problems. I believe that a top marginal tax rate of 95% on income and on capital gains exceeding five million dollars annually will result in improved investment in corporate and public infrastructure. I believe that it should be extremely difficult for any company to purchase a competitor or a supplier. In other words, I believe

23: Health and Wholeness

that everyone has a right to prosper. I do not believe that anyone has a right to be a billionaire.

At this point, one may respond with shock, "Do you mean to tell me that I may have to work hard for twenty or thirty years in order to accumulate my fortune; and even then I won't be a billionaire capable of buying multiple Congressmen!?" to which I answer, "Yes, comrade, I do."

There is a perfectly persuasive argument against my view, though (which I admit is even further left than that of the rightly revered Bernie Sanders). If Elon Musk hadn't pulled in multiple millions of dollars from the success of PayPal, he couldn't have started Tesla and SpaceX. That is a fair argument and yet I dispute it on two counts. Firstly, it is very likely that Elon Musk could have pulled together enough independent investors to fund Tesla anyway. He could have started with money from a relative, like he did for his first enterprise or he could have sold the idea to a few more unrelated investors. Those time-honored ways of starting a company worked fine for Ford Motor Company, Westinghouse and Apple. Musk easily has enough business acumen to pull that off. Secondly, a society that depends on the charity of the wealthy is subject to their demands. The ancient Greeks rewarded their benefactors with accolades and, in some cases, godhood. We reward our benefactors with special laws that favor their business fortunes. All of the good that benefactors like Musk may do must be weighed against the enormous harm done by such wealthy advocates of ignorance and regression as the Koch brothers and Sheldon Adelson. I would happily (and apologetically) make Mr. Musk's job more difficult in exchange for hobbling his more nefarious peers.

———•———

Whether a menial delivery driver or a renowned musical composer, the machine has not yet been developed that can surpass the capabilities made manifest by the human being. This is important. Corporations are not job creators. Corporations are profit creators. They hire human beings only when all non-human options have been exhausted. As automation improves, jobs will become more and more sparse until, at some point in the near future, automation will make full employment impossible. R. Buckminster Fuller refers to this as *ephemeralization*[Fuller_1963]. It is often summarized as the ability of technological advancement to do "more and more with less and less until eventually you can do everything with nothing."

Karl Marx said essentially the same thing but we'll stick with Fuller to avoid that controversy. What should become evident to a serious observer is that we will eventually have to simply accept that manufacturing has become automated to such a degree that a large number of humans will not have the option of working for an employer. Automation will supplant the worker in all mundane occupations. The only remaining option will be the creative endeavor.

Thomas Jefferson's dream of every citizen farming their own plot in order to supply their family's needs will be equally impractical due to a shortage of arable land for the Earth's bloated population. If we were all to turn back to the land, we would find it bleak and unyielding: soil exhausted, water distant and animals uncooperative and fickle.

When that happens, we will need to entirely rethink our attitude toward work[32]. Old concepts like *if you don't work you can't eat* and *there's no such thing as a free lunch* will go the way of the expired agrarian economy, the industrial revolution and the labor union. In a world where automation has mastered all mundane occupations, humans will appear to be obsolete actors in the industrial economy. Nonetheless, people will have to eat and even the wealthy will yearn for the company of others (even those who do not directly contribute to their fortunes).

In those days, the human must be reassessed. It will become more and more obvious that the human being, providing no means to the ends of the powerful, will have to be considered again as an end in itself. Emmanuel Kant in *Groundwork of the Metaphysics of Morals*[Kant_1785] wrote:

> *In the kingdom of ends everything has either a price or a dig-*

---

32 See http://newworknewculture.com for Frithjof Bergmann's reasoned review of this issue along with proposals for its resolution.

23: Health and Wholeness

> nity. *What has a price can be replaced by something else as its equivalent; what on the other hand is above all price and therefore admits of no equivalent has a dignity.*
>
> *What is related to general human inclinations and needs has a market price; that which, even without presupposing a need, conforms with a certain taste, that is, with a delight in the mere purposeless play of our mental powers, has a fancy price; but that which constitutes the condition under which alone something can be an end in itself has not merely a relative worth, that is, a price, but an inner worth, that is, dignity.*

Thus humans, while valuable, are unique because of their *dignity*. They are irreplaceable. If we are to recognize the dignity of the human being, we must direct our actions toward an environment that emphasizes the exploitation of humans as creative beings.

I use the word *exploitation* in the sense of *applying boldly*. The humans with whom I have had the pleasure to work were in their element, happy and joyous, when boldly challenged to do the impossible. In those roles, they yielded great value and also experienced great satisfaction. This is what humans do best. Companies, of late, are very timid in their use of human beings because of an apparent fear that humans, when wielded without restraint, will challenge the bounds of the world understood by management, that they will disrupt the status quo with which the wealthy and settled have become comfortable and that they will challenge the existing protocols of power by which the world is governed.

Despite this, the ever-expanding technologies of automation and expert systems make Fuller's prediction inevitable. Eventually, 10% of the human population will be sufficient to supply all of the goods required by the rest of us. When that begins to happen, what will we do? Will we discard the non-workers as refuse leading to a failed consumer-free economy or will we instead discard our antiquated notions regarding a salary defining the value of the individual and turn instead to an economy of relentless creation wherein the populace has been educated and acclimated to construct ingenious solutions as a matter of course? Indeed, why would we not begin fostering that now?

In such an economy, housing and food will be unquestioned necessary privileges provided by a rational and civilized society. Many things we now consider technologies will be trivial commodities available to all, such as means of communication, access to data and access to home-based manufacturing facilities. Human beings will be challenged through programs, established by communities from towns to nations, to resolve persistent problems: not merely for money but for the sheer joy of doing what no one else can do.

Freed from the profit motive, diseases will be cured and not just monetized. Energy will be spontaneously generated from innumerable small sources around the world. The asteroid belt will be mined and access to space will be trivial as space elevators launch tourists and workers to points of interest throughout the solar system. Solar power will be conducted easily and efficiently using a mass produced room-temperature super-conductor, from the poles and the sunny side of the earth to the dark side leaving restoration of the ecosystem a prime and achievable priority.

How, then, should we prepare for this eventuality? We begin by accepting creative problem-solving as a key value provided by human beings. Any commerce that trades in human production of value demonstrates its good health by periodically allocating resources during each employee's tenure to encourage the practice of astounding challenge. Not all people will find this challenge satisfying, and so every employee must have the option to refuse with impunity. Those employees bring value in more subtle ways; but, the innovators will withstand the inevitable stints of dull drudge work with fewer complaints knowing that their potential will again be fully exercised in the foreseeable future.

An organization that challenges its personnel to do great things will reap the benefits of a happier workforce and also of the trove of useful solutions provided by the true potential of their workers. This seems fairly obvious, but then this seems obvious too: when you install solar cells, they provide energy with minimal maintenance for twenty five years; when you drill for oil, you have to transport it, refine it and transport it again through multiple distribution points until you deposit it at

23: Health and Wholeness

the place where it will finally be converted into usable energy. Despite this, oil company executives prefer oil to solar or wind.

What is also obvious is that people who are in charge of institutions are basically people. They are not extraordinary. The recent failures of various banks and global corporations[33] should constitute convincing evidence that super powers do not accompany career advancement. People who guide companies are driven by the same prejudices, fears and preconceptions that drive the rest of us. Therefore, they may be swayed by reason or salesmanship and inspired to explore new pathways.

•

I will try, in this latter part of this final chapter, to summarize the normative conclusions that seem to arise from our analysis. A review of the evidence seems to suggest concrete actions that may be taken individually or together to move an institution into a position that will more fully utilize the potential of its constituent humans. As with the rest of this book, my most recent experience is within the software industry. If you are not in that industry but you have read to this point, the observations I have made must seem familiar enough that you have taken an interest. I trust that these suggestions should be as applicable to electronics or retail sales as they are to software. Since Scrum-style practices are being applied to service industries as well as manufacturing, I would guess that hospitals and insurance companies may find these conclusions useful as well.

These, of course, are my conclusions. As with any complex project, the investigator is too close to fully evaluate the problem. That fact has limited my comprehension, which means that your conclusions will likely go beyond these and that is reason for rejoicing. Good engineering is a team endeavor. My humble work, expanded and corrected through your disciplined review, may deliver concepts beyond my understanding. Such concepts are yours and not mine and you will have an obligation to write your own book correcting me and explaining the actual solution to the problem of desolation.

---

33 I assume this statement is and will remain meaningful into the foreseeable future.

Famine In the Bullpen

I will summarize my ideas here and I invite you to carry the research beyond my initial concepts. I propose the following:

1. Isolate Scrum.

    Use Scrum, if you like it, for conventional tasks. Fixing bugs or adding simple predictable features is supported well by Scrum and you can demonstrate features to management in a manner they may find comforting. Specific departments within your company may be well served by the Scrum process; but isolate it to those departments wherein the product is simple and the effort to produce it is easily guessable. For simple guessable goals, the collaborative story-pointing process progressively improves the ability of a fixed and stable group of active participants to predict resource requirements over even fairly long work periods.

2. Encourage proposals.

    Provide a mechanism with which anyone may propose a project and an impartial means for selecting proposals for execution based upon company goals. Excellent senior people are able to generate a corporate vision but that vision is rarely filled out with all of the important components. The creativity of the individual in the field is required to identify the actual problem space and to propose actual solutions. Even the humble janitor is seeing problems to which the CEO is oblivious. The proposer must be recognized for his contribution and must have the option to participate in the project.

3. Provide worker privacy.

    Invest in cubicles that can close out noise or, if you can bring yourself to believe the fact-based calculations made by Geoffrey James in 2016[34], save some money by building small offices. The cubicle was developed in 1967 by Robert Propst to solve the ongoing problem of *desk farms* where even employees of *that* era were finding themselves distracted and unable to perform to the

---

34 https://business.linkedin.com/talent-solutions/blog/hr/2016/open-office-plans-are-a-lot-less-cost-effective-than-you-may-think

23: Health and Wholeness

best of their ability. Now the desk farm is called an *open-plan office* but the original problem didn't go away: people doing creative work – and that should mean most people – need some privacy to think, muse and take risks. Given that freedom, the value and productivity of each employee is increased.

4. Don't settle for good enough.
When confronted with a disappointing but acceptable result, I would often remark, "Good enough is, by definition, good enough." This is funny only because it is clearly not true. There are a lot of ways to generate a working product. The problem is figuring out the problem. Take the time to understand the problem, burrow down to the root cause and fully resolve that. Take the time to specify the solution. Submit it for critical review and take the time to craft a solution that actually addresses the problem class. Write your own test harness if you don't like what's available. Set up a system that allows extensive automated verification. Rigorously test for *optimal* and accept nothing less.

5. Prepare for innovation.
Accept that in any corner of the organization, innovation may be profitable. Allow the innovator to function with minimal tracking. Construct a culture of innovation and bring all teammembers into that culture. The more you inspire humans to participate in the worthy goals of your organization, the more profound will be your success. Minimize procedure and maximize the unbracketed possibilities of method.

6. Make the boredom endurable.
Yes, there is boring stuff to do. Every employee has to accept that and endure; but, pains must be taken to challenge people to take on difficult problems to which no one knows the solution. Everyone taking on a boring routine task must know that the pain will end. Those who avoid the impossible problem due to a natural tendency to fear the unknown, must be incrementally exposed to the unknown and allowed to glory in its gradual subjugation. Those cautious actors may be gently introduced to

the wonders of innovation. It won't always work but from time to time, you will unearth a fantastic nugget of creativity.

7. Use popular tools only when appropriate.
Discourage the use of popular tools and frameworks unless the internal creative process develops a solution into which a given tool happens to fit well. In the software arena, the services performed by most modern frameworks were accomplished fifteen years ago at Sun Microsystems using ksh scripts and standard UNIX utilities. Such tools, built in-house, are not as cool but they are specialized to your needs. They are more easily modified as needs change and they contribute to true agility.

8. Be agile everywhere.
Agility is always good. Use Scrum, if you like, for projects that are appropriate to Scrum. Use a more formal approach for projects with more critical quality requirements. Free up your options for projects requiring serious creativity. Trust no consultant to teach you the procedure for engineering. There is no procedure that will yield engineering. Instead, build a culture of innovation. Promote and socialize engineering method. Make problem-solving the attitude of the organization and watch with satisfaction as it yields its beneficent fruit.

9. Actively campaign for constructive government policies.
Play your part in the political process. Promote candidates at all levels who appear to understand the problems we have discussed and are open to policies that support a solution. Governments can stifle or promote innovative cultures through various means including tax accommodations, enforcement of existing anti-trust laws or simply advocating creative business practices. Craft a government that promotes a culture of innovation.

———— • ————

So, after all of this, where are we? This started out with a review of what has happened to tamp down the threat of problem-solving in the software industry. A rigid complex has arisen, backed by moneyed in-

23: Health and Wholeness

terests, to establish a veritable church of the mundane. Religious adherents, like newly converted Scientologists, celebrate their unnatural restrictions: no design, inadequate languages and restrictive test methodologies. They submit themselves to the conditioning and accept the common teaching: noncommentarianism, "OO is a failed experiment", "integration tests may not be run locally".

The religion seems to be an outgrowth of, or at least encouraged by, a larger cultural change that prefers simple easily-acquired profits above real accomplishment. This cultural change may be influenced by public policy; but, it does not appear to be essential to the current policy framework, having flourished through a variety of policies from no taxes to high taxes, from low inflation to high inflation, from minimal technology to current technology.

Despite this, we have reviewed modern companies that still value innovation and bring new and meaningful solutions to market even without special tax incentives. We have marveled at what could drive such a decision by these innovative entrepreneurs and we have explored what value is inherent in innovation under such circumstances. We cannot be driven to genius by capricious politicians. Genius thrives because it is beautiful. Like so many beautiful things, it may be born, thrive and die without ever being witnessed. We, as a people, benefit every time we bring beauty into the open, nurture it and manifest its treasure in our everyday lives.

What could keep us from this joy but the delusion that it is not accessible? Why would a healthy organization not tap the creative energy of every team-member but by the delusion that humans are merely clever machines? How could people submit themselves to the science of desolation except by the delusion that there is nothing else? This is not our only option. This is not the way the world must be. Turn back the clock only a handful of decades to the 1950s and we will see a world where innovation was valued and encouraged. At the turn of the Twentieth Century, when monopolies were rampant, there were still entrepreneurs taking on problems that no one believed could be resolved. Imagine a modern world where impossible problems are tackled as a matter of routine; where the genius of the human being is amplified and tapped through a system where innovation is the natural product of a benign mechanism offering people the reward commensurate with their inherent magnificence.

As an individual, take on a personal project that taxes your intellect. As a lowly programmer, look for the most challenging stories and emphasize, to your colleagues, the joys of accomplishing the impossible. As a manager, challenge and trust your people. Bend the formal methods in favor of creativity and try to go beyond the basic request to the root cause. As a director, move toward informal methods and challenge yourself to take on problems for which there is no clear solution. As a CEO, consider building a culture of innovation. Take a fair salary and no more. Reinvest in the company and nurture your own internal expertise. Compete rather than assimilate.

Why would you do this? Do it because enough is plenty and too much is a gaudy embarrassment. Do it because the companionship of competent team-mates is more fun than you will ever deserve. Do it because you can maximize your wealth or you can maximize your character and your character has greater value in more interesting markets. Do it because you have a soul and you should be able to point to its worthy effects.

Do not merely survive in a professional wasteland. Your impending death will not cower at your cautious approach. Live and accomplish great things *now*. Find every opportunity to invent and create. As you nurture your internal innovative culture, you will be driven to bring that energy to your workplace. Join with others to question the state religion and explore new ways of thinking.

Let us not be satisfied with the routine assembly of standard parts. Let us not believe the things that others believe. Let us not accept others' solutions just because they are convenient. Let us join forces and manufacture a world of unique creation: a world whose boundless glory will cast down the priesthood of this feeble faith and rightly corrupt its laity.

Appendix A: The Toyota Way

The Toyota Way is based on fourteen principles. Compare them to the Agile Principles in Chapter 5.

1. Base your management decisions on a long-term philosophy, even at the expense of short-term financial goals.
2. Create a continuous process flow to bring problems to the surface.
3. Use 'pull' systems to avoid overproduction.
4. Level out the workload (work like the tortoise, not the hare).
5. Build a culture of stopping to fix problems, to get quality right the first time.
6. Standardized tasks and processes are the foundation for continuous improvement and employee empowerment.
7. Use visual controls so no problems are hidden.
8. Use only reliable, thoroughly tested technology that serves your people and process.
9. Grow leaders who thoroughly understand the work, live the philosophy, and teach it to others.
10. Develop exceptional people and teams who follow your company's philosophy.
11. Respect your extended network of partners and suppliers by challenging them and helping them improve.
12. Make decisions slowly by consensus, thoroughly considering all options; implement decisions rapidly.
13. Become a learning organization through relentless reflection and continuous improvement.
14. Go and see for yourself to thoroughly understand the situation.

Bibliography

Beck_2000: Kent Beck, "eXtreme Programming eXplained," Addison-Wesley, 2000

Bergström_2015: Jessica Bergström, Michael Miller & Eva Horneij, "Work environment perceptions following relocation to open-plan offices: A twelve-month longitudinal study," Work, 2015

Berns_2005: Gregory S. Berns, "Neurobiological Correlates of Social Conformity and independence During Mental Rotation," Biological Psychiatry, 2005

Berns_2010: Gregory Berns, MD, PhD, "Iconoclast," Harvard Business Press, 2010

Boehm_2004: Barry Boehm & Richard Turner, "Balancing Agility and Discipline," Addison-Wesley, 2004

Bohm_1980: David Bohm, "Wholeness and the Implicate Order," Routledge, 1980

DeMarco_1999: Tom DeMarco & Timothy Lister, "Peopleware," Dorset House Publishing, 1999

Desai_2012: Mihir Desai, "The Incentive Bubble," Harvard Business Review, 2012

Dunning_2003: David Dunning, Kerri Johnson, Joyce Ehrlinger & Justin Kruger, "Why people fail to recognize their own incompetence," Current Directions in Psychological Science, 2003

Fuller_1963: R. Buckminster Fuller, "Nine Chains to the Moon," Southern Illinois University, 1963

Garousi_2015: Golara Garousi, Vahid Garousi-Yusifoglu, Guenther Ruhe, Junji Zhi & Mahmoud Moussavi, "Usage and usefulness of technical software documentation: An industrial case study," Information and Software Technology, 2015

Ghanbari_2016: Lyda Ghanbari & Michael D. McCall, "Current Employment Statistics survey: 100 years of employment, hours, and earnings," Monthly Labor Review, 2016

Graves_2010: Philip Graves, "Consumer.ology," Nicholas Brealey Publishing, 2010

Kadlec_1999: Charles W. Kadlec, "Dow 100,000: Fact or Fictoin," Prentice Hall, 1999

Kant_1785: Immanuel Kant, "Groundwork of the Metaphysics of Morals," Cambridge University Press, 1785

Kim_2013: Jungsoo Kim & Richard de Dear, "Workspace satisfaction: The privacy-communication trade-off in open-plan offices," Journal of Environmental Psychology, 2013

Martin_2009: Robert C. Martin, "Clean Code: a handbook of agile software craftsmanship," Prentice Hall, 2009

Mednick_1962: Sarnoff A. Mednick, "The associative Basis of the Creative Process," Psychological Review, 1962

Meyer_1997: Bertrand Meyer, "Object-Oriented Software Construction," Prentice Hall, 1997

Murray_2010: Allan Murray, "The End of Management," Wall Street Journal, 2010

Phelps_2013: Edmund S. Phelps, "Less Innovation, More Inequality," The New York Times, 2013

Porter_2013: Michael E. Porter, Jan W. Rivkin & Rosabeth Moss Kanter, Competitiveness At a Crossroads, 2013

Rubin_2015: Richard Rubin, "Pfizer Piles Profit Abroad," Wall Street Journal, 2015

Sheinert_2012: Rachel B. (Speisman) Scheinert, Asha Rani, Ashok Kumar & Brandi K Ormerod, "Environmental enrichment restores neurogenesis and rapid acquisition in aged rats," Neurobiology of Aging, 2012

Tuomaala_2009: A. Kaarlela-Tuomaala, R. Helenius, E. Keskinen & V. Hongisto, "Effects of acoustic environment on work in private office rooms and open-plan offices - longitudinal study during relocation," Ergonomics, 2009

Weinberg_1985: Gerald M.Weinberg, "The Secrets of Consulting," Dorset House Publishing, 1985

Whitehead_1925: Alfred North Whitehead, "Science and the Modern World," The Free Press, 1925

Wittgenstein_1922: Ludwig Wittgenstein, "Tractatus Logico-Philosophicus," Routledge, 1922

Index

Agile
- -as Scrum 45
- -documentation 45
- -eXtreme Programming 45, 252p.
- -open-plan office 60, 64p.
- -pair programming 45, 260
- -testing 45, 58
- -The Agile Principles 72
- -YAGNI 92p., 262

Bentham, Jeremy 63p.
Berns, Gregory S. 67, 213p., 216
business cowardice 11, 76, 83, 101
Coding War Games 61
competence 211
configuration singleton 52, 138

Culture
- -inspiring the employee 222
- -of innovation 83, 125, 229, 239, 241, 244
- -part of a complex 12
- -PROSE 245

DeMarco, Tom 61p.
engine vs. motor 4

Engineering
- -as commodity 83
- -design document 48
- -design for anything 54, 261
- -documentation 170p., 173
- -engineer vs. technician 2pp.
- -etymology 3
- -form 93p., 256, 262
- -functional specification 117, 167, 171pp.
  - --Definitions 175
  - --Exposed Interfaces 176
  - --Provisions 175, 179
  - --Related Documents 175
  - --Scope 175
  - --Use Case Scenarios 176
- -hardware vs. software 116
- -method 4p., 12, 54
- -origins 1p., 4
- -problem definition 5, 171
- -requirements document 167, 172
- -root cause 2p., 5, 53, 94, 97, 153, 164, 189, 207, 255
- -side-effect 5, 94, 97p., 136, 187
- -simple mapping 10, 12, 98
- -step-by-step 7, 9, 13, 53

feature factory 55p., 73p., 148, 250, 252, 259
Fish, Barry 36p., 76
Flemming, Alexander 3
Florey, Howard 3

Formal Methods
- -Adaptive Software Development 80
- -Crystal 81
- -Dynamic System Development Method 82
- -eXtreme Programing 80
- -Lean Development 82
- -Scaled Agile Framework 79p., 183
- -Scrum 79p.
- -Waterfall 78p.

Framework
- -Akka 12, 50, 113
- -and OOM 137
- -as panacea 184
- -Hibernate 50, 156
- -limitations 111
- -MyBatis 50
- -safe choice 111, 113
- -so you can innovate 137
- -Spring 12, 49pp.

Gosling, James 98, 119p., 162

Grand architecture for doing stuff with things 173p.
Henry, Joe 100, 221
Hui, Willy 253
Imhotep 1p., 4
incompetence 211
Informal Methods
    -at Sun 251, 253
    -focus on form 256
    -justification 81
    -Red Flag Review 257
    -the right questions 255
    -word emphasis 255
Innovation
    -and evolution 223, 231, 237
    -and public policy 264
    -and Scrum 59
    -argument for 230
    -at Apple 187
    -at select companies 229
    -at Sun 31, 33p.
    -communication 247
    -control of 65, 78, 83p., 193, 263
    -culture of 83
    -executive compensation 185
    -in Agile Scrum 99
    -in the U.S. 185, 190p.
    -is a drug 217
    -randomizing agents 198
    -unexpected innovators 100, 204, 219pp., 264
Inversion of Control 12, 49pp., 121, 133, 138
Java Complex 49p., 98, 125
Kettering, Charles 5
Language
    -bash 110, 114
    -C 115, 127, 129
    -C++ 44, 118p., 124
    -Clojure 115
    -Eiffel 118, 124, 126p., 162
    -Erlang 115
    -Haskell 114

    -Java 49, 127, 131
    -Python 49, 110, 124pp.
    -Ruby 115
    -Sather 126
Leong, Terence 204, 253
Lister, Timothy 61p.
Mallikarjuna, Mahima 253
Martin, Robert C. 89
McDermott, Erin 99
McNealy, Scott 32p., 35
Methodology
    -functional 85
      --side-effect 85
    -object-oriented
      --and Java 163
      --and Scrum 148
      --example 135pp.
      --failed experiment 123pp.
      --like electronics 44
      --necessary objects 147
      --Object Oriented Software Construction 118p.
      --objections 138
      --philosophical underpinnings 144
      --principles 85
    -procedural 85
Meyer, Bertrand 85
motor vs. engine 4
Neoconservatism 192pp.
Neoliberalism 191p.
Paine, Cecil George 3
panopticon 63p.
penicillin 3
Principles
    -Information Expert Principle 135
    -Law of Demeter 85
    -Open-Closed Principle 85, 146
    -Rule of Three 85
    -Single Choice Principle 85, 136
    -Uniform Access Principle 86, 136
Problem Solving
    -engineering solution 2, 5p., 165
    -technical solution 2, 5, 158, 161

Religion
   -etymology 44
   -in software 44
   -noncommentarianism 88
revision 16
Rist, Jason 100
Schwerdt, Brooke 99
Scrum
   -against innovation 78
   -alpha developer 66pp.
   -as Agile 45, 57
   -as religion 46, 48
   -backlog 58
   -best case 47
   -customer engagement 70p.
   -developer 58
   -documentation 72
   -industry 46
   -innovation sprint 65, 83
   -limitations 48
   -minimize documentation 65
   -no one does it 57, 75
   -origin 13
   -planning poker 66
   -problem-solving 47
   -procedure 46, 58, 259
   -Product Owner 58p., 66p.
   -Scrum Master 58
   -spike 59
   -story 59
   -story points 58, 66
   -technical lead 66
   -time-boxing 59

Software
   -declarative 114
   -imperative 114
   -uniqueness 44
   -updates 56
Sun Microsystems
   -advertising hiatus 38pp.
   -agility 45
   -Architecture Review Committee 34p., 98, 173, 231, 233pp.
   -beer bust 197
   -business vs. engineering 34, 37
   -Change Review Team 35, 96
   -crash 38
   -culture 32, 34p., 38, 64p., 96, 110
   -failure 31, 33
   -growth spurt 37
   -open-source 38
   -Parade of Bozos 35, 197
   -Scrum adoption 46
   -Software Development Framework 33p., 96p.
   -Solaris 31, 34
   -two projects per developer 64
Testing
   -integration test 90p.
   -JUnit 90p.
   -mocking 90p.
   -Selenium 90
   -Test it like you fly it. 91
   -unit test 90p.
Veblen's Principle 255
version 15
Weinberg, Gerald 254p.